Virginia Colonial Abstracts
Series 2, Volume 1
Northumberland County, Virginia
1678–1713

by
Lindsay O. Duvall

Southern Historical Press, Inc.
Greenville, South Carolina

Copyright 1979 by:
The Rev. Silas Emmett Lucas, Jr.

All rights reserved. No part of this publication may be reproduced, stored in a retrieval system, transmitted in any form, posted on to the web in any form or by any means without the prior written permission of the publisher.

Please direct all correspondence and orders to:

www.southernhistoricalpress.com
or
SOUTHERN HISTORICAL PRESS, Inc.
PO BOX 1267
Greenville, SC   29601
southernhistoricalpress@gmail.com

ISBN #0-89308-062-4

Printed in the United States of America

Northumberland County Orders

Court Orders 21 Aug. 1678

Page 1

Present: Lt. Col. Sam Smyth, Capt. Peter Knight, Mr. William Presly, Maj. Thomas Brereton, Capt. John Mottrom, Justices.

Last Will of William Showters proved by the oaths of James Johnson and Hugh Harris.

Mr. Matthews Present.

Roger Onsale freed from Levy.

Graves Garrett sonn of Thomas Garrett, dec'd., bound to Clement Aldridge.

Last Will of Hannah Bridgeman proved by the oaths of Mr. John Haynie and James Nepper.

George Hamilton who marryed Elizabeth the servant of Hannah Bridgeman entered a caviate vs. her.

Dorothy Cotanceau ye Attorney of Jacob Cotanceau sued by Sam. Typton.

Page 2

Commission of Administration to Mrs. Mary Thomas on the estate of her dec'd husband Mr. William Thomas. Mr. William Downing, Senior, Samuel Goch, Mr. Edward Coles and Thomas Webb to appraise Estate of Mr. William Thomas. Edward Sanders chose his Mother Mrs. Mary Thomas guardian. Ebenezer Sanders to be possessed with his land.

Petition of Mrs. Joane Garlington Relict of Mr. Xpher Garlington for her thirds and for dividing Estate between said Joane and the children of the said Garlington.

George Wale who married Mary the Daughter of Mr. Robert Jones, dec'd, and Estate of Mr. Jones to be divided and portion to George Wale in right of his wife by the Last Will of his wife's father.

Page 3

Thomas mould freed from Levy. James Jones freed from Levy.

Mr. John Harris to survey his land.

Page 4

Cert. to William Sheares for 600 acres of land, trans. of 12 persons: Katherine Cadany, Samuel Wills, Peter Richards, Symon Walker, Walton Dassey, Thomas Dukes, Robert Michael, William Cask, John Cout, Elizabeth Thomas and Edward Smyth.

Page 5

Adam Yarrett in behalf of Rachell his wife admx. of Augustine Rhodes, dec'd vs. Edward Barnes referred.

George Hutton who marryed the Relict of Henry Lynton vs. Anthony Lynton for land of his son Henry Lynton.

Court Oct. 6, 1678

Present: Col. St. Leger Codd, Mr. Wm. Presly, Capt. Peter Knight, Mr. Peter Presly, Mr. Nicholas Owen, Mr. Thomas Matthews, Capt. John Mottrom, Justices.

Northumberland County Orders

Page 6

Mrs. Mary Thomas Security for Com. of Adm. on her husband's Estate, Mr. William Thomas. Mr. William Downing and Mr. Christopher Neale bound with Mrs. Thomas. Samuel Mahen and William Flowers to App. Estate of Mr. William Thomas.

Whereas Mr. James Gaylord has informed the Court that the Honorable ye Secretary is dead, and whereas Mr. Thomas Hobson ye Clerke of this Court had commission for his place from the dec'd Secretary, he is to continue in it.

Samuel Nicholls freed from Levy.

Com. of Adm. to Sarah Lee the Widdow of John Lee, dec'd, on her husband's Estate. Mr. William Downing, Senior, Mr. William Downing, Junior, John Robinson and John Hudnall to App. Estate of John Lee, decd.

Com. of Adm. to John Atkins on Estate of Will Perriman.

Page 7 (none)

Page 8

William Walker having accidentally killed Daniell Crosby and said Walker freed, but he to pay costs.

Court 17 Oct. 1678

Present: Capt. Peter Knight, Mr. William Presly, Maj. Thomas Brereton, Mr. Nicholas Owen and Mr. Thos. Matthews.

Page 9

Mr. John Waugh vs. Dominic Rice for defamation.

Page 10

Whereas William fflower ffeofer in Tenet for the children of Widdow Sanders (dec'd) vs. the Estate of Mr. William Thomas, dec'd.

Mr. Edward ffeilding vs. John Oldham, he not appearing, judgement to Mr. ffeilding vs. the Sheriff.

Page 11

Mrs. Rebecca Travers adm. of Col. William Travers vs. Adam Booth.

Court 20 Nov. 1678

Page 12

Present: Capt. Peter Knight, Mr. Wm. Presly, Mr. Peter Presly, Maj. Tho. Brereton, Mr. Phillip Shapleigh, Justices.

Mr. Edward Feilding vs. John Oldham.

Page 13

Com. of Adm. to Patience Howard on the Estate of Thomas Howard her (Dec'd) .... (Note: As it is in the text.)

Mr. John Harris who married Grace ye Relict of Mr. Thomas Hopkins, decd and Maj. Thomas Brereton and Mr. Phillip Shapleigh to App. Estate of sd. Hopkins.

Court 21 Nov. 1678

Northumberland County Orders

Page 14

Present: Capt. Peter Knight, Mr. Wm. Presly, Maj. Tho. Brereton and Mr. Thomas Matthew, Justices.

Page 15

Cert. to John Harris for 700 acres, trans. of 14 persons: John Harris, Isaac Hudson, William Briffin, Elizabeth Wright, Ann Paine, John Mordey, Gennett Taylor, Elizabeth Murrow, Alice Grant, John Hill, Samuel Oakeley, Alexander Lloyd and Luy Howard.

Page 16

Ann Alexander vs. Estate of John Williams.

Page 17 (none)

Court 15 Jan. 1678/9

Page 18

Present: Col. St. Leger Codd, Capt. Peter Knight, Maj. Thomas Brereton, and Mr. Phillip Shapleigh, Justices.

Capt. John Mottrom, Mr. Xpher Neale and Mr. Richard Kenner to divide Estate of William Cotanceau, dec'd, between Katherine Cotanceau Exx. of William Cotanceau and Jacob Cotanceau son.

Mr. Edward Coles in right of Elinor his wife the Relict of Thomas Dorrell, dec'd. Mrs. Edward Coles with William Wildey and Thomas Hobson, bond for adm. Mr. Phillip Shapleigh, Mr. William Tigner and Thomas Webb and James Austin app. Estate of Thomas Dorrell, dec'd.

Page 19

Thomas Adams vs. Estate of William Adams.

Page 20 (none)

Court 19 ffeb. 1678/9

Page 21

John Higgins who married the Relict of James Pope has impaired the Estate of the Children of the sd. Pope, and Higgins to appear in the next court.

Tho. Robinson and Richard Hales runaways from the Province of Maryland are to be returned to Maryland.

Page 22 (none)

Page 23

Mr. Philip Bish of Bristoll Merch't vs. Lt. Col. Samuel Smyth.

Com. of Adm. to Elizabeth Typton ye Relict of Mr. Joseph Typton on his Estate. Elizabeth Typton, John Hughlett, Senior, William Downing, Senior their bond.

Edwin Conway to survey his land.

Page 24

Mr. Ellin Howson att. of Mr. Williamson Howson vs. Mr. James Gayland.

Northumberland County Orders

Page 24 (cont'd)

Elizabeth Heard relict of Walter Heard vs. Estate of Thomas Howard.

Page 25 (none)

Page 26

Thomas Smyth one of the orphans of Richard Smyth, dec'd. chose his brother William Smyth guardian.

Page 27

Caviate of Lt. Col. Samuel Smyth let noe will be proved or adm. granted on Estate of Samuell Elliott, Cooper dec'd until ye sd. Col. be called.

Court 19 March 1678/9

Page 28

Present: Col. St. Leger Codd, Lt. Col. Sam Smyth, Mr. Wm. Presly, Maj. Tho. Brereton, Mr. Nich. Owen and Mr. Edward ffeilding, Justices.

Page 29

Cert. to John Downing for 100 acres, trans. of Charles Blackwell and Margaret Harley.

Page 30

Adm. to Elizabeth Dennis ye Relict of John Dennis on his Estate. Elizabeth Dennis, Mr. Bartholomew Dameron, bond for Estate. Mr. George Dameron, Mr. Xpher Garlington, Mr. John Pinkard and Mr. Thomas Waddy to app. Estate.

Page 31

William Moy freed from Levy.

Page 32

ffra. Hunter vs. Anthony Steptoe who marryed with the Relict of Tho. Howard, dec'd.

William Bledsoe and William Hobson vs. Mr. Henry Burdett.

Cert. to Mr. Xpher Neale, 1200 acres, trans. of 24 persons: Tho. Haberfeild, Jno. Hutton, Luke Mannon, Peter Blackley, Joan ffrancis, Joan Sanders, Nich. McGennis, John Itrey, Ann Robinson, will and Diane, negroes, Stephen Sallows, James Jersey, George Pedley, Elizabeth Hawkins, Ann Brooke, Thomas and Henry and Robert Saddler, ffran. Discoll, John Powell, Elizabeth Musgrane and mingo a Negro.

Court 21 May 1679

Page. 33

Constables: Richard Bradley for Matapony, Mr. Daniel Neale for Newmans Neck, Thomas Harwood for Capitt's Creek and John Downing for ffairfields.

Cert. to Dennis Carty, 350 acres., trans of 7: Dennis Carty, Jno. Woolard, Tag. Adamough, Tho. Oldoell, Margaret May, Mary Olliver and Gilbert Osford.

------ English Relict of John English P/A (Power of Attorney) to Rich. Rice.

Northumberland County Orders

Page 34

Col. Samuel Smyth adm. of Estate of Samuel Elliott vs. Katherine Ingram, who has a mare in her possession belonging to Elliott's Estate. Thomas Winter and Katherine Ingram vs. Elliott's Estate.

John Parker freed from Levy.

William Perciffold sued by Mr. George fflower.

Page 35

Upon petition of Col. Samuel Smyth who married Joane the Relict and admx. of Christopher Garlington, dec'd, a quietus est is granted from the decd's Estate.

Page 36

Lt. Col. Smyth sworn High Sheriff.

Court 7 June 1679

Page 37

Present: Capt. Peter Knight, Mr. William Presly, Capt. John Mottrom, Mr. Nicholas Owen, Maj. Thomas Brereton, Capt. Leod. Howson, Mr. Thomas Matthew and Mr. Phillip Shapleigh, Justices.

John Taylor freed from Levy.

Sworne Justices: Capt. Xpher Neale, Mr. Rich. Kenner, Capt. William Downing.

John Kyrke constable for Southside of Great Wicocomoco in the place of Edward White.

(Note: the following take the rest of pages 37 and all of page 38; They are given in lists with tithables totaling 48, except for one list of 16; THESE ARE NOT INCLUDED IN THE INDEX AT THE END OF THE BOOK.)

Lyst of Tythables

Thomas Adams, Edward Algood, William Allen, Maj. Isaac Allerton, Telif Alverson, John Atkins, James Austen, Ja. Babury, Thomas Banks, Edward Barnes, Thomas Barnes, William Barry, Edmund Basey, John Bayles, William Beane, Daniel Beathan, Jas Bee, Edward Bennett, William Bersham, John Bird, George Bledsoe, William Blundell, John Boaz, Henry Boggins, ffran. Boon, Adam Booth, John Bower, ffran. Bowsley, Richard Bradley, Thomas Brewer, John Bridgeman, Clement Bridger, Mr. Broardfold, John Browne, Jno. Bryant, Robert Byerly, John Bysick, William Cammell, Walter Carter, John Champion, Samuel Churchill, Thomas Clarke, ----- Claughton, John Claughton, John Clowes, John Coan, John Cockerall, Col. St. Leger Codd, William Coppidge, John Corbell, William Cornish, George Courtnell, John Courtney, Goerge Courthouse, Jacob Coutanceau, Mr. John Coutanceau, Richard Cox, John Craford, James Creen, George Crosby, William Cummings, Bartholomew Dameron, George Dameron, George Dawkins, Henry Dawson, William Dawson, Widdow Dennis, John Downing, William Downing, Jr., Phil Drake, Walter Dunn, John Edwards, Mr. Eustas, Phil Evans, Thomas Evans, George Everard, Dennis Eyes, William Eyes, Mr. John Farnefold, Thomas ffearne, Mr. Edward ffielding, Richard fflynt, Henry ffranklin, John Freeman, Christopher Garlington, William Garner, Henry Gaskins, Josias Gaskins, Ezekiel Genesis, Thomas Gilbert, Thomas Gill, Samuel Goch, Walter Grady, John Graham, Jno. Greensted, Col. Samuel Griffin, James Hadwell, Thomas Hall, John Hallum, Hugh Harris, Mr. John Harris, Gilbert Harrold, Josias Harrison, William Hartland, Thomas Harwood, Mr. John Haynie, Richard Haynie, William Hayward, Thomas Hickman, Thomas High, James Hill, William Hill, Robt. Hobbs,

Northumberland County Orders

List of Tithables, cont'd:

Thomas Hobson twice, Thomas Hopper, Will Howard, John Howell, Mr. Leod. Howson, Henry Hudnall, John Hudnall, John Hughlett, John Hull, Richard Hull, Henry Hurst, George Hutton, Katherine Ingram, Dr. Isarian, Walter Jenkin, Widdow Jones, Richard Jones, William Jones, Abraham Joyce, William Keen, Richard Kenner twice, Edward Kerby, Thomas Kesterton, Capt. Peter Knight, John Knott, Christopher Kyrk, Richard Lamprey, Nicholas Lancaster, Clement Lattimore, Bartholomew Leasure, Mr. Han. Lee, Richard Lewis, ffran. Little, Andrew Lovershard, Richard Lugg, Richard Lunsford, John Lynn, Anthony Lynton, Samuel Mahen, Thomas Mallard, Thomas Matthew twice, Alexander Mattraine, Peter Maxwell, Henry Mayes, Henry Medcalfe, Thomas Miller, John Mitchell, James Moon, Anthony Morris, Capt. John Mottrom, ----- Muttom, Mr. Christopher Neale, Mr. Daniell Neale, Mr. Nelms, James Nipper, John Nichols twice, Ph. Norgate, Mr. Richard Nutt, William Nutt, -----Offoulks, John Oldham, Robert Oldig, Thomas Opye, Mr. Nicholas Owen, John Paine, John Palmer, Joseph Palmer, Azritam Parker, John Parker, Through Good Pate, Charles Paule, Dr. Pemberton, Thomas Perryn, Geo. Pickens, John Pinkard, James Plercond, John Powell, Mr. Peter Presly, Mr. William Presly, Nen. Proverb, John Read, John Reason, Dominic Rice, John Roach, John Robson, Capt. John Rogers, John Rogers, William Rogers, Anthony Roper, Henry Ross, John Rotherum, Richard Rout, John Royston, John Samson, Robert Seth, Phillip Shapleigh, William Sheares, Robert Sheppard, Thomas Shirley, Thomas Short, Thomas Simons, Walter Sims, Richard Smyth, Lt. Col. Sam. Smyth, William Smyth, John Southerly, John Stanley, Ralph Stephens, Hugh Steptoe, John Swaine, John Symons, James Taylor, John Taylor, Mr. John Taylor, William Taylor, Mrs. Mary Hudnall, John Throppe, Thomas Thorp, Mr. William Tignor, Richard Thomson, Thomas Towers, Cloud Tullos, Elizabeth Typton, Richard Underwood, ffran. Vsllond, Ralph Waddington, Mr. John Waddy, Thomas Waddy, William Walker, Mr. John Warner, John Waters, Mrs. Watts, Widdow Way, John Webb, Thomas Webb, William Web, Richard Wells, Stephen Wells, Edward White, Joseph White, William Wildey, Erasmus Wilkes, Edward Williams, Howell, Williams, Richard Williams, Mr. Thomas Williams, Robert Wilson, Thomas Winter, John Wood, John Wornam, William Wrotton, Adam Yarrett.

Court 10 June 1679

Page 39

William Rogers sworne Constable.

Page 40

Cert. to John Robyson for 100 acres, trans. of Ashmelew Jewell and Annie Robinson.

The Division of Constables given.

Page 41

George Bledsoe vs. John Harris, John Waddy and Thomas Ingram.

Adam Booth a constable for Mattapony.

Court 20 Aug. 1679

Thomas Harding Son of Thomas Harding, dec'd, that his Mother Ann Harding might be his guardian.

Page 42

Cert. to Thomas Hobson, 1200 Acres, trans. of 24 persons: Thomas Rowland, William Tharte, Richard Caule, William Betts, Ellias Merritt, John Butler, Elizabeth Salmon, Elizabeth Doggett, Margaret Leypott, Samuel Limock, Hugh Broughton, Allice Argile, Alexander Camell, Phillip Pitts, Ma-

Northumberland County Orders

Page 42 cont'd:

ry Evans, Hugh Cannon, Peter Platt, Mary Pledjoel, Joseph Holt, ffran. Wares, Thomas Joanes, William Clay, Mary Shortman and Henry Samlers.

ffrances Adams Quietus est as ye admx. of William Adams, her dec'd husband.

Page 43

William Cornish freed from Levy.

Christopher Garlington is appointed Constable in the room of Mr. Thomas Winter.

Page 44

20 Aug. 1679: memorandum that Edy Way the Relict of Richard Way, dec'd and adm. to her on his Estate.

Court 15 Oct. 1679

Page 45

Cert. to Sam. Mahen, 250 acres, trans. of John Dodd, Thomas Howard, James Gilbert, James Tosse and ----- Bloomfield.

Page 46 (none)

Page 47

Surveyers of the Highways: George Hamilton, and John Hallum; Surveyers in the room of Adam Yarrett and James Nipper.

Court 22 Oct. 1679

Present: Col. St. Leger Codd, Mr. William Presly, Maj. Thomas Brereton, Mr. Nicholas Owen, Capt. John Haynie, Mr. Peter Presley, Capt. John Mottrom, Mr. Thomas Matthew, Mr. William Downing, Mr. Christopher Neale, Justices.

Pages 49 and 50 (none)

Court 19 Nov. 1679

Page 51

Anne Smyth Daughter to Richard Smyth, dec'd, chose Richard Lugg guardian.

Court 3 Dec. 1679

Petition of Joane Joanes Relict of Hugh Jones, dec'd, Com. of Adm. William Smyth and Thomas Gill, bond on it. Thomas Webb, William Downing, Junior, John Downing and William Palind app. Estate.

Order to build a Court House at Coane.

Page 52 (none)

Court 21 Jan. 1679/80

Page 53

Com. of Adm. to Edy Way on Estate of dec'd Husband Richard Way. She, John Symons and William Barry bond for it. Edward Olds, Thomas Webb,

Northumberland County Orders

Page 53 cont'd:

William Tignor and John Corbell App. Estate.

Page 54

Com. of Adm. to Richard Cox on Estate of George Knight, dec'd. He, Thomas Mathhew and Richard Flynt, bond on it. William Bowsham, Thomas Adams and William Lawson, App. Estate.

John Taylor, Henry Mayse, Josias Gascoyne, Henry Gascoyne in behalf of the orphans of Thomas Gascoyne, dec'd, vs. John Pinkard who marryed ye Relict of Thomas Gascoyne, and being since dead, the five children of Thomas Gascoyne mentioned, and the 5 children be delivered to Taylor, Mayse, Josias and Henry Gascoyne.

Cert. to Richard Rice for 300 acres, trans. of 6 persons: Daniel Hay, John Butler, John Lowes, Roger Hayer, Ann Hay, and Elizabeth Lowell.

Petition of George Barrett, shipp Master of the good Ship Mary of Carolina, by Mr. Edward Middleton, Mr. John ffowell, owners, from the sd. port of Carolina to Va. and to Carolina again. A leak in the vessell & runaway help rendered him helpless to buy provisions, or to hire men, only Mr. John Pinkard said I should lack for nothing. Petition for wages and costs. Court opinion was that this Business was out of their jurisdiction, being no Estate to satisfy wages.

Page 55 (none)

Court 18 Feb. 1679/80

Page 56

Estate of Thomas Keen, dec'd, indebted to Mr. Jarvis Squire.

Cert. to Mr. Thomas Matthew for 3800 Acres, trans. of 76 persons: Tho. Matthews and 10 negroes from Barbadoes, Mr. Tho. Matthew from London, Mr. Tho. Matthew and 3 negroes, from New England, Robert House, John Whittington, Stephen Sallows, Xpher Byerly, Thomas Curtis, Thomas Dew, John Houghton, John Doulson, JOhn Cope, James Jonn, Mathew Neale, Daniel Knoton, Mary Cooper, Ann Cleaves, Stephen Proctor, Xpher Clarke, James Deabary, Thomas ----, Mary ----, Mary Packman, Edward Grosman, John Hendy, Edward Watts, Matt. Peterson, John Rumly, Mary Downes, Thomas Morris, Lan. ffulbrook, Thomas Holley, JOhn Turrane, William Wiggan, Sarah Statham, Susanna Ofild, John Bamford, Patrick Maly, Robert Mundy, William Parker, Peter de Jerry, Robert Dunn, Anthony Pan, William Sage, Miles Crawley, Thomas Owen, George Lyle, Stephen Walton, Hawett Ignatius, Thomas Kea, Joseph Beeton, David Hughes, Oliver and Mary ----, Phil Welsh, Arthur Rickett, Daniel Shea, Turner ----, James Olesander, Michael Dorsmundy, Mary Covernough, Henry Burk, Mary ----, Samuel Cnibley Mr. Mathew had cert. for 24 of these rights March 18, 1679/80.

Page 57

Sarah Moore who has consent of Walter Moore her ffather bound to Tho. Hobson until 17 years old.

Page 58

Ezekiel Genesis guardian to Peter Byram.

Page 59

Thomas Webb vs. Estate of Thomas Coppage.

Mr. George Hosier P/A from James Twyford of Citty of Bristoll, Merch't petitions in behalf of sd. Twyford attachment in behalf of Joseph Typton,

Northumberland County Orders

Page 59 cont'd:

dec'd, who was impowered by sd.Twyford to make sale. Mr. Hobson to meet at house of Maj. Tho. Brereton to audit the accounts between George Hosier, Att. of Twyford and Elizabeth Typton, Relict and admx. of Joseph Typton.

Page 60

Richard Lugg stabbed William Smyth and Lugg to pay Doctor's charges.

Maj. Brereton, Adm. of Estate of George Dunn, dec'd, vs. Mr. James Austen.

Court 17 Mar. 1679/80

Page 61

Alexander English vs. Estate of Michaell Bayley.

Page 62

Whereas Mary Webb, servant to Thomas Coppage, tobacco due to Thomas Webb from ye sd. Coppage. Court needs more evidence.

Whereas Mary Peannot now being free and four men to judge the time of the servant's service and serve Webb for his debt. Henry Mayse, Sam. Goch, William Tignor and James Austen App. the Servant to serve saide Webb.

Maj. Brereton Att. of John Boy vs. George Barratt who marryed Isabel Pettigrew, security for John Salisbury to Boy.

Page 63 (none)

Court 29 March 1680

Page 64

Dr. William Harcum vs. Edyth Way, Relict of Richard Way.

Court 14 April 1680

Provisions to be carried to the garrison in Potomac.

Cert. to John Hughlett for 300 acres, trans. of 12 persons: John Williams, John Porkey, Sarah Huch, John Church, Richard Banister, James Gording, Edward Ellis. Assigned to William Coppedge.

Page 65 (none)

Court 19 May 1680

Page 66

Com. of Adm. to Anne Short on Estate of Thomas Short, her dec'd husband. She, William Sheares and John Knott, bond on it. James Johnson, Anthony Lynton, William Hill and George Hutton app. Estate.

Thomas Gaskeyne chose Josias Gaskeyne guardian.

John Man vs. Estate of John Fowell.

Constables: Phil Norgate for Matapony, Tho. Miller for Cherry poynt, Thomas Towers for Chitacon, John Southerland for upper parts of Fayrefield parish, John Warner for Newman"s Neck, Wm. Smyth Junior for lower part of ffayrefield, William Barry for Southside of Gr. Wicocomoco, and

Northumberland County Orders

Page 66 cont'd:

Mr. William Jones for lower part of County.

Page 67

    Capt. Leonard Howson sworne Sheriff.

    Maj. Richar Lee, Esq. and Mrs. Dor. Lawrence Ye Relict of Capt. Edm. Lyster referred to next Court.

Page 68

    John Webb vs. John Hughlett tried by Jury: Robert Barklett, servant to John Webb and John Church, servant to John Hughlett, alleged that Barklett was not servant to John Webb and Jury to decide moyety of what plank was sawyed by Robert Barklett and Jury resolved that Robert Barklett is servant to John Webb. Judgement: order Hughlett to deliver to Webb one moyety or half part of what Planck was sawyed by their servant and clothes for Barklett and other costs.

    Cert. to Phil Evans, 350 acres, trans. of 7 persons: Hannah MacGuire, Owen Maley, Prissilla, Dam. Flamagon, Mary Whitehead, William Treskale, Mos. Hart.

    Com. of Adm. to Joane Rogers on Estate of her dec'd Husband John Rogers. She and William Rogers bond on it. William Klyne, Henry Boggas, Phil Poggas and William Webb App. Estate.

Page 69

    Cert. to Thomas Waddy for 300 acres, trans. of 6 persons: Elizabeth Walters, William Green, Mary Smyth, Amb. Tanner, Jeremiah Gibson, and Margery Rowley.

Court 21 July 1680

Page 70

    Last Will of Capt. John Rogers proved by oaths of Dan. McGlaughlin & Thomas Eycock.

Page 71

    Edward Coles Guardian to Thomas Hayes Junior, he being husband to ye sd. Child's Grandmother. Whereas Thomas Hayes Sen'r by last will devised to Aug. Knotten (who marryed ye Relict of ye sd. Hayes) by several deeds of gift made over to Thomas Hayes Jun'r one mare, one mare ffilly, 2 cows, furniture, chest, table, of which cattle and goods Knotton is gott devised, and hath departed this county; attachment granted Edward Coles Guardian of sd. Thomas Hayes Jr.

Page 72 (none)

Page 73

    Towne for this County to be laid out, to be on Chicacoan River behind Maj. John Mottrom's Orchard to ye Creek it divides ye land from ye land of Mr. John Coutanceau and so up ye Creek.

Court 16 Aug. 1680

None

Court 15 Sep'br 1680

Page 74

    Ann Short gave Inventory of her dec'd Husband's Estate, having 5 small children and from Est. for clothing of children.

Northumberland County Orders

Page 75

Mr. William ffox sonne to Capt. David ffox, dec'd, chose his brother Capt. David ffox to be his guardian and Col. St. Leger Codd to have possession of Estate of sd. William ffox, to desist from sowing seed on the said land and Col. St. Leger Codd to have timely notice.

Page 76

Thomas Evans made over all his Estate to John Harris for debt and he is departed this colony and Harris to possess Estate.

Page 77 (none)

Court 20 Oct. 1680

Page 78

No. Adm. nor will to be proved on Estate of Robert Jeffery until Mr. Kenner be called. Mr. Kenner to secure the Estate of Robert Jeffery. Bond of Richard Kenner and Phillip Shapleigh.

Court 17 Nov. 1680

Page 79

Richard Nutt sonne to Capt. William Nutt chose Mr. Richard Nutt for his guardian.

Page 80 (none)

Page 81

Com. of Adm. to Mrs. Elizabeth Morgan on Estate of Mr. Charles Morgan her dec'd husband. Capt. Leonard Howson and Capt. John Haynie bond on it

Court 15 Dec. 1680

Page 82

Richard Craton orphant of Richard Caton chose Dennis Eyes guardian.

Court 2 Mar. 1680/1

Page 83-84

Cuthbert Span, Petitions that the Estate by a deed of guift given unto his Brother Richard, and him (his Brother Richard being dead) might be divided and he to live on his plantation.

Page 85

Cert. to Thomas Waddy, 300 acres, trans. of 6 persons: Amos Jeffard, John Raney, Peter Morning, Anne Smythgill, Adam Hawker and Peter Damison.

Dep. of Thomas Staney, aged 30, in the cause of Mr. Teaborne vs. Alex. Brodie. Dep. of William Keyne, aged 38, same.

Pages 86-89 (none)

Court 20 April 1681

Page 90

Last Will of John Ashton proved by Mr. Nicholas Owen and William Burdett.

Northumberland County Orders

Page 91 (none)

Page 92

Robert Hunter kept unseeming company with Anne Goddart wife of Thomas Goddart, custody of Sheriff.

Henry ffranklin Constable in place of John Southerland, in the parish of Gr. Wicocomoco.

Court 21 April 1681

Page 93

John Lewis who married ffrances the daughter of John Mottoone, dec'd. The sd. J. M. by last will bequethed legacies to the rest of the children and nothing to his Lewis' said wife. Ordered that Thomas Williams, Samuel Goch, Ezekiel Genesis and Clement Lattimer make Inquiry into the Estate, giving the said ffrances at her marriage, by her said ffather, and they make equal portions of the rest of his daughters, out of the whole estate, and put an end to differences.

Capt. Thomas Smith sued by Richard Thompson for entertaining John Stone Chirurgeon late of the said Capt. Smith his ship six weeks.

Court 15 June 1681

Page 94

N.C. Will of Erasmus Whithers by William Jones and Gervase Hatfield. Dep. of Will Chapman, aged 40, that Erasmus Whithers bequethed all his estate to ffrances his wife, and his ffour children and Erasmus Whithers his sonn a gold seale Ring and made 21 Nov. last and sworne before Mr. Peter Knight Dec. 29, 1680. Dep. of Hatfield and William Jones the same.

Page 95

Thomas fferne to be Constable for Lower points of Potomac in the place of William Jones. George Courtness in place of Thomas Miller for Cherry point Neck. Thomas Harmond in place of John Warner for Newman's Neck. John Bayles in place of William Smith for lower points of Potomac and the Northside of Gr. Wicocomoco. William Hill in place of Phill. Norgate for Matapony.

Edward Jones, aged, freed from Levy. Robert Mahallam, impotent, freed from Levy.

Page 96.

Last Will of Mr. William Wildey oroved by Owen Bradley and Mr. James Gaylord.

Mr. Thomas Matthew sworne High Sheriff.

Page 97

Jane Wildey exx. of Mr. William Wildey vs. Estate of Charles Morgan.

Court 16 June 1681

Page 98

William Sheares (who marryed the Relict of John Tingey) vs. Daniell Bearchamp, the Tenant of William Thornbury, was seated within the bounds of John Tingey his pattent.

Mrs. Mary Harris vs. Ezekiel Genesis.

Northumberland County Orders

Page 99

Ann Gaylord Adm. of Mr. James Gaylord vs. George Bledsoe.

Court 17 Aug. 1681

William Leach orphan and noe Estate, bound to Clement Aldridge.

Cert. to William and Charles Betts, 400 acres, trans. of 8 persons: Thomas Trip, James Dumlay, Edward ffeild, Mary Williams, Sarah Anderson, Elisha Howell, Thomas Barber, Lydia -----.

Page 100

William Thornbury in behalfe of the heire of Mr. Thomas Robinson to enjoy the 1000 acres, held in pattent 4 July 1664, according to the bounds of the said pattent and of Thomas Broughton of 20 acres and seated by Mr. John Tingey, as appears by a deed, April 1664.

Page 101

Com. of Adm. with will annexed to Mrs. ffrances Withers on Estate of her deceased Husband Erasmus Withers.

Court 18 Aug. 1681

Page 102

Edward Barnes in behalfe of Mary his wife vs. Richard Cox referred to next Court.

Page 103

George Crosly vs. Estate of Hugh Sheldon.

John Harris vs. Estate of James Glynne.

Court 19 Oct. 1681

Page 104

Mr. Joseph Lewis vs. James Moor.

Page 105

Deborah Adams to serve Anthony Morris and his wife.

Cert. to Mrs. Jane Wildey, 250 acres, trans. of 5 persons: Thomas Spilman, Mary Spilman, Benjamin Ricketts, John Cuning, Owen MacGoam.

John Downing guardian to John Cockrell son of Andrew Cockrell, dec'd.

Page 106

Edward Barnes and Mary his wife vs. Richard Cox and sd. Cox detained a child of sd. Mary and petitions Court to deliver sd. child to them. Sd. Mary Mother of ye sd. child did 6 weeks to 2 months after the death of ye father send to sd. Cox to demand the child of him, but was denyed ye delivery of him and ordered child to Edward Barnes.

Thomas Waughop vs. Estate of Thomas Barker, an attachment.

Pages 107-109 (none)

Court 2 Nov. 1681

Page 110 (none)

Northumberland County Orders

Court 21 Dec. 1681

Page 111

Mrs. Elizabeth Hull Admx. of Anthony Lynton obtained judgement of Rappa. County Court dated 4 Sept. 1678 vs Lt. Col. Sam. Griffin, adm. of Mr. Henry Ashton.

Pages 112-113 (none)

Court Dec. 22.....

Page 114

Page 115

Edward Tarleton vs. James Blinco.

Dennis Eyes guardian of Richard Eaton.

Elizabeth Brittaine to take the Estate of ffrances Brittaine, ye orphant of ffrancis Brittaine, dec'd.

Page 116 (none)

Page 117

Estate of Mr. Richard Flynt, dec'd to be audited.

Court 18 Jan. 1681/2

Jane Elinor Mother to John Matthew doth bind her sd. son to Henry Dawson for 13 years.

Elizabeth Clark, Mother to ffran. Brittain, doth bind her sd. daughter to Rachell ye wife of Adam Yarrett until 17.

Page 118

Anne Cammell wife of William Cammell abused Anne wife of John Bryant, saying she was a whore and Sheriff to take her to his custody.

Page 119

William Clark, who maryed ye Relict of ffrancis Brittaine, to give security for Brittaine's Estate. Dennis Carter security for William Clark.

James Jones vs. Estate of Alexander Pattison.

Page 120

Madam Elizabeth Hull vs. Henry Boggas adm. of Estate of George Knott.

Thomas Hughlett to be keeper of the prison.

Court 15 ffeb. 1681/2

Sam Mahem vs. William Coppage; whereas Rog. Nusam lays claym to ye land in dispute between sd. Mahem and Coppage; by virtue of a pattent granted to William Nusam and William Totton, 18 Sept. 1665.

Page 121

Elizabeth wife of Azariam Parker vs. Mr. Edward Husband.

Mr. Edward Tarleton vs. Mr. James Blinco, who marryed ye Relict of Thomas Keyne.

Northumberland County Orders

Pages 122-127 (none)

Court 17 May 1682

Page 128

Constables: Henry Gascoyne for Upper Wicocomoco Parish, Dennis Conway for upper fayrefield parish, Thomas Barnes for Newman's Neck, John Claughton for Matapony, Fran. Little for Cherry Point.

David Williams Sonne to Roger Williams about aged 7, with consent of his ffather bound to John Wornam until 20.

Mr. William Rogers sworn Justice of Peace and High Sheriff.

Last Will of William Garner proved by Edward Williams and Thomas Timmons.

Charles Jackson, poor and lame, freed from Levy; Rowland Bushell, poor and impotent, freed from Levy.

Page 129

Anthony Manby servant to Mr. Thomas Opye, aged 14 years.

Page 130

Dorothy Meredith, Mother to Abr. Byram, by guift dated 11 July 1670 and by order of Wicocomoco vestry 21 Oct. 1671 and John Champion who marryed ye sd. Dorothy indebted to Abr. Byram. John Champion appeals to next General Court.

Page 131 (none)

Page 132

John Grinstone, aged and impotent, freed from Levy.

Page 133

Col. Thomas Brereton vs. Estate of Owen Gradie.

Page 134

Dennis Eyes guardian to Richard Eaton Jr. did in Court show ye will of Richard Eaton Sr., his dec'd father, a yearling steer, 2 steers of 3 yrs., one payre of blankett, one Iron pott of one gallon, one iron pot of 5 gallon, one frying pan, five wedges, one froc'a (?), one grindstone, one Chayr-table, half ye pewter, one ticking, 2 barrows 2 yrs. old; William Clark who maryed the Admx. of sd. Brittaine forthwith to deliver.

Court 19 July 1682

Page 135

James Waddy Constable for lower part of County.

Page 136

Last Will of George Courtnall proved by Nicholas Owen and ffran. Bryery.

Richard Nelms vs. Mr. George Knight.

Page 137 (none)

Page 138 (see following page)

15

Northumberland County Orders

Page 138

    Cert. to John Walters, 350 Acres, trans. of 7 persons: John Walters, Hester Walters, Phoebe Walters, Diana Walters, Mary Walters, Easter Walters and John Walters.

Court 16 Aug. 1682

Page 139

    Probate to Christian Bickby, Exx. to ffrancis Bickby of the Last Will of her dec'd Husband by oaths of Howell Williams and John Topping.

Pages 140-143 (none)

Page 144

    Cert. to Thomas Winter for 1500 Acres, trans. of 30 persons: Robert Maursh, Robert Ash, John White, John Moore, Mary Godding, John Thomas, Robert Chilcock, Thomas Tap, Thomas Camplaine, John Pithard, Edmond Wheadon, Thomas Williams, Lawrence Miller, John Dabbs, John Lee, Robert Barry, Richard Cook, John Tipto, Ann Lee, James Edney, William Wood, John Varley, Xpher Varley, Jun. and James Varley.

Court 18 Oct. 1682

Page 145

    Abraham Shears who maryed Elizabeth ye daughter of Thomas Brewer prayed Judgement to possess ye land of George Courtmell Sen. producing ye Last Will and Testament of ye sd. George. Wherein ye sd George did devise unto his sonne George all ye lands he should be seyzed of and his sonne should fayle of showing lawful issue, then he did devise ye sd. lands unto ye sd. Elizabeth. Appealed to George Courtnell Jun. to be possessed according to ye intent of ye sd. Will unto which Mary, Late Widdow of ye sd. George Jun. did plead it. Ye Widdow ought to enjoy ye thirds of her dec'd Husband's lands.

    Last Will of Edward Coles, dec'd, proved by William Barry and John Nicholls. Col. Brereton, Thomas Hobson, Thomas Webb and John Worman to App. Estate.

Page 146 (none)

Page 147

    John Russell vs. John Champion who maryed Edyth Way.

Pages 148-149 (none)

Page 150

    Mr. Robert Lyndsay vs. Estate of William Webb.

Page 151 (none)

Court 8 Dec. 1682

Page 152

    N.C. Will of Rowland Bushell proved by Dav. Griffin, Math. Edwards & John Royston. Dav. Griffin aged 25 dep. that Rowland Bushell gives all his Estate to Rich. Smyth. The oaths of Math. Edwards and Jonathan Royston the same.

Page 153
    Petition of Hen. Boggas Exor. of Fran. Little, dec'd, Probate of Will

Northumberland County Orders

Page 153 cont'd:

granted by oaths of Nicholas Owen and John Julian and Robert Bryery.

Court 3 Jan. 1682/3

Page 154

Dorothy, Widdow of Anthony Morris, A Com. of Adm. on Estate of her dec'd Husband.

Henry De Boyes, a poor orphan in ye Parish, to serve William Bashaw and he aged 12.

Court 17 Jan. 1682/3

Page 155

George Hughs, a poor orphan child, to serve George Hambleton.

Page 156

.Cert. to Leo. Howson, 500 acres, trans. of 10 persons: William Harcum, Lidia Harcum, James Harcum, Mary Harcum, Thomas Chandler, Thomas Smyth, Mary Webb, Will Williams and Abigail Harcum.

Page 157 (none)

Court 18 Jan. 1682/3

Page 158 (none)

Pages 159-161 (none)

Court 21 Feb. 1682/3

Page 162

Cert. to Richard Kenner, 1359 Acres, trans. of 27 persons: Th. Crosse, Dor. Hurst, Eliz. White, Jone Francis, Th. Winston, Xpher Wade, Mary Wade, Th..Newman, Robt. Tewes, Th. Thewes, Jno. Janes, Jno. Osborne, Mac. Sparhatt, Jon. Maghby, Benj. Johnson, Tho. Jones, Ann Gill, Jam. Crosse, Math. Winberry, More Moughby, Sus. Tinoth, Rowl. Oslen, Tamb. a negro, Rachell a negro.

Page 163 (none)

Page 164

John Lewis in behalfe of his wife ye Relict of George Courtnall did move the Court for judgement for a third of ye lands belonging to Courtnell and one third due him in the right of his wife, widdow of sd. Courtnall, ye other third as purchased by her sd. Husband of Phoebe ye Relict of George Courtnell Sen'r vs. Sheares.

Page 165

John Webb vs. the Estate of Mr. Sam. Jefferson.

Court 21 Mar. 1682/3

Page 166

Peter Flynt, who marryed Mary ye Relict of John Knott, dec'd, Com. of Adm. on his Estate Peter Flynt, Richard Flynt and Jam. Johnson the bond. William Bashaw, Henry Dawson, William Dawson and Jno. Oldam App. Estate.

Northumberland County Orders

Page 166 cont'd:

Petition of Elizabeth ye Relict of Phil. Evans a probate to her of the Last Will of her dec'd Husband.

Page 167 (none)

Page 168

Ezekiel Genesis, on ye behalfe of Rebecca his wife, daughter of John Shaw, dec'd, vs. Capt. John Haynie, adm. of sd. Shaw.

Pages 169-172 (none)

Page 173 (Day 22)

A deed of guift by Barbara Salisbury, now wife of Thomas Frarnce, gave to her daughter Mary now ye wife of Barth. Scriver.

Page 174 (none)

Page 175

Thomas Hickman vs. Michaell Chin ye Att. of Isaac Colton.

Henry Rider complayneth to this court yt his father in law Walt. Moor by his last will gave him his plantation; John Moor came to age, and Richard Hull, overseer, and Henry wishes to occupy his land.

Court 18 April 1685

Page 176

Probate to Thomas Williams Jun'r, ye Exor. of Thomas Williams Sen'r, dec'd of ye last Will.

Col. Brereton sworn High Sheriff and John Topping subsheriff.

Page 177

Jonathan Royston freed from Levy, aged and impotent.

Robert Bonus being poor, freed from Levy.

Page 178

William Harcum vs. Josias Long, who marryed X'tian (Christian), ye Exx of ffrancis Posakly.

Pages 179-183 (none)

Court 20 June 1683

Page 184

Constables: Henry Boggas for Cherry Poynt, Cloud Tullos for Chicacon, Richard Bradley for Metapony, Zach. Thomas for Newman's Neck, Thomas Rout for ye Upper pts. of Fayrefeild Parish and Jn'o Coles for the lower pts thereof, Xpher Bayles for Southside of Gr. Wicomaco and Jn'o Eustace for ye Lower Precincts of this County.

Petition of Hannah ye Exx. of Jno. Raskall, dec'd, probate on Last Will by oath of Thomas Jones.

Petition of Mary, Exx. of William Downing, dec'd, probate of will by oaths of William Southing and Jno. Atkins.

Northumberland County Orders

Page 184 cont'd:

Richard Burgess, poor, to be freed from Levy.

Page 185 (none)

Page 186

Widdow Elizabeth Walters freed from Levy.

Page 187

Court 18 July 1683

Page 188

Com. of Adm. to Miriam Sadler of ye Estate of Thomas Sadler, her decd Husband.

Quietus Est. on Estate of Mr. Peter Presly dispensed from this order.

Cloud Tullos, ye sonne of Cloud Tullos, being both deaf and dumb, is freed from Levy.

Pages 189-190 (none)

Page 191 (Day 19)

Henry Rider moved this Court (on ye behalf of Anne his wife, daughter of Walter Moor, dec'd, for a portion of his Estate, vs. Richard Hull,Exor; said Moor gave to his daughter Sarah, one portion and to Anne another portion, or if short to be divided equally.)

Page 192

Thomas Goldsmyth vs. Edward Fielding Adm. of Mr. Ambrose Fielding,decd.

Page 193 (none)

Court 12 Sept. 1683

Page 194

Present: Capt. Peter Knight, Mr. Peter Presly, Maj. John Mottrom, Mr. Phillip Shapleigh, Mr. Christopher Neale, Capt. John Haynie and Mr. Edw. Feilding.

Andrew Morton by will did leave his daughter Mary to Mr. Thomas W:ms, who being dead and ye child small, John Ford, who marryed ye Aunt of ye sd. child to be guardian.

Page 195

Petition of Mrs. Margaret Downing Exx. of Mr. William Downing a probate is granted on said will by oaths of Christopher Kirk and William Polundoll.

Page 196 (none)

Page 197 (none)

Page 198

Com. of Adm. with Will annexed to Mary Downing of ye Estate of her dec'd Husband, William Downing. Securities are Mary Downing, John Hughlett and Dennis Eyes. John Hughlett, Tho. Webb, Jno. Worman and John Atkins App. Est.

Northumberland County Orders

Page 198 cont'd:

Court 17 Oct. 1683

Present: Mr. Peter Knight, Maj. Jno. Mottrom, Capt. Tho. Matthew, Cpt. John Haynie, Mr. Rich. Kenner, Mr. Xpher Neale and Mr. Wm. Rogers.

Page 199

Capt. John Haynie in behalfe of Jane, ye Heyre of Anthony Morris, decd. and Mr. Cuthbert Span (in ye behalfe of his wife, Dorothy, ye Relict of Anthony) petitions for a division.

Page 200 (none)

Court 1 Nov. 1683

Page 201

Thomas Hobson Sworn High Sheriff.

Page 202

Com. of Adm. to Elizabeth Gerrard on the Estate of her Husband Samuel Gerrard, and she and James Claughton give bond. James Johnson, William Sheares and George Hutton to App. Estate.

Pages 203-204 (none)

Page 205 (Day 2)

Thomas Hobson Jun'r sworn Clerk. John Topping subsheriff.

Thomas Askley, poor, freed from Levy; also John Lawrence.

Page 206 (none)

Court 19 Dec. 1683

Page. 207

Com. of Adm. to Allice Hudnall on Estate of her dec'd Husband John Hudnall. Allice Hudnall and John Downing sign the bond. Mr. Richard Nutt, John Dunaway, George Dawkins and Roger Hambleton to App. Estate.

Pages 208-209 (none)

Court 16 Jan. 1683/4

Page 210

Com. of Adm. to Alice Peryne on Estate of her dec'd Husband Thomas Peryne. She, James Claughton and George Hudson give bond.

Page 211

Petition of Mr. Ebenezer Sanders and Mr. Edward Sanders, ye sons of Mrs. Mary Thomas, dec'd, Com. of Adm. They, Thomas Hobson, Thomas Webb, John Cockrell and John Symmons.

A Com. of Adm. to Josial Pitts, who maryed Rebecca, daughter of Mr. Wm. Thomas, dec'd, on ye Estate of sd. Thomas. Joseph Pitts, James Claughton, and James Johnson give bond.

Page 212

Cert. to John Downing, 350 acres, trans of 7 persons: Jer. Harris,

Northumberland County Orders

Page 212 cont'd:

John Farigon, Henry Clarles, Dor. Howard and Shoo Sland.

Pages 213-214

Page 215 (Day 17)

John Hughlett Jun'r who maryed Mary ye Relict of William Downing indebted to William Bonoway.

Page 216

Mr. John Hughlett Sen'r and John Palmer to App. Estate of George Hughes, now in the hands of George Hambleton.

Page 217 (none)

Court 19 Mar. 1683/4

Page 218

Mr. Peter Flynt in ye behalf of himself and B'r Thomas Flynt arrested Mr. Peter Presly and Mr. Thomas Hobson sen'r, Exors. of the Last Will of Mr. Richard Flynt, dec'd, their father for an accounting.

Pages 219-226

Court April 1, 1684

Page 227

Two Daughters Mary and Jane Dukes of Isreal Orge, Mary being 10 years old and Jane, 3, to serve Peter Maxwell, and Mary his wife until 21.

Page 228   Court 4 June 1684

Thomas Hobson Sen'r sworn High Sheriff.

Constables: Thomas Ashton for Cherry Poynt Neck, Thomas Hopper for Metapony, William Smetnan for Jerico and lower precincts of Bowtracey Parish, Richard Lamprey for Newman's Neck, Josias Long for Lower pt. of Fayrefield Parish, Patrick Pollick for Upper pts. of Wocomoco Parish.

Edward Barnes and Thomas Davies, two aged, impotent and poor men free from Levy.

Petition of Alice Hudnall, Exx. of Ezekiel Genesis, dec'd, Probate on Will to her by oaths of John Hughlett and Edward White.

Anne, Relict of Samuel Goche, dec'd, a probate on the Last will by oaths of James Moor and Elinor Reynolds.

Page 229

Petition of Thomas Trip yt his wife being principall Legatee, a Probate is granted him of ye Last Will and Testament of Thomas Nelmes, decd, by oaths of Isaac Hester and Margaret Hester and James Moor.

Andrew Nonner, poor, freed from Levy.

Edward Williams vs. James Johnson, Richard Pemberton and William Howard: a tract of land formerly belonging to Robert Bradshaw and sold by Bradshaw to Edw. Williams his father and ye sd Williams to James Claughton and by Claughton to Johnson, Pemberton and Howard, under pretence of a deed, wherein ye sd Bradshaw did oblige himself to get a patent for ye

Northumberland County Orders

Page 229 cont'd:

sd. Land, in ye name of Temperance, ye Mother of ye first mentioned Edw. Williams and attradged (?) yt ye Edward Williams Sen'r ye plt's father sold ye sd. Land unto ye sd. Claughton without consent of ye sd. Temperence, ye Plt's Mother, in whom ye right of ye sd. Land laye, and land not affected by this. The suit dismissed.

Page 230

Richard Lamprey declared yt Barth. Yoomans was lately dec'd at his house leaving no known relatives; he to take Estate.

Page 231

Mr. Thomas Brereton produced the Will of Col. Thomas Brereton, dec'd. John Jenny and Peter Platt, witnessed it. Thomas Brereton to have Probate of his dec'd father's will.

Pages 232-234 (none)

20 Aug. 1684

Page 235

Petition of Thomas Trape, a Com. of Adm. to him on Estate of Thomas Nelmes als Maddox, dec'd. Bond by Mr. Richard Haynie and John Wornon.

Charles Harris petitions for license as attorney.

Page 236

Mrs. Elizabeth George, adm. of Mr. Thomas George, dec'd, vs. Thomas Barnes.

Petition of William Beane, a Probate granted on the Last Will of Wolthian Bonas, by oaths of Samuel Buckley and James Genn. The deceased by will disposed of her three children: Her sone Robert Bonas to William Beane until of age, Her Daughter Elizabeth Bonas to Mrs. Rebecca Mathew until of age, and Her Daughter Anne Bonas to Thomas Miller.

Page 237

James Moor att. of James Foules vs. Peter Bryam as marrying ye Exx. of Samuel Goch, referred to the next Court.

Page 238 (none)

Court 17 Sept. 1684

Page 239

Petition of Mary Swanson, a Probate on the Will of John Swanson, her dec'd Husband by oaths of Samuel Mahen and George Barrett. Com. of Adm. to her. Bond by Samuel Mahen and John Lunce. Mr. Xpher Garlington and Clement Lattimore App. Estate.

Pages 240-241 (none)

Page 242 (Day 19)

Ezekiel Genesis by will bequeathed to Ezekiel Hill and Partin Hudnall 5,000 lbs. Tobacco which Mr. Isaac Hester was to pay him, for a tract of land. Alice Hudnall Exx. of Ezekiel Genesis to have Hill and Hudnall to pay debts. Thomas Trip petitions that Ezek. Genesis did by will bequeath several things to Thomas Nelms als Mattocks and Tho. Nelms als Mattocks

Northumberland County Orders

Page 242 cont'd:

by will did bequeathe the greater part of his Estate to ye sd. Trip and his wife (Mother of ye sd. Thomas, dec'd.)

Page 243 (none)

Page 244

Ebenezer and Edward Sanders, Adm'rs of Mrs. Mary and Adm. of Mr. William Thomas arrested by Edward White and Ben. Cotman Husbands to Mary and Eliza daughters of sd. Mary.

Page 245 (none)

Court 19 Nov. 1684

Page 246

Petition of Nich. Parris, a Probate on the Will of Elinor Walters, decd to him by the oaths of James Blackerby and Thomas Berry.

Pages 247-250 (none)

Page 251

10 Dec. last John Robinson and John Wornam met at the house of Nich. Parris and then devided cattle devised by the Last Will of Elinor Walters among her grandchildren, and Nich. Parris carefully look after ye cattle given to his wife's children and he to give an account.

Joane Rogers, Relict of John, not educating and caring for the children properly, to appear at next Court.

Cert. to Mr. William Rogers, 500 acres, trans. of 10 persons: John Althorp, Henry Taylor, Thomas Ecock, Kath. Bryant, Dan. A. Dooly, Phil. Gammonds, Israell Berry, Anne Sprag, Judith Kanne and Dominic Rice.

Pages 252-253 (none)

Court 1 Jan. 1684/5

Page 254

Petition of Elizabeth Algood, Exx. of her Husband, Edward Algood, Probate of the Will granted to her by oaths of Richard Smyth and Charles Harris.

Petition of Ann Condon, Exx. of Edm. Condon, dec'd, Probate of Last Will by oaths of Dav. Lyndsay and Wm. Warwick.

Court 18 Mar. 1684/5

Page 255

Petition of Richard Nutt, Exor. of Mr. Richard Nutt, dec'd, Probate to him on Last Will by oaths of James Montgomery and John Edgar.

Petition of Nicholas Owen, Exor., of Mr. John Julian, dec'd, Probate to him on Last Will by oaths of John Batcheler and John Baker.

Petition of Ruth Boggas Exx. of Henry Boggas, Probate to her of Will by oaths of Henry Medcalf, Henry Masey and William Parker.

Petition of Thomas Brewer, Exor. of Thomas Brewer, Probate to him of Will by oaths of John Turberville and John Sparkes.

Northumberland County Orders

Page 256

Thomas Searle, poor and impotent, freed from Levy.

Ann Greenston, daughter of John Greenston, 9 years old, with consent of her father, to serve William Yarrett and Jane his wife. Thomas Grinstead, aged 7, and John Grinstead, aged 4, with consent of William Grinstead their father, to serve William Taylor until 20.

Page 257

Thomas Bennett lately dec'd at the house of Thomas Adams, left no known relatives, and Adams to take Estate.

Thomas Quick, poor, died, and William Dawson to be compensated for his burial.

Page 258

Petition of Cuthbert Span, a division of ye Estate between him and his Br'thr John.

Page 260-261 (none)

Page 262 (Day 19)

Thomas Hughes pet. yt ye landes devised unto him by will of his dec'd father to his Br. John Hughes might be divided between them.

Pages 263-265 (none)

Page 266

Nicholas Lancaster vs. Estate of Charles Paul. Mr. John Farnefold vs. Estate of Mr. Thomas Matthew.

Court 19 March 1684/5

Page 267

Robert Oldis "broke" prison and his Estate siezed.

Court 20 May 1685

Page 268

Present: Lt. Col. Sam. Smyth, Mr. Peter Presly, Sen'r, Capt. Leonard Howson, Mr. Thomas Howson, Mr. Nicholas Owen, Capt. John Haynie, Mr. Richard-Kenner, Mr. Thomas Brereton, Mr. Peter Presly, Jr., Mr. Richard-Rogers.

Mr. William Lee sworn High Sheriff.

Petition of Elizabeth Keen, a Probate of the last Will of her dec'd. Husband Mr. William Keen by oaths of Mr. Nich. Owen, Mr. Rich. Rogers, & Mr. Jno. Cralle.

Page 269

Petition of ffran., ye Exx. of Robert Bryerly, Probate to her of the Last Will of her sd. dec'd Husband by oaths of Ben. Brown and Jno. Laurams.

Petition of Anne Hill, Probate of Will to her on her dec'd Husband William Hill by oaths of Richard Pemberton and George Hutton and James Moor.

Northumberland County Orders

Page 268 cont'd:

Petition of John Smith of a Probate of Will of Richard Lugg, dec'd, by oaths of William Tignor and Mr. Azricam Parker.

John Nelmes, Lame, freed from Levy.

Constables: Michael Vanlandagham for Chickacoane, John Lewis for Cherry Point, Peter Constant for Mattapony, Joseph Palmer for Upper parts of Gr. Wiccocomoco Parish and Richard Lattimore for lower parts, George Hambleton for Upper parts of fairfield's Parish, Henry Rider for Newman's Neck and Hull's Creek and Mr. Cuthbert Span for Lower parts of ffairfield Parish.

Page 270

Com. of Adm. to John fflowers on Estate of his dec'd father William fflowers.

Pages 271-272 (none)

Page 273 (Day 21)

Whereas Peter Presly, Jr., heir to Mr. William Presly, dec'd, vs. Mr. William ffarmer ffeeffe in trust for ye Estate of Maj. John Mottrom,1504 lbs. tob., due to his sd. father in part of what levyed for him the year 1677 for Burgess charges and due from sd. Mottrom to sd. Presly. Farmer appeals to the General Court.

Page 274 (none)

Court 15 July 1685

Page 275

Present: Lt. Col. Sam. Smyth, Mr. Peter Presly, Sr., Capt. Leon. Howson, Mr. Tho. Howson, Sr., Mr. Chas. Lee, Mr. Nich. Owen, Capt. Jno. Haynie, Mr. Rich. Kenner, Mr. Tho. Brereton, and Mr. Peter Presly, Jr.

Petition of Dorothy Exx. of Thomas Towers, dec'd, Probate of Will of her sd. Husband by oaths of Edw'd Williams, Wm. Dawson, Mr. Chris'per Neale and Mr. Rich. Pemberton.

Petition of John Walters exor. of Richard Jones, dec'd, Probate of Will to be his by oaths of Jeffery Addamson and Ester Walford.

Page 276 (none)

Page 277

Nicholas Rhodes, poor child, aged 3 years, given by his Mother to serve John Freeman.

Richard Rice att. of Edward Williams heire unto Temperance Bradshaw vs. Robert Bradshaw, who marryed Anne, daughter and heire of Robert Bradshaw, dec'd, judgement for 345 acres.

Page 278

Robert Bradshaw appeals to the next General Court.

Page 279

William Betts petitions to the Court complains yt his father by his last Will gave and his Bro. Chas. Betts an Estate and his brother had impaired it and he seeks damages.

Northumberland County Orders

Page 280 (none)

Page 281 (Day 16)

Harrold Gilbert Constable in the place of Peter Constant of Mattapony.

Page 282

John Evans vs. William Percifull. Mr. Thomas Hobson vs. Estate of Wm. Percifull.

Pages 283-286 (none)

Page 287

Peter Byram complained yt Jeffery Johnson (being Brother to his wife), treatment of Byram and his wife and children while at his house. Damages for plaintiff.

Pages 288-290 (none)

Court 16 Sept. 1685

Page 291

Petition of Samuel Sanford who marryed Eliza Exx. of Edward Elliott, Probate to him on the Last Will by oaths of Francis Boon and yt ye sd. ffrancis did see ye Testator signe, seale and deliver ye sd. Will as doth appear under ye hand of William Hatton one of his Ld's Justices of ye peace for ye County of St. Mary's in ye p'vince of Maryland dated ye 24th June 1681. The other witness names William Hooke being dec'd.

Pages 292-294 (none)

Page 295

Eliz:a Ye Relict of Azricam Parker, dec'd, a Probate is granted her of his Last Will, being her dec'd Husband.

Petition of Thomas High, Com. of Adm. to him of Last Will of Edward Maxwell, dec'd.

Pages 296-297 (none)

Page 298 (Day 17)

Com. of Adm. with will annexed to Mr. James Austen on Estate of Thomas Morris, dec'd and bond by him and Mr. Richard Haynie.

Page 299

Petition of Henry Rider who maryed Anne ye daughter of Walter Moor, yt Mr. John Graham and Peter Maxfield make a division of ye Estate of Walter Moor.

John Lyver who married ye Exx. of Edward Algood, dec'd, to have Algood's Estate.

Pages 300-301 (none)

Page 302

Richard Smyth overseer of John Nelms complains yt Richard Nelms obliged himself for a cow and a calf.

Pages 303-304 (none)

Northumberland County Orders

Page 305 (Day 18)

Mr. William Rogers vs. Estate of George Knight.

Court 18 Nov. 1685

Page 306

Timothy Green, orphan of Timothy Green, dec'd, chose Mr. James Johnson Guardian.

Page 307

Richard Orland complained that whereas David Orland his father dyed intestate and Stephen Sallees intermarryed with his Mother, about ten years since never adm. upon his dec'd father's Estate and denying him a child's part. An inventory ordered.

Page 308

19 March 1681, Hon. Nicholas Spencer, Esq., commended Mr. William Farmer ffeoffe in trust for Estate of Maj. John Mottrom. William ffarmer being dead, ye Hon. Nich. Spencer recommended Mrs. Anne ffarmer to be admitted ffeoffe in trust of sd. Estate.

Page 309 (none)

Court 19 Nov. 1685

Page 310

Mr. John Webb and William Taylor to view damages by William Swetman unto ye Estate of ffran. ye orphan of ffrancis Brittaine.

Pages 311-314 (none)

Page 315

John Bee and Rice Williams to App. Estate of Thomas Morris, dec'd.

Court 21 Dec. 1685

Page 316

Probate to Richard Hull of last Will of Henry Willoughby, dec'd, by oaths of Mr. Charles Harris and Edward Nesbitt.

Page 317

Richard Jones chose John Walters guardian.

Pages 318-333 (none)

Court 25 ffeb. 1685/6

Page 334

Mr. William Harcum on ye behalf of Hannah his wife vs. Thomas Smyth.

Pages 335-336 (none)

Court 7 April 1686

Page 337

Probate to James Waddy of the last Will of his dec'd father, John Waddy, by oath of Eliza Eliphant and other dec'd.

Northumberland County Orders

Page 337 cont'd:

Cert. to John Davis, 200 acres, trans. of 4 persons: John Davis, Sr., John Davis, Jr., Hester Davis and Matthers Davis.

Page 338 (none)

Court 19 May 1686

Page 339

Mary Maxwell, Exx. of Peter Maxwell, dec'd, Probate of Last Will to her of her said dec'd husband.

Constables: Stephen Wells for Mattapony, Mr. William Parker for Cherry Point, John Greensted for Chiccacoane, George Dawkins for Upper parts of ffairfield, John Liver for Newman's Neck, Thomas Berry for lower pa'ts of ffairfield, Thomas Williams for Upper pts. of Gr. Wiccocomoco precincts, JOhn Lewis for lower.

Page 340

Petition of Sarah Bayles Exx. of Thomas Bayles, dec'd, Probate of Will of her dec'd husband, by oaths of Alex'r Brodie. John Mutton and Isaac Hester.

Page 341 (none)

Page 342

William Lee sworne High Sheriff.

Court 21 July 1686

Page 348

William Reynolds, poor and impotent and decripett, freed from Levy.

Page 349

James Waddy vs. Estate of Thomas Chandler.

Page 350 (none)

Page 351

Stephen Wells who marryed Anne ye Widd. and Exx. of William Hill, late dec'd, to give bond for the Estate.

Page 352 (none)

Page 353

Thomas Hobson vs. Estate of Thomas Wilkes.

Page 354

Henry Bently vs. James Waddy: John Waddy, father of James, granted him 250 Acres of Land dated 1651, sold 1651 to Andrew Boyer, assigned to Jno. Gamlen, ye 13: 9ber: 1652; that he hold the land in right of his wife, daughter and heir of ye sd. Patter. Appeal of Waddy to the General Court.

Page 355 (none)

Court 17 Nov. 1686

Page 356 (following page)

Northumberland County Orders

Page 356

Bartholomew Yeomans indebted to Angel (ye Widdow of Richard) Lamprey.

Page 357

William and Ruth Parker arrested at the suit of William and Susanna Webb, nonsuited.

Page 358

Cert. to Mr. Cuthbert Span for 850 Acres, trans. of 17 persons: Edward Harvey, Joseph Amee, Edward Bennett, Eliza Bennett, Thomas Hilman, David Davis, Howell Propert, Kath Hughlett, Owen Brady, Richard Stephens, Edmund Poiselle, Andrew a Scotsman, Thomas ----, Samuel Batesman, Tony a negro, Judith a negro, Maple a negro.

Page 359

John Moor son of Walter Moor late of this County, dec'd, chose Richard Hall guardian.

Cert. to Richard Hull, 600 acres, trans. of 12 persons: George Hill, Dorothy Sabrice, Gerv. Ellistone, Arthur Oneale, James Macloughan, John Willey, Grace Warnaw, Andrew Waddy, Edmond Maudley, Jane Maudley, Sarah an Indian, Tom a negro.

Pages 360-362 (none)

Court 1 Dec. 1686

Page 363

Petition of Charles Betts, Ex. of his dec'd father William Betts by oaths of Alexander Mulraine and William Smyth, a Probate is granted.

Petition of -----, ye Exx. of Henry Medcalfe, late of this County, dec'd, a Probate granted her of the Last Will of her dec'd husband by oaths of Thomas Miller and Benjamin Boggis.

Court 2 Dec. 1686

Page 364

Mr. William Rogers complained vs. Joan Rogers, ye Widdow of John Rogers, late dec'd, and she is now dec'd, that he now have the Estate in his hands.

Pages 365-372 (none)

Court 20 Jan. 1686/7

Page 373

Adam Yarrett, guardian of ffrances, ye orphan of ffrancis Brittaine, ordered that Dennis Eyes become security for William Clark who marryed Eliza ye Widd. of ye sd. ffrancis.

Page 374 (none)

Court 16 ffeb. 1686/7

Page 375

John ye sonne of Benjamine Wall did with consent of his Mother Ruth (ye Relict and Widdow of ye sd. Benjamine) Wall, aged 6 years, to serve Mr. William Yarrett.

Northumberland County Orders

Pages 376-379 (none)

Court 16 Mar. 1686/7

Page 380

Ruth Widdow of Benjamin Wall, dec'd, bound her Sonn Joseph Wall to John Boaz and Elizabeth his wife until 20.

Page 381

John Coutanceau Exor. of the Last Will of his father John Coutanceau. Probate to him by oaths of Mr. Richard Kenner and Mr. Robert Lee.

Pages 382-388 (none)

Court 17 Mar. 1686/7

Page 389

William Algood orphant of Edward Algood, dec'd, chose Thomas Barnes guardian. Eliza orphant of Edward Algood, decd, chose Mr. Christopher Neale.

Petition of John Webb, Probate to him of the Last Will of his dec'd. Mother Elizabeth Watts by oaths of William Anderson and Thomas Larson the other witness being sick.

END OF PART ONE
****

PART TWO

Page 390 (date carried over from last Book)

Children of Elizabeth Evans to continue with her until they attain age of 21.

Pages 391-392 (none)

Page 393

John and Richard (the Orphants of Edward) Algood, dec'd, to serve Peter Flynt until 21, trade of carpenter.

Court 18 May 1687

Page 394

Constables: William Knott, Mattapony; Ralph Stephens, Cherry Point; Samuel Poole, Cone; Jacob Coutanceau, Newman's Neck; William Yarrett, for Upper ffairfeild; Joseph Moult, Lower ffairfield and John Evans for Upper pr'cincts of Gr. Wicc:o parish.

Henry Oague, Orph:t to John Oague, dec'd, to serve Thomas Barnes, he being 12 years of age, to be by trade a weaver.

Petition of John Lewis for Probate of the Last Will of Thomas Tapp, by oaths of John Carew and Mary Lawrence.

Page 395

Mr. William Lee to collect dues.

Page 396

Mr. John Curtis and George Bledsoe to be surveyers of highways and al-

Northumberland County Orders

Page 396 cont'd:

so Henry Butler. John Robinson and Joseph White to replace John Wornom and Thomas Hamm:t of ffairfields.

Page 397

John Higginson to take Inventory of William Allenson, dec'd.

Court 20 July 1687

Petition of Lucy ffurnett, Com. of Adm. with Will annexed to her on Estate of Richard Cox, dec'd. Bond of James Johnson and Thomas fflynt.

Page 398 (none)

Page 399

Eliz:a an infant daughter of Edmund Maudly's, servant to Richard Hull, ordered to serve Howell Williams and Ellinor his wife, with consent of the father until 21. Richard Hull appealed to the General Court.

Page 400

Mr. William Jones and Mr. John Eustace vs. Mr. John Curtis who marryed ye Admx. of Mr. Erasmus Wither dec'd.

Page 401 (none)

Court 5 Oct. 1687

Page 402

Petition of Thomas Ham't who marryed Mary Exx. of William Cornish, Probate of the Will to him by oaths of James Hadwell and Edward Lewis.

Page 403

Richard Smith and Thomas Barnes Security of John Lyver, dec'd, to have Estates of orphants of Edward Algood, dec'd, in their custody until further care might be taken at the following Court, and sd. orphants since have been ordered to Mr. Chr. Neale, Peter Flynt and Thomas Barnes and Estates of John and Richard orphants of Edw. Algood.

Page 404

Richard Smyth and Thomas Barnes Bond for William Algood, orphan of Edward Algood.

Page 405

Elizabeth (Admx. of Thomas) Wilkes vs. Mr. Peter Knight.

Pages 406-407 (none)

Court 6 Oct. 1687

Page 408

Richard Rout as marrying ffrances Adams sued by John Downing att. of Samuel typton.

Page 409 (none)

Court 16:9ber:1687

Page 410 (on following page)

Northumberland County Orders

Page 410 cont'd:

John Way son of Ricard Way late of this County, decd, chose his Bro. in law Richard Smyth to be his guardian.

Court 17:9ber:1687

Page 411

Charles Edwards Constable for Newman's Neck sworn.

Page 412

Daniel Webb molatto serv't of Maj. John Mottram freed.

Court 18 Nov. 1687

Page 413

Elizabeth Betts, Widd. and Relict of William Betts to have her thirds surveyed by petition of Charles Betts.

John Downing Att. of Samuel Typton Merch't in Bristoll sued by James Jones.

Page 414

Edward ffurnett in behalfe of his wife Lucy ffurnett vs. John Mynor, nonsuit to Edward ffurnett.

Richard Kenner in behalf of his son Rhoden Kenner vs. Daniel Sullvant, trial by Jury.

Page 415 (none)

Court 28 Dec. 1687

Page 416

Dorothy Jackman to take Inventory of Estate of Thomas Dyer, dec'd.

Petition of Mr. Phillip Shapleigh, Com. of Adm. on Estate of Richard Pearce and Morgan Powell who marryed Elizabeth, Widdow and Relict of sd. Pearce on behalf of sd. Pearce orphants. Mr. Phillip Shapleigh and Mr. Christopher Neale give the bond.

Page 417

Mr. Phillip Shapleigh for funeral expenses of Thomas Morris vs. James Austen, Adm. of sd. Estate.

Page 418

James Austen appeals to the General Court.

Page 419 (none)

Court 29 Dec. 1687

Page 420 (none)

Page 421

Thomas Harwood, John Paine and Joseph Hoult take Inventory of Estate of Robert Oldis.

Page 422 (on following page)

Northumberland County Orders

Page 422

James Wattson to be constable for Mattapony.

Page 423 (none)

Court 21 March 1687/8

Page 424

John Bayles brought an inventory on Estate of Robert Oldis, and Eliz. wife of the sd. Robert being dec'd leaving two children the youngest whereof is suspected to be begotten by Joseph Carr. Children to be in custody of John Bayles.

Page 425

John Hull petitions for Adm. of Estate of Howell Williams and Ellinor Williams, Widdow, to sd. Howell concerning her thirds.

Page 426

John Hull, Richard Hull and Thomas Barnes give bond.

Court 28 Mar. 1688

Page 427

Joseph Carr who marryed Ann the daughter of John Warner, petitions for adm. on Estate of Warner and Charles Edwards who marryed Prudence Widdow to ye sd. John Warner being absent, he to appear at next Court.

William Richardson who marryed ye Widdow and Relict of Thomas Hopper, Adm. to him. James Johnson and William Sheares give bond.

Page 428

Cert. to John Haynie for 100 Acres, trans. of 2 persons: John Maxwell and Joseph Bland.

Court 20 June 1688

Page 429

Probate to Eliz. Exx. of her dec'd Husband John Bowller, proved by oaths of James Austen and Josias Long.

Petition of Mary (Exx. of her husband Joseph) ffeilding, Probate to her of the Last Will by oaths of Josias Long and Nich. Lancaster.

Page 430

Constables: Peter Byram, upper and Thomas Brewer, lower precincts of Gr. Wiccocomoco; James Montgomery, upper and Stephen Chaukerett, Middle and Henry Butler, lower precincts of ffairfeild; William Beane, Cherry Point; and Will Taylor Jun., lower B-wtracy.

Mrs. Eliz. Parker's Estate to be inventoried by Petition of Thomas Baker.

Page 431

Thomas Downing orphan of Mr. William Downing chose John Downing his guardian.

Page 432

Mr. William Lee sworne High Sheriff.

Northumberland County Orders

Page 432 cont'd:

Petition of Cha. Edwards for division of John Warner's Estate.

Court 15 Aug. 1688

Page 433

Present: Mr. Thomas Hobson Sen., Mr. Han. Lee, Mr. Nich. Owen, Mr. Chr. Neale, Mr. Pet. Presly, Mr. Rich. Rogers.

Petition of Jno. Downing and Tho. Hobson Jr. overseers of the Last Will of Mr. Wm. Downing, ordered that Henry Mayze, Jno. Wornom and Jos. Palmer App. Est. of Edwd. Typton.

Page 434

Probate of the Last Will of Wm. Eves, Dec'd, by oaths of Jno. Bryan Thomas and Mary Dutton.

Court 16 Aug. 1688

Page 434 cont'd:

Jos. (ye son of Robt.) Oldis, being aged 7, to serve Jno. Bayles. Jno. Hull and Jno. Bayles bond for indenture.

Page 435

Sarah Oldis Infant Daughter of Eliz Oldis, dec'd, aged 1 year on 4 June last, to serve Jno. James and his wife.

Page 436

Custody of Jno. Greensted ordered, suspected of being guilty of the violent death of his late deceased wife Eliza. Greensted.

Court 5 Oct. 1688

Petition of Richard Vanlandegham, Probate on the Last Will of his decd Mother Eliza. Evans, Widd., proved by the oaths of Cloud Tullos and Ester Walters.

Page 437

John Downing and Daniel Neale and Richard Smyth to sell Estate of Gervase Hattfeild.

John Greensted to be carried to James Citty for the General Court..

Page 438 (none)

Court 17 Oct. 1688

Page 439

Petition of Mary Royston, Widd. of Jonathan Royston, Probate of the Last Will of her dec'd Husband by oaths of John Corbell and Samuel Batson.

Page 440

Petition of Azricam Parker, Com. of Adm. on Est. of his dec'd Mother Eliz. Parker. Bond of John Turberville and Tho. Baker. Fearnot Parker, Daughter of Eliz. Parker, dec'd, chose Tho. Baker guardian.

Page 441

Angel Lamprey guardian of Jno. Cockrell vs. Thomas Maize.

Northumberland County Orders

Page 441 cont'd:

Jno. Downing and Tho. Hobson overseers of the Will of Wm. Downing for the Est. of Wm. Downing belonging to Est. of Edwd. Tipton ye same being attached and left in custody of Margaret (wife of ye sd. Edwd.) Tipton and Downing orphans to possess their Est. Bond of Jno. Downing and Jn. Coles.

Court 21 Nov. 1688

Page 442

Richard Smyth as greates creditor to Estate of Gervase Hattfeild, a Com. of Adm. to him, and Richard Smyth and Phillip Shapleigh and John Graham give bond.

Page 443

Thomas Sims servant to Mr. James Johnson to be free.

Petition of John Charles and William Nelms to survey their land.

Court 22 Nov. 1688

Page 444

William and Susanna Webb vs. William Parker, 60 Acres of land became due to them by right of inheritance from ffrancis Little, late of this County, dec'd, brother to the sd. Susanna Webb and ffrancis Little by Will bequeathed the 60 Acres to Henry Boggas for life only, who being likewise dec'd, Sheriff to possess William and Susanna Webb with the Land.

Page 445

Capt. William Lee, Capt. Richard Kenner and Capt. Thomas Brereton, a Motion concerning the Militia.

Page 446 (none)

Court 19 Dec. 1688

Page 447

Edmund Maudley servant to Richard Hull to be free.

Page 448

George (orphan of Thomas) Hughs, dec'd, to continue at the house of Richard Smyth until the next Court.

Page 449 (none)

Court 20: Xber: 1688

Page 450

Mary Roper Admx. in her wrong to the Estate of Anthony Roper sued by Capt. Thomas Jones.

Pages 451-452 (none)

Court 20 Feb. 1688/9

Page 453

John Goch son of Sam'l Goch, dec'd, to choose a guardian.

Northumberland County Orders

Page 454 (none)

Page 455

Com. of Adm. to Richard Smyth on Estate of George Hambleton (he having marryed Eliz. Widd. to ye sd. Geo.).

Henry Weeks, poor, aged and impotent, freed from Levy.

Pages 456-460 (none)

Court 17 Apr. 1689

Page 461

Probate to James Waddy on the Last Will of his Brother Thomas Waddy by the oaths of John Harris and Mr. Thomas Winter.

Petition of Mrs. Elizabeth Howson by her son Mr. William Howson, a Probate of the Will of her dec'd Husband Capt. Leonard Howson by the oaths of Capt. William -----, Mr. Hancock and Charles Lee and John Southerland.

Page 462

Robert Hill brother and heir of Ezekiel Hill vs. Partin Hudnall dismissed.

Court 15 May 1689

Nicholas Powell son of Edmund and Sarah Powell, being 3 years ye 13th of December next, with the consent of his Mother, to serve John Lewis & his wife until 21.

Constables: Samuel Mahon, Jun'r for lower and Stephen Sallows for upper precincts of Gr. Wiccocomoco; William Richards, Mattapony; Michaell Gilbert for Cherry Point; John Adams for Jerrico; John Jones, lower fairfield and Joseph Carr, Newman's Neck.

Page 463

John Hull Adm. of Howell Williams vs. Capt. Thomas Jones.

Page 464

Patrick Michleroy as marrying Elizabeth Admx. of Richard Yowell, dec'd vs. Evan Jones.

Court 22 May 1689

Page 465

Mr. William Yarrett son and heir of Adam and Rachel Yarrett vs. Dorothy Jackman, referred to next Court.

Page 466

Elizabeth Richardson wife of William Richardson fined for not appearing in Court.

Page 467

Mr. Phillip Shapleigh sworne High Sheriff.

Richard Thompson, an aged, sickly and impotent, freed from Levy.

Page 468 (following page)

Northumberland County Orders

Page 468

John West, an order to survey a tract of land of 94 Acres, bequeathed by the Last Will of Richard Cox, dec'd.

Page 469 (none)

Court 15 July 1689

Page 470

Present: Capt. William Lee, Mr. Nicholas Owen, Capt. Richard Kenner, Mr. Christopher Neale, Mr. Peter Presly, Jr., Mr. Richard Rogers.

Ester Butler daughter of John Butler, aged 3 years the 4th of April last, by consent of her said father, to serve Thomas Whitehead and Mary his now wife until 17.

Petition of Robert Bradly Exor. of the Last Will of John Roach. Probate to him by oaths of Edward Williams, John West and Thomas Shirley.

Pages 471-472 (none)

Court 18 July 1689

Page 473

John Bayles vs. Walter Curtis for trespassing on a tract, bounding upon Potomack river and Herring pond and land of James Austen, formerly belonging unto Elizabeth Oldis Sister to ye sd. John Bayles, bequeathed to her for life only by her dec'd father John Bayles as by his will appears and Elizabeth is dec'd, and John Bayles the petitioner to possess the land. Petition of Walter Curtis for hearing in chancery the next Court.

Page 474

Capt. Thomas Opie vs. Thomas Harwood as marrying Ann ye relict and admx. of John Leaver.

Pages 475-476 (none)

Court 6 Nov. 1689

Page 477

Petition of Mrs. Jane Lynton Exx. of the Will of her dec'd Husband Mr. Anthony Lynton. Probate to her by oaths of George Hutton and Samuell Gerrard the other witness being dead.

Petition of Mary (Widdow and Exx. of Capt. Richard) Lynsfeild, dec'd, Probate to her of the Last Will by oaths of Thomas Winter and George Bledsoe.

Thomas Swain son of John and Frances Swain, being born 28th day of Aug. 1679, to serve Richard Rice, Sr.

Page 478

Joseph Waterman ye son of Thomas and Isabella Waterman, aged 4 the 30th of Jan. next, to serve Richard Nutt until 21.

Thomas Bushrod Exor. of the Will of Nicholas Owen. Probate to him by oaths of John Lewis and Thomas Banks, Mrs. Elizabeth Banks and Elizabeth Smyth.

Thomas Webb by P/A of Sarah ye wife of Thomas Hobson, Sr. ack. her

Northumberland County Orders

Page 478 cont'd:

right of Dower to a certain land made over to George Cooper by deed of guift from her sd. Husband.

Page 479

Ezekiel Genesis, dec'd by Will dated 2 April 1684 bequeathed to Partin Hudnall and Ezekil Hill a tract on the Southside of Great Wiccocomico river. and Ezekiell Hill being since dec'd, Robert Hill, brother & heir of ye sd. Ezekiell Hill hath brought his action to this court vs. the sd. Partin Hudnal for Equal portion of the laid land. Partin Hudnal appeals to the General Court. James Hill and William Harcum bond for Robert Hill for the appeal.

Page 480

John Haynie and Richard Haynie give bond for Partin Hudnall for appeal

Page 481

Jacob Countanceau, brother and heir of William Coutanceau vs. John Coutanceau, referred to the next Court.

Pages 482-483 (none)

Court 20 Nov. 1689

Page 484

Mary Eves (ye daughter of William and ------ Eves, dec'd.) being aged 10 ye next June, to serve Richard Nutt until 18.

Page 485

Petition of Mr. Robert Soch, a Probate on the Last Will of Mr. Robert Scott by oaths of Mr. William Alden and Charles Browne.

Court 21 Nov. 1689

Page 486

Petition of Thomas Downing son of Mr. William Downing dec'd, and he to have his lands and Mrs. Margaret Downing, Exx. of sd. Mr. William Downing her Third part.

Pages 487-488 (none)

Court 22 Nov. 1689

Page 489

Henry Bruce as marrying Mary ye Daughter and Heir of Andrew Morton, dec'd, vs. Clement Lattemore and Thomas Williams son and heir of Thomas Williams dec'd, overseers of ye sd. Andrew Morton's Estate.

Page 490

William Lee vs. Alexander Mulraine as marrying Mary ye Exx. of Joseph ffeilding.

Pages 491-493 (none)

Court 15 Jan. 1689/90

Page 494 (on following page)

Northumberland County Orders

Page 494

Mr. Spencer Mottrom son and heir of Maj. John Mottrom, dec'd, chose Mr. Peter Presly, Sr. and Mrs. Anne ffarmer trustee to ye Estate of ye sd. Maj. John Mottrom having made choice of Thomas Hobson, Jr. for an audit of Estate.

Page 495

Henry Bruce as marrying Mary daughter and heir of Andrew Morton, dec'd vs. Clement Lattimore and Thomas Williams son and heir of Thomas Williams dec'd and sd. Morton's Estate to two Daughters under management of sd. Williams and Lattimore, viz.: Elizabeth (since dec'd.) and Mary ye plaintiff's now wife, whole Estate to sd. Mary.

Page 496

Mary Oague daughter of Isreall Oague, 6 yrs. of age in April next, to serve by the Mother's consent Henry ffranklin.

Pages 497-498 (none)

Court 16 Jan. 1689/90

Page 499

Richard Smyth ye son and heir of Thomas Smyth late dec'd vs. Cloud Tullos.

Page 500 (none)

Court 19 Mar. 1689/90

Page 501

Petition of Sarah Palmer, Relict and Widdow of John Palmer dec'd for App. of Estate.

Pages 502-503 (none)

Court 25 May 1690

Page 504

Constables: Thomas Hickman, Jun'r for Mattapony; Thomas Bearcroft for cherry Poynt; Benjamin Price, Jerrico; Henry ffranklin, upper ffair feild; Nicholas Kingwell, Newman's Neck; Mr. Peter Hack, lower ffairfeild; Isaac Hester, upper Wiccocomocco; Thomas Knight, lower Wiccocomoco.

Robert Shepherd, poor, aged and decrepid, freed from Levy.

Pages 505-506 (none)

Court 18 Jn. 1690

Page 507

Mr. Phillip Shapleigh sworne High Sheriff.

Page 508

John Langsdale to be constable for upper ffairfeild and Henry ffranklin be released.

Page 509 (following page)

Northumberland County Orders

Page 509

Petition of Ann Bradly to have land laid out, which was bequeathed by John Roach late dec'd to James Bradly Son of Robert Bradly.

Pages 510-511 (none)

Page 512

George Marshall in behalfe of his wife Rachel vs. Josias Gaskins, she having served Gaskins.

Pages 513-519 (none)

Court 17 Sept. 1690

Page 520

John Flower and Hannah his wife fine for contempt of Court.

Court 19 Nov. 1690

Page 521

Petition of James Jessey Exor. of Will of Andrew Shaw, dec'd, Probate to him by oaths of James Claughton and James Crean.

Petition of ffrances (ye Widd. of Isaac) Wall, dec'd, Comm. of Adm. with ye Will annexed, to her on her dec'd Husband's will by oaths of Wm. Percifull and John Webb.

Ann Towers daughter of Dorothy McClanichan, aged 10 years ye 7th day of April next, who has consent of Mother, to serve John Boaz and his wife Ann.

Page 522

John Davis son of Joan Alexander with consent of his Mother to serve John Adams until 21.

Court 20 Nov. 1690

Page 523

Petition of William Alden, Com. of Adm. to him on Estate of Walter Grady, dec'd. William Sheares and he give the bond.

Pages 524-528 (none)

Court 21 Nov. 1690

Page 529

Henry and John Harding made choyce of their brother Thomas Harding to be their guardian.

Pages 530-532 (none)

Court 17:Xber:1690

Page 533

John Lawrence has 3 children of Owen Dermott's bound to him and the oldest is hugh being heir to sd. Owen's land and being one of the said three, John Lawrence to possess land.

Page 534 (none)

Northumberland County Orders

Court 18 Dec. 1690

Page 535

George Knott vs. William Sheares: George Knott declared that his grandfather George Knott dyed seized of 400 Acres of land in Mattapony and the sd. Shears marrying Eliza grandmother of the sd. Knott, and Geo. Knott petitions the Court as heir of his grandfather for the land.

Page 536 (none)

Court 18 ffeb. 1690/1

Page 537

Petition of John Nickless Exor. of the Will of James Young, dec'd, Probate to him by oaths of John Turberville and Mrs. Katherine Junn.

Page 538

Richard Rice as marrying Joan Berkeley sued by Thomas Clarke.

- John Wheeler who marryed ffrances (Admx. of Isaac) Wall, quietus est on Estate.

Page 539 (none)

Court 19 ffeb. 1690/1

Page 540

Richard Smyth and Elizabeth his wife plaintiffs vs. Mr. John Haynie, land claimed by plaintiffs scituate near head of Great Wiccocomoco river and a survey ordered.

Pages 541-543 (none)

Court 18 Mar. 1690/1

Page 544

John Reason, aged and impotent and poor, freed from Levy.

Page 545

Elizabeth Pinkard P/A to Capt. Thomas Jones; Elizabeth Pinkard Exx. of Capt. John Pinkard vs. Thomas Hulks.

Page 546 (none)

Court 19 Mar. 1690/1

Page 547

James Jarsey petitions for a survey of land bequeathed by the Last Will of Andrew Shaw, dec'd, to sd. Jarsey.

Page 548

Thomas Bushrod vs. William and Eliza Leech.

Court 20 May 1691

Page 549

Constables: Thomas Harding, Mattapony; William Warwick, Jerrico; Richard Eaton, upper ffairfeild; John Cockerell, Newman's Neck; Chris.

Northumberland County Orders

Page 549 cont'd:
Newton, ffairfeilds; Partin Hudnall, upper Wiccocomoco; Thomas Hayden, lower Wiccocomoco.

Page 550

Petition of Ann Bradly, App. of Estate of Robert Bradly.

John Standly, aged and failure in his eyes, freed from Levy.

Pages 551-552 (none)

Court 17 June 1691

Page 553

Mr. Rodham Kenner sworn High Sheriff.

John Lawrence appointed Constable for Cherry Point.

Page 554

Survey of Land of John and Richard Hull, and division made.

Pages 555-556 (none)

Court 18 June 1691

Page 557

Nicholas Algrove and Elizabeth his wife vs. Mr. William Harcum.

Petition of William Paine, a Com. of Adm. to him on Estate of John Ball, dec'd, and bond of William Paine and Mr. Thomas Banks.

Page 558

John Lewis and Mary his wife vs. Mr. Thomas Bushrod.

Court 1 July 1691

Andrew Marcry vs. Mr. Charles Ball.

Pages 559-560 (none)

Court 19 Aug. 1691

Page 561

Thomas Seddon, infant child a year old last ffebruary, with consent of his father Thomas Seddon, to serve John Bird.

John Mattley complains vs. his guardian Ralph Steephens and he chose Mr. Thomas Banks as guardian.

Pages 562-565 (none)

Court 2 Sept. 1691

Page 566

Ralph Stephens to give security for rendering an account of the Est. of John Mosely ye orphan of William Mosely dec'd.

John Haynie Sen. Petitions the Court that Thomas Harding dec'd. dyed Intestate and had issue by sd. Hanie's daughter, dec'd, also a son named Thomas Harding who hath from his birth being three years since been sus-

Northumberland County Orders

Page 566 cont'd:

tained by him and prayed for guardianship of sd. child, to exhibit inventory on Estate.

Petition of John Donaldson yt he have guardian ship of William Grady ye orphan of Walter grady, dec'd.

Pages 567-569 (none)

Court 19 Nov. 1691

Page 570

Present: Lt. Col. Samuel Smyth, Mr. Peter Presly, Capt. Richard Kenner, Capt. Thomas Brereton, Mr. Peter Presly, Jr., Capt. George Cooper, Mr. Daniel Neale, Mr. Thomas Banks, Mr. Ebenezer Sanders and Capt. William Jones.

Thomas Hobson Exor. of the Last Will of Mr. Thomas Hobson, dec'd, Probate to him by oaths of Capt. Peter Hack and Mr. Joseph Hoult.

Pages 571-573 (none)

Court 16 Dec. 1691

Page 574

Petition of Charles Vollon, Exor. of Richard Welsh, Probate to him on last Will, proved by oaths of James Montgomery and John Mottrom and ye Will is returned to Rappa. County.

Page 575 (none)

Court 20 Jan. 1691/2

Page 576

Petition of Mrs. Elizabeth Kenner Exx. of Capt. Richard Kenner, dec'd and Probate of the Last Will by oaths of Richrd fflynt and John Joanes.

Petition of Cloud Tullos, a Probate to him of the Last Will of John Davis, dec'd, by oaths of Richard Smyth and Sarah Montgomerie.

Mr. William Nutt and Mr. Cuthbert Span to be guardian of the orphans of John Coles, dec'd and they to have ye sd. Estate (who dyed intestate) into their possession.

Thomas Browne son of David Browne is bound with his father's consent to John Garner until 21.

Petition of William Yarrett Exor. of Adam Yarrett, dec'd, a Probate to him of the Last Will by oaths of Thomas Hughlett Ellinor Bassett and John Hawkins.

Court 17 ffeb. 1691/2

Page 578

Present: Lt. Col. Sam. Griffin, Capt. Geo. Cooper, Mr. Peter Presly, Jr., Mr. Dan. Neale, Mr. Tho. Banks and Mr. Ebenezer Sanders.

Thomas Hayes orphan of Thomas Hayes, dec'd, chose Mr. John Downing guardian.

Petition of Jane Joyce, wid. of Abraham Joyce, dec'd a Probate of his last will by oaths of John Hicks and _____.

Northumberland County Orders

Pages 579-582 (none)

Court 16 Mar. 1691/2

Page 583

Petition of Thomas Miller for Com. of Adm. as greatest creditor on Estate of Jonathan Gould, dec'd.

Page 584

John Butler son of Henry and Susan Butler, being aged 10 next June, with the consent of his Mother on her death bed, to serve Mr. Cuthbert Span and his now wife.

Petition of Richard Rice, Jun'r Exor. of his dec'd father Richard Rice, Sen'r, Probate of the Last Will to him by oaths of Capt. John Haynie, Mr. Richard Haynie and Mr. Michael Milton.

Court 17 Mar. 1691/2

Page 585

William Woodland to take the Estate of Susanna Butler, dec'd, unto his possession.

Petition of John Parris att. of Richard Haynie, Com, of Adm. on Est. of David Whitford.

John Pearce orphan of Richrd, dec'd, chose William Parker guardian.

George Hughes orphan of Thomas Hughes chose John Trimlett guardian.

Ralph the orphan of ffrancis Bickley, dec'd, chose Mr. John Wornom.

Page 586 (none)

Page 587

Petition of Cloud Tullos, Com. of Adm. to him on the Est. of John Davis, dec'd.

A nonsuit to Richard Oldham vs. Cloud Tullos as heir of John Davis, dec'd.

Page 588 (none)

Court 10 May 1692

Page 589

Mr. Thomas Jones Att. of Capt. Richard Willis and Robert Leefield, a Probate to them on the Will of Mr. Michaell Grigge, proved by the oaths of Mr. Charles Lee and Mrs. Elizabeth Lee.

Constables: Mr. Christopher Neale, lower Mattapony; Mr. William Keene, Cherry Point; Anthony Lynton, upper Mattapony; Mr. Peter Coutanceau, upper fairfeild; John ffeilding, Newman's Neck; Christopher Newton, lower fayrfield; Patrick Pollick, upper and Thomas Baker, lower Lee Pish (parish)

Rim Garrison, aged and Impotent, freed from Levy.

Christian, Relict and Widdow of ffrancis Bickley, dec'd, made over to her sone Ralph Bickley two cowes and Mr. John Wornom guardian to be possessed with the sd. cowes.

Northumberland County Orders

Page 588 cont'd:

Richard Pearce, orphan of Richard Pearce, dec'd, to serve Thomas Harwood for 10 years.

Peter Flynt on behalfe of himself and Mrs. Mary Flynt his wife Exor. of the Last Will of Mr. Robert Sech (Soch?), dec'd, Probate to them, proved by the oaths of Mr. Charles Harris, Mich'll Dermott and Peter Howell.

Court 19 May 1692

Page 590

Edward Williams, an ancient and impotent, freed from the Levy.

Spencer Mottrom sworne Justice of the Peace. Capt. Rodham Kenner sworne High Sheriff.

Page 591

James Moore, aged and decrepid, freed from Levy.

Joseph Auston vs. James Austen, unlawfully detaining him as servant, he to appear at next Court for hearing.

Nicholas Edwards vs. Mr. Sam. Warcupp.

Page 592

John Graham, Walter Dunn, Joseph Hoult and Richard Nutt or any three to meet at the house of William Simpson who marryed the Relict of Nicholas Kingwell and App. the Estate.

Court 15 June 1692

Present: Mr. Peter Presly, Capt. Thomas Brereton, Mr. Peter Presly, Jr., Capt. George Cooper, Mr. Daniel Neale, Mr. Thomas Banks, Mr. John Downing and Capt. Spencer Mottrom.

Mr. John Turberville and Capt. Peter Hack take oath to Justice of the Peace.

Page 593

Henry Hudnall, impotent, poor and distempered, freed from the Levy.

Page 594 (none)

Page 595

George Cooper surveye before next Court lay out the Land of Capt. Sp. Mottrom comonly called Black Point.

John Rice orphan child son of Richard Rice, Sr., dec'd, in custody of Sam'll Poole, having a parcel of land bequeathed to him by his sd. dec'd father, upon petition of Richard Rice Exor. of sd. dec'd, and next Court to take care of sd. child, and management of his Estate.

Court July 1692

Page 596

Graves Eves orphan of William Eves, dec'd, chose Isaac Hester guardian.

Page 597 (following page)

Northumberland County Orders

Page 597

Petition of Thomas Byram, Isaac Hester, Richard Lattimore, William ffletcher, and Richard Smyth or any three to App. Estate of Sarah Bayles, dec'd, and John Bayles who has Estate in his possession to exhibit an Inventory.

Edward Woolridge and Elizabeth his wife vs. John Eaton.

Capt. Samuel Travers vs. John Thomas.

Page 598

Petition of Mr. Peter Flynt and Mary his wife Exx. of Mr. Robert Sech Mr. Richard Rogers Mr. Thomas Banks and Mr. Chr. Neale or any two to make a divison of the Est. of sd. Robt. Sech between sd. Mary and her daughter Jane Knott.

Court 21 Sept. 1692

Page 599

Petition of Mr. Richard Hutt Exor. of John Bayles, dec'd, Probate of the Last Will, proved by the oaths of Richard Ayry and Roger Oneale.

Mr. John Turberville and Capt. William Jones or either of them to take an inventory of the estate of Mr. Richard ffarington.

Page 600 (none)

Court 20 Oct. 1692

Page 601

James Moore died intestate, Patrick Pollick and Alexander Weatherstone to take an inventory.

Pages 602-604 (none)

Court 16 Nov. 1692

Page 605

Lawrence Whitehouse binds his daughter a base begotten child begotten on the body of Susanna Jackson borne 3 July last past to serve Capt. Rodham Kenner until 21.

Pages 606-610 (none)

Court 22 Dec. 1692

Page 611

William Man vs. John Webb and Rachel his wife alleged due from Adam Yarrett dec'd husband to the sd. Rachel, nonsuit to plaintiff.

Page 611a (none)

Court 15 ffeb. 1692/3

Page 611b

Petition of ffrancis Selfe and Rebecca his wife relict of Ralph Stephens, a Com. of Adm. to them.

Court 16 ffeb. 1692/3

46

Northumberland County Orders

Page 611c

Mathew Swelter and Mar. his wife relict of William Gatton, Com. of Adminstration to them.

Concerning a Survey of Land of Andrew Shaw dec'd, in a difference between James Jarsey and Samuel Mahen --- (Note: the blanks are in the manuscript) who married Barbara Salisbury child of Thomas Salisbury dec'd. Memorandum: Thomas Salisbury and Thomas Mayze did this day in court acknowledge to have received full satisfaction from Mr. Thomas fferne for their portions of Thomas Salisbury's Estate or child's portion.

Page 611d (none)

Pages 612-614 (none)

Page 615

Thomas Salisbury son of Thomas Salisbury late dec'd and Thomas Maize who married Barbara daughter of the sd. dec'd, acknowledged to have rec'd of Mr. Thomas fferne who marryed the sd. dec'ds widdow full satisfaction for their portions of the sd. dec'ds Estate. (Note: the above two records are not only complicated, but corrections are not altogether clear)

Court 15 Mar. 1692/3

Page 616

Mr. Thomas Banks and Mr. William Parker to take an Inventory of the Estate of John ffouks, dec'd.

Pages 617-618 (none)

Court 19 Apr. 1693

Page 619

William Collins, impotent and aged, freed from Levy; also William Morgan, ancient and impotent; Edward Paine, ancient and poor; Alexander ffleming, ancient; Abraham Johnson, ancient and poor.

Petition of Eliz. Sanders Exx. of her dec'd husband Mr. Ebenezer Sanders, Probate to her of the Last Will, proved by the oaths of Mr. Peter Presly and Mr. William Githagie.

Mr. Peter Presly and Thomas Gebson overseers of the Last Will of Mr. Peter Presly late dec'd on the behalfe of Peter Presly an infant Sone Exor. to the sd. dec'd, Probate to them, proved by the oaths of Mr. Dan. Neale and Tho. Hobson.

Petition of John Merrydith who marryed Mary the relict of William Barry dec'd, Com. of Adm. to him.

(Page 619a a duplicate of last two)

Page 620

John Cralle to be Constable for Cherry Point and John Haynie, Jun'r for upper ffairfield.

ffrancis Woods, aged and impotenet, freed from Levy.

James Johnson has served as overseer of highways for 12 months in Mattapony and to be released, and Stephen Wills overseer in his place.

William Hill Constable for Mattapony.

Northumberland County Orders

Court 18 May 1693

Page 621

Present: Lt. Col. Sam. Griffin, Capt. Geo. Cooper, Mr. Jno. Turberville, Capt. Wm. Jones, Mr. Dan'l Neale, Mr. Jno. Downing, Capt. Peter Hack and Capt. Spencer Mottrom.

Chas. Betts Constable for lower ffairfield; James White, Newman's Neck; Tho. Hurst, upper Wiccocomoco.

Jno. Atkins, ancient and decrepid, freed from Levy.

Madam ffrances Spencer Exx. of the Last Will of Hon. Nicholas Spencer, Esq., dec'd, vs. Estate of Lt. Col. St. Leger Codd.

Pages 622-623, 623a and 624 (none)

Court 22 June 1693

Page 625

James Moore has considerable Estate and exclusion from Levy revoked. The same for Richard Key.

Pages 626-629 (none)

Court 20 Sept. 1693

Page 630

Mr. Thomas Bushrod and Anne his wife vs. Edward Henly. Plaintiff appealed to the General Court.

Page 631

William Woodland and Mary his wife vs. Joseph Amee.

Page 631a (duplication of above, except the following:)
Deposition of Mary Stethan, aged 25, worked hard as a servant of Adam Yarrett and sworne before mee 8ber 15, 1664 John Roper.

William Berkeley appoints Edmund Lister Commissioner of Northumberland County and asigned in the hand of William Berkeley, 20 April 1667.

Page 631e:

Anth. Lynton late of this County died intestate. John Lynton his brother. (Note: the insertions are included in this book, and it is obvious they belong to earlier books.)

Page 632 (date as above, 20 Sept. 1693)

Charles Vollon vs. Dennis Cameron as Intermarrying with Jane the Widd. of Walter Welsh dec'd.

Court 15 Nov. 1693

Clement Aldridge and Elizabeth his wife vs. William Beane, nonsuit, and C. and Eliz. his wife to pay damages.

Page 633

Rich. Hilliard and Joane his wife Relict of William James dec'd, an App. of his Estate is Petitioned for.

Page 634 (none)

Northumberland County Orders

Court 16 Nov. 1693

Page 635

Capt. George Cooper vs. William Rout.

Pages 636-638 (none)

Court 17 Jan. 1693/4

Page 639

Richard fflynt to be trustee of Estate of Adam Booth, dec'd.

Vestry of Wiccocomoco vs. Estate of John Kelly and John Kelly transported out of this County one Neale MacKenny guilty of begetting a bastard child.

Page 640

John Hughlett Jun. brought action vs. Rodham Kenner Grand Sherr. of this County upon ye Statute of 23 Henry 6th Cap. ye 15th for one hundred pound for default in not duely returning the Burgess to an Assembly held at James Citty in March 1693, and the matter being debated whether it lay within the Jurisdiction of this court to try ye sd. Cause or not,--- This Court are of the opinion that ye sd Cause doth not lye within their Jurisdiction and doe therefore order the suit to be dismissed. Mr. John Turberville and Capt. William Jones dissent for yt they are of the opinion ye sd. action will lye (being brought an action of it) that of ye 23 Henry 6th Capt. ye 15. John Hughlett Jun. appealed to the Genral Court.

Page 641 (none)

Court 18 Jan. 1693/4

Page 642

James Larkins Merchant, dying intestate at ye house of William Parker, Mr. Flynt to take an inventory.

Pages 643-645 (none)

Court 19 Jan. 1693/4

Page 646

Capt. John Haynie guardian of Thomas Harding vs. William Harvey.

Court 20 Jan. 1693/4

Page 647

Clement Lattimore surviving overseer of the Estate of Andrew Morton, dec'd sued by Henry Bruce.

Court 12 Mar. 1693/4

Page 647a

Whereas Edward Randolph Esq. Surveyor Gen"ll of their Maj'es Customs in America, and Christopher Wormeley Esq. Coll'r of the Potomac vs. John Emerson Master of Ship Elizabeth of Berwych in Cone River for not shipping in English vessels according to Act of Parliament. (More on this case in the following pages.)

Court 21 Mar. 1693/4

Northumberland County Orders

Page 648

Petition of Ann fflynt relict of Thomas fflynt, dec'd, Com. of Adm. to her.

Page 649

William Lewis sone of Edward Lewis and Ann Lewis through ye charity of Thomas fflynt and Anne his wife maintained two years, the sd. Anne (now widd. of the sd. Thomas fflynt) moved that the child might serve her until 21.

John Pendrill orphan child of John Pendrill, dec'd, aged 4, to serve William ffletcher until aged 21.

Page 650

Anne Pendrill orphant of John Pendrill dec'd to serve Thomas Maize until aged 18.

Petition of Peter Presly, Capt. Peter Hack and Mr. Charles Harris in behalfe of Richard Hull an infant Exor. of Richard Hull dec'd, Probate to them, proved by the oaths of George Ellistone and Thomas Hobson.

Petition of James Nipper, Probate of the Will of John Crawford, dec'd proved by the oaths of John Bridgeman, Arthur Marsh and Charles Moorhead.

Thomas Byrom petitions this Court yt Sarah Bailes Exx. of Thomas Bayles dec'd dying intestate and left Estate that it might be divided amongst her children with one of whom he intermarryed and concieved (?) in her right a child's portion to be due him, their several portions to them by John Bailey Sone of the sd. Sarah who hath ye Estate in his possession.

Petition of Partin Hudnall to take the personal Estate of Henry Hudnall late dec'd into his possession.

John Patter, poor, aged and impotent, to be freed from Levy.

Page 651

Mary Round infant daughter of John Round to serve John Squires until 18 years of age.

Court 16 May 1694

Motion of Katherine Coutanceau (Exx. of John Coutanceau dec'd) by her Sone Mr. Peter Coutanceau, Probate to her of last Will, proved by oaths of Mr. Henry Rosse and Mary Walker.

Petition of Elizabeth Bently Exx. of the Last Will of her husband Henry Bently, dec'd, Probate, proved by the oaths of James Waddy and William Harvatt.

Page 652

Petition of Edward ffeilding Exor., Probate to him of the Last will of Mr. Thomas Jones, de'cd, by the oaths of Thomas Downing and Thomas James.

Clement Aldridge appointed Constable for Cherry Point Neck; Thomas Bushrod, lower Bowtracy; James Pope, upper Wiccocomoco; Rbt. Christopher upper ffairfield; Wm. Wildy, middle ffairfield; Thomas Hayes, lower ffairfield.

John Lynum, impotent and poor, freed from Levy.

Page 653 (following page)

Northumberland County Orders

Page 653

Petition of John Trimlett and Hannah his wife relict of Thomas Staynie, dec'd, Com. of Adm. to them.

John Thomas infant child base son of John Thomas Serv't to Mr. James Johnson bound with the consent of his father to James Johnson until 21.

John Booth (orphan Sone of Adam Booth dec'd) being about 9 or 10 yr's old, bound to John Claughton until 21; Anne Booth (daughter of Adam Booth dec'd) about 6 or 7 years old, is bound to Mr. Richard Kenner until 18. Richard Booth aged 13 and Adam Booth aged 5, orphans of Adam Booth dec'd, are bound to Mr. Richard fflynt until 21.

Capt. George Cooper sworn High Sheriff.

Court 18 May 1694

Page 654

Richard Vanlandeghan appointed Constable for Mattapony.

John Crawford Orphan Sone of John Crawford, dec'd, with the consent of his grandfather James Nipper bound to John Trimlett.

Page 655

Mr. Alexander Spence Att. of Mr. David Henderson ffactor of Mr. John Boreland of Boston in New England vs. Col. Samuel Griffin.

Pages 656-657 (none)

Court 18 May 1694

Page 658

Edward Lewis petitions that Mrs. Anne fflynt deliver up to him his sone named William Lewis.

Page 659

Richard Flynt as trustee of the Estate of Adam Booth declared that Rawleigh Travers unlawfully possessed 11 head of cattle belonging to the Estate of Adam Booth and the Court ordered sd. Mr. Travers to deliver the cattle. Mr. Rawleigh Travers appeals to the General Court.

Page 660

John Lewis and Mary his wife Exx. of George Courtnell, dec'd, vs. Roger Williams.

The Sheriff to summon Mr. William Parker and Mr. Peter fflynt to render an account of the estate of Mr. James Larkins.

Court 20 June 1694

Petition of Anne Waddington and Geo. Waddington, Exors. of ---- Waddington, dec'd, Probate of the Last will of sd. dec'd. proved by Mr. Phillip Shapleigh and Mr. Sam. Smyth.

Page 661

Anne Alexander daughter to William and Joan Alexander (ye sd. William being absent) with the consent of her Mother, to serve John Oldham and Abigail his wife until aged 18.

Page 662 (none)

Northumberland County Orders

Court 20 June 1694

Page 663

John Crawford dec'd, his Estate being this day produced to this court sold at outcry, and payment to James Jarsey and Richard Adams (in trust and to ye use of each orphan or orphans or other persons.) James Jarsey and Henry ffranklin bond on Crawford's estate. Richard Adams and Thomas Rout on the Estate (bond).

Page 664 (none)

Court 21 June 1694

Page 665

Thomas Berry and Ester Robeson wife of ffrancis Robeson did not appear in Evidence of John Way vs. William Harcum.

Page 666

Mrs. Eliza ffeilding surviving Exor. of Mr. Edward ffeilding of Bristol, dec'd vs. Mr. Peter Knight.

Court 15 Aug. 1694

Page 667

John Embry, John Kent for his wife Katherine, Richard Clapman and Wm. Embry sued by Capt. Wm. Jones; Margrett Reine serv't to the sd. Capt. Jones said she had a false key to her masters Storehouse door and in May last did persuade her sd. Master's daughter to take the false key and draw an Earthon jugg of rume; William Embry and Rich. Clapman were given the rume, and went to the house of John Kent, and sd. Margrett later went to John Kent and Katherine Kent asked her to get some sugar. It is ordered to take William Embry, Rich. Clapman and Katherine Kent into custody and sd. Margrett to be punished and by request of Capt. Jones the punishment remitted on condition of good behaviour.

Pages 668-669 (none)

Page 670

Sarah Dickinson entered Mr. Charles Harris her Att.

Page 671 (none)

Court 19 Sept. 1694

James Austen, Tho. Harwood, Jno. Graham and Joseph Hoult or any three to take Inventory of the Estate of Ralph Waddington.

Court 21 Nov. 1694

Page 673

Sarah Pendrill orphan Daughter of John Pendrill dec'd, aged 10 ye first day of March, to serve Chris. Garlington.

Jonathan Dabinett, aged 14, chose Charles Harris guardian.

Thomas Berry who married Margaret the Relict of Thomas Smyth, dec'd, Com. of Adm. to him.

Page 674

Mary Maclanahan orphan of John Maclanahan to serve Dennis Oneale and his wife.

Northumberland County Orders

Page 675

Estate of John Pendrill sold at outcry and Christopher Garlington, Thomas Maize and William ffletcher (to whome one of sd. dec'd orphans is bound) to receive the estate.

Page 676 (none)

Court 22 Nov. 1694

Page 677

Jno. Dudly as marrying Eliza. the daughter of Erasmus Withers dec'd vs. John Curtis.

Page 678 (none)

Page 679

Edward Kirkpatrick and Anne his wife late Relict and Widdow of Mr. Wm. Smyth dec'd, Com. of Adm.

Page 680 (none)

Court 23 Nov. 1694

Page 681

Richard Wells, poor, indigent and aged, freed from Levy.

John Lankester intermarryed with ffrances ye Relict and Widdow of Ralph Warrington dec'd, dying intestate, and he to give an account of the Estate.

Sam. Webb als Day begotten of the body of Mary Day, a Molatto child, apprenticed to Wm. Yarrett.

Court 16 Jan. 1694/5

Page 682

John Nickless who marryed ffrances Exx. of John Lewis dec'd, Probate is granted her of ye will, proved by oaths of Wm. Havett and Jno. Nickless witt. to sd. Will.

John Sharp to take Inventory of the estate of Wm. Brooks, dec'd, who dyed a poor man at the house of the sd. Sharp.

John Trussell dec'd died intestate leaving diverse children and his relict and widdow hath since his decease marryed with Henry Hatson; Hatson and Eliz. his wife late Eliz. Trussell, wid. of ye sd. dec'd to exhibit an inventory.

Court 17 Jan. 1694/5

Page 683

Petition of James Nipper exor., a Probate to him on the Last Will of James Jarsey, dec'd, proved by the oaths of John Hughlett and William Murrow.

Pages 684-685 (none)

Court 20 ffeb. 1694/5

Page 686

Petition of James Lockman, a Probate of the will of Walter Allen, decd

Northumberland County Orders

Page 686 cont'd:

by oaths of Charles Dodson and John Thomas.

Motion of Anne fflynt, Admx. of Tho. fflynt dec'd, William Parker, Th. Bushrod, James Creane and Jno. Cralle or any three to Appraise the Est.

Moor ffantleroy Sone of Mr. Wm. ffantleroy late of Rap. Co., dec'd, has chosen his grandfather Col. Samuel Griffin to be his guardian.

Court 20 Mar. 1694/5

Page 687

Eliza. Eaton, Relict of Richard Eaton, a Probate of the last will of Rich'd Eaton to her, ye Will being proved by the oaths of Tho. Hughlett and Anne Christopher.

Petition of Abigail ye Relict and Widdow of James Seabury, Com. of Adm. to her.

Petition of John Sharp, Com. of Adm. on ye Estate of Wm. Brooks, decd.

Pages 688-692 (none)

Court 15 May 1695

Page 693

John Way appointed Constable for lower, William Woodland for middle and Richard Rice for upper ffairfield; Henry Masie for Cherry Point; and Edward Smyth for Mattapony.

Abraham Griffin a saylor who belongs to ye Ship Adventure (Mr. Thomas Opie commander) was accidently struck overboard with ye boome of a shallop at or neer ye mouth of Coan river thereby receiving his death, and a Jury of inquest was impanelled (the coroner being lately dec'd) and sworne by Capt. Peter Hack, the dec'ds goods are in possession of Mr.Th. Opie, and Mr. Opie to pay fee to Capt. Hack out of the dec'ds Estate.

Patrick Grady orphan child about aged 13 bound to Jno. Reason 'til 21.

Charles Downing Sone of Mr. Wm. Downing, dec'd, chose Jno. Downing guardian.

Petition of Anne Taylor relict and Exx. of Wm. Taylor dec'd, Probate to her of the Will, proved by the oaths of Edw. Williams, Henry Dawson, Wm. Dawson and James Wilson.

Page 694

Gannah Chankerett infant daughter of Stephen Chankerett, aged ye 1st of October last one year, to serve James White until 18.

Page 695

Luke de Merritt and Mary his wife attended one day in evidence in behalf of Andrew Salisbury vs. Samuel Mahem.

Court 19 June 1695

Stephen Chankerett infant son of Stephen Chankerett, a year old ye 1^s day of Oct. last, by his father's consent to serve Jno. Moor until 21.

Petition of Katherine Relict and Widdow of Jno. Dunaway, Com. of Adm. with will annexed to her.

Northumberland County Orders

Page 696 (none)

Court 19 June 1695

Page 697

Arthur Marsh, Rich'd Nutt and Robert Nash or any two to App. Est. of John Lord dec'd in possession of Edw. ffeilding.

Peter Coutanceau to be overseer of highways.

Joseph Hoult and Tho. Barnes to continue as overseers of ye highways. Thomas Berry also an overseer of ye highways and also Jno. Greensted.

Pages 698-702 (none)

Court 21 June 1695

Page 703

Wm. Smyth and Eliza his wife vs. Jno. Hughlett and Mary his wife Adm'ts of Wm. Downing dec'd, and defts. not appearing, the plts. vs. Capt. Geo. Cooper former Sheriff.

Court 21 Aug. 1695

Page 704

Pet. of Jno. Thomas, Exor., a Probate to him of the Last Will of Edw. Jones, proved by the oaths of Joseph Hoult, Edmund Mandly and Tho. Hobson.

Pet. of William Cornish Exor. of Wm. Alden, dec'd, Probate to him of the last will of sd. dec'd, proved by the oaths of Capt. Rodham Kenner and Mr. Peter Coutanceau.

Jno. Price an infant child son of Eliza Price, aged 6 yrs ye 3^d of this instant, to serve Andrew Bashard and his wife until 21.

Page 705

Katherine Williams an orphan child, aged 14, to serve Hugh Stathen and his wife until 18.

Court 22 Aug. 1695

Page 706

Jno. Baker Adm. of Dennis McCarty vs. Rich'd Flynt.

Page 707 (none)

Court 14 Sep. 1695

Page 708

Pet. of Jane Wilkins Relict and Widd. of Jno. Wilkins dec'd, Com. of Adm. to her.

Pages 709-710 (none)

Court 16 Oct. 1695

Page 711

Pet. of Mrs. Hannah Neale Exx. of Mr. Christopher Neale dec'd, Probat to her of sd. dec'd Husband's Last Will, proved by oaths of Capt. Rodham Kenner, Mr. Thomas Bushrod and Clement Aldridge.

Northumberland County Orders

Page 711 cont'd:

Mr. Dan'l Neale and Patience his wife vs. Edw. ffeilding Exor. of Tho. Jones referred to next Court.

Mary Chankeret, aged 6 next Jan., is by the consent of her ffather Stephen Chankerett to serve Henry ffrankling until 18.

Page 712

Elizabeth Chankerett, aged 8, with the consent of her ffather Steph. Chankerett to serve Joseph Hoult until 18.

Court 17 Oct. 1695

To. Capt. Rodham Kenner for Burgess charges.

Page 713

Mr. Dan'l Neale, Coroner, on a dead body of Jno. Moon's Sone, Moon to pay fees.

Court 18:Xber:1695

Page 714

Pet. of Alexander Mulraine, Exor., Probat to him of the Last Will of Josias Long, proved by the oaths of Thomas Webb and Eliza his wife.

Pet. of Elizabeth Browne Relict and Widdow of Wm. Browne dec'd, Com. of Adm. to her.

Pages 715-718 (none)

Court 15 Jan. 1695/6

Page 719

Mrs. Jane Wildy vs. the Estate of William Norris.

Court 18 Mar. 1695/6

Page 719 cont'd:

Elizabeth Smith wife of Richard Smith relinquishes right of Dower in land sold by her sd. husband to Mr. John ffarnefold.

Anne Hull Exx. Probat to her of the Last Will of John Hull, dec'd, proved by oaths of Charles Harris and Zachar. Thomas.

Pet. of John Million, Com. of Adm. to him on the Est. of John Tolson, dec'd.

Pet. of Alexander Mulrane Exor. of Joseph Long, dec'd, App. of the Estate.

Page 720

Nicholas Harrold, son of Walter and Priscilla Harrold, 11 years old last ffeb., to serve Capt. Tho. Brereton until 21. John Harrold, ditto, 7 years old last Dec., to serve John Erimlett and his wife until 21. Hugh Harrold, 7 last Dec. to serve Wm. Woodland.

Mr. Peter Presly vs. Thomas Barnes and Jane his wife Admx. of John Wilkins dec'd.

Court 15 Apr. 1696

Northumberland County Orders

Page 720 cont'd:

Pet. of Mr. Peter Coutanceau, Probate to him of the Last Will of Mrs. Catherine Coutanceau, dec'd, proved by the oaths of Henry Rosse and Mrs. Eliz. Banks.

Page 721

Probate to Andrew Salisbury for Geo. Berratt Exor. of the Last Will of Isabella Berratt.

Court 20 May 1696

Page 722

Tho. Trape, poor and aged and impotent, freed from the Levy.

John Weeks son of Henry Weekes, who is now absent by consent of his Mother Anne Weekes to serve Tho. Webb or Wm. Yarrett until he is 21.

Page 723

. John Turberville sworne High Sheriff. Benj. Vanlandegham sworne Constable for Metapony. Thomas Hughlett and Rich'd Lattimore sworne Under Sheriffs. Ignatius Oliver Constable for Cherry Poynt; Mr. Dan. Neale Jr., upper Cone; Joseph Gendall, upper Wiccocomoco; Jos. Humphrey, upper ffairfields; Garvase Ellistone, lower ffairfields.

Mary Bennett, 6 years old, 11th March last and Daniell Bennett, 12 months old 3 Jan. last, by consent of the Mother to serve John Downing and Eliz. his wife; Mary until 18 and Dan until 21.

Susannah West Relict of John West dec'd, Est. to be App.

Est. of Benjamin Tolson to be App.

Court 21 May 1696

Page 724

John Harris Adm. of David Whitford vs. John Gouth Son and Heire of Sam'l Gouth; the Mother of Sam'l Gouth marryed Peter Byram.

Page 725

Jane Nipper Widow and Relict of James Nipper, dec'd, Com. of Adm. to her.

John Dunaway, dec'd, indebted to Katherine Dunaway his Relict and Adm. for funeral expenses.

Page 726

John Trimlett and Hannah his wife vs. Thomas Staynie.

Matthew Groth, poor, impotent and distempered, freed from Levy.

Page 727

Peter Presly, Capt. Peter Hack and Charles Harris Exors. of the Last Will of Richard Hull, dec'd, vs. Turles Conner.

Page 728

John Alverson and Jane his wife as evidence in behalf of Wm. Jones vs. Telif Alverson.

Northumberland County Orders

Court 22 May 1696

Page 729

Henry Hutson and Elizabeth his wife vs. Capt. Rodham Kenner dismissed.

Page 730

Jno. Allen was arrested at ye suite of Peter Presly, Capt. Peter Hack and Charles Harris Exors. in trust of Rich'd Hull dec'd during the minority of Rich'd Hull.

Court 15 July 1696

Page 731

Pet. of Rich'd Shirley, Probate to him of the Last Will of Thomas Shirley, proved by ffrancis Billingham and James Gaynes.

Pet. of Anne Danks, Probate of the Last Will of John Dankes her husband, proved by William Elliott and Tho. Bushrod.

Page 732

To Peter Presly the greatest Creditor, Com. of Adm. on Est. of James Pope, dec'd, unless someone who is next of kin shall take the privilege.

Page 733

Cert. to John Hanye for 450 acres, trans. for: Richard Burgesse, John Beard, Joseph Bland, Thomas Harley, Abigail ----, Jane Peterson, John Margill, Luke Demeratt and Tho. Hope.

Cert. to Rich'd Hanye for 200 acres, trans. for: Morris Bassill, Mary Stephens, Elinor Crinsby and Joan Gurrill.

Cert. to Dennis Eyes for 550 acres, trans for: Tho. Aldwell, Jane Thompson, Barbara Jackson, George Mackdanell, Gilcrist Oheart, Sam'l Camell, Margt. May, Wm. Gunson, Isabell Mason, Kath. Smith and Jno. Ogan.

Cert. to John Harris for 250 acres, trans. for: James Ward, Neale McCarty, Henry Armstrong, James Milligan and George Runkin.

Pages 734-735 (none)

Court 16 July 1696

Page 736

Difference between Edward Saunders Plt. and John Cockerall and Eliz. his wife Exx. of Ebenezer Saunders, dec'd, concerning land devised by the sd. Ebenezer Saunders to his son Edward his daughter Elizabeth and his said Brother Edward the plt.

Pages 737-739 (none)

Court 16 Sept. 1696

Page 740

Sam'l Smith Exor. a Probate of the Last Will of Lt. Col. Sam'l Smith to him, proved by the oaths of James Austen and Thomas Hobson.

Pet. of Mary Simons Exx. of the Last Will of her dec'd husband John Simons, proved by Thomas Brewer.

Pet. of Judith Leazure Exx. , A Probate to her of the Last Will of Bartholomew Leazure, proved by Geo. Hutton and Sarah Hutton.

Northumberland County Orders

Page 740 cont'd:

Pet. of Mary Screver for Mary Heath Exx. of the Last Will of Captain William Lee, Probate to her, not witnessed and ordered.

Pet. of Joyce Trape, Com. of Adm. on the Est. of Thomas Trape, dec'd, (John Wornom Exor. in Court relinquished his Exor'ship) the said Will being proved by Thomas Hobson and William Woodland.

Pet. of Bartholomew Scriver and Mary his wife Exx. of Capt. William Lee, App. of Est. ordered.

Pet. of Charles Betts in behalfe of his Daughter Mary Betts a minor, a Probate is granted her of the Last Will of Sam'l Batson, the Will N.C. proved by the oaths of Mary Royston and Margaret Hamons.

Motion of Richard Rogers, Probate of the Last Will of John Rogers, dec'd, proved by Tho. Bushrod and Peter Presly.

Pages 741-742 (none)

Court 17 Sept. 1696

Page 743

The Est. of John Lee, dec'd, to be sold.

Court 18 Sept. 1696

Page 744

Wm. Nutt vs. Edward Sanders: land on Gr. Wiccocomoco in ffairfields Parish, part of 10,000 (1,000?) acres granted to Roger Walters (now decd) by Pattent, and said 200 acres sold out of the said Pattent to William Nutt ffather to the Plt. by the said Walters as by deed 2 May 1657 and Saunders unlawfully holds it.

Pages 745-746 (none)

Court 19 Nov. 1696

Page 747

Motion of Elizabeth Henly, Probate of the Last Will of her dec'd husband Edward Henly, proved by Richard Thompson and George Allen and App. of the Est. is ordered.

Page 748

Est. of Benjamin Tolson to be App.

John Algrove 5 years old the 26th of May Next Son of Nichilas Algrove, to serve Tho. Hughlett and Mary his wife until 21.

Page 749

Thomas Algrove son of Nicholas 8 yrs. old the 8th of May next with the consent of his Mother Eliza Algrove to serve Thomas Gill until 21.

To Rawley Travers as chiefest Cred'r, a Com. of Adm. on the Est. of James Shipard, dec'd, who dyed intestate.

Court 20 Nov. 1696

George Crosby and Charles Betts sworne Surveyers of the Highway; also John Wornom. Richard Hanye and Richard Smith to be overseers of the hiways. Dennis Conway and Henry ffranklin also overseers; also John Carbell and James White; also Charles Harris and Thomas Harwood.

Northumberland County Orders

Page 750 (none)

Page 752

Thomas Bushrod is nominated Trustee in the Last Will of Robert Sech represented to the Court that Jane Knott orphan of John Knott dec'd having an Est. and non qualified to serve the Land, it is ordered that Capt. Rodham Kenner and Thomas Bushrod take the Est. until the next Court.

Court 16 Dec. 1696

Richard Orland and Margrett his wife by John Turberville her Att. ack. assignment of Land to Robert Davis.

Thomas Dutton and Mary his wife by John Turberville their Att. ack. assignment of Land to Richard Orland.

Page 753

Jane Knott orphan of John Knott dec'd chose Capt. Rodham Kenner guardian.

Pet. of Henry Harding, Com. of Adm. to him on the Est. of Wm. Harding.

Court 17 Dec. 1696

Page 754

Richard Hanye and Elizabeth his wife ack. a Deed to their children.

Thomas Webb and John Wornom to App. Est. of John Paulson.

Pages 755-756 (none)

Court 18:Xber:1696

Page 757

Pet. of Richard fflynt Exor. of Peter fflynt dec'd, Probate to him of the Last Will, proved by Hugh Harris and Richard fflynt, Jr.

John Sharpe wrote the Will of John Simons and entered himself witness.

By the Will of Peter fflynt, he appointed his Bro't Richard fflynt Ex. the the said Richard assumes the payment of all the Orphan's Estates in possession of his brother.

Motion of William Harvy, Probate to him of the Last Will of John Sanders, proved by William Bashaw and Andrew Bashaw.

The Last Will of William Greensted proved by ffrancis Billingham, Jno. Bowe, Sr. and John Bowe, Jr.

Jesse Bayles and Mary his wife by her Att. Richard Smith ack. a deed of sale of Land to Samuel Lunte.

Court 17 Mar. 1696/7

Page 758

Motion of John Hughlett and Susanna Relict of John Hulett, dec'd, the Probate to them of the Last Will, proved by John Farnefold and Mary Chapman.

Motion of John Lewis Exor., a Probate of the Last Will to him of Ralph Holmes, by oaths of David Straughan and John Mcray.

Northumberland County Orders

Page 758 cont'd:

The N. C. Will of Thomas Harwood proved by Richard Prichard and Martha Clarke.

Page 759

Lucretia Lewis daughter of Edward and Ann Lewis, 7 years old the 9th of June last, to serve by the consent of her Mother, Thomas Hughlett and Mary his wife.

William Allen who marryed Margarett the Daughter of John Sharpe, decd, Com. of Adm. with Will annexed to him.

Motion of John Craven, a Probate to him of the Last Will of Rim Garrison, dec'd, proved by John Webb and Wm. Carpenter.

Elizabeth Aldridge wife of Clement Aldridge Jun. relinquishes rights of dower to 64 acres of land sold to Tho. Miller. She also relinquishes Dower in their sale of 60 Acres to John Cralle.

Page 760

Ester and Sarah Sanders daughters of John Sanders dec'd, Ester being 10 years and Sarah being 4 years, to serve John Boaz and Elizabeth his wife until 18.

Pet. of Elizabeth Wornom Relict of John Wornom, dec'd, Com. of Adm. to her and App. of Est. ordered.

John Nickless ack. deed of gift to his son John Nickless.

Est. of Tho. Harwood to be App.

Peter Presly orphan of Peter Presly dec'd, chose Thomas Hobson guardian.

Daniell James Orphan of John and Mary James dec'd, 9 years old about next Christmas, to serve Mary Graham until 21.

Motion of Jane Mahen Exor. by Richard Hanye her Att., a Probate to her of the Last Will of her dec'd husband Samuel. Mahen, proved by Robt. Robinson and Katherine Pollick.

Page 761

Hannah Bee orphan of John Bee, 10 years old last Sept., to serve Thos. Berry.

Motion of Mary Graham and John Graham Exors., Probate to them of the Last Will of John Graham, dec'd, proved by Tho. Hobson and Richard Clark.

Motion of William and ffrancis Cursone Joint Exors., Probate to them of the Last will of ffrancis Cursone, proved by Peter Hammon and John Emberson.

Zachariah Sanders, orphan of John Sanders, dec'd,, chose William Harris guardian.

Pet. of Mary Rowland, Relict of Luke Rowland, dec'd, a Com. of Adm. to her. (See page 736, Court 16 July 1696, Capt. Jno. Haynie guardian to the Orphans of Thomas Harding, dec'd, vs. Luke Rowlands who marryed Anne Admx. of the sd. Harding.)

Motion of Richard Prichard Exor., Probate to him of the Last Will of William Ward, proved by Alexander Mulraine and Mary Whitehead.

61

Northumberland County Orders

Page 761 cont'd:

Pet. of Mary Woodland Relict of William Woodland, Com. of Adm. to her.

By consent of Richard Prichard and Mary Ward Relict of Wm. Ward, decd, Est. to be sold.

John Sanders, 10 years old, orphan of John Sanders, decd. to serve John Dawson until 21.

Page 762

Anne Grady orphan of Walter Grady dec'd, to serve Peter fflynt and Mary his wife until 18.

John and Richard Algood orphans of Edward Algood dec'd, to serve Peter fflynt until 21.

Motion of Richard Lankester and William Parker Exors., Probate of the Last Will of George Waddington to them proved by Edward Watkins, Thomas Hobson and the codicil by the sd. Thomas Hobson and Ralph Pearie.

Page 763

Motion of Andrew Bashaw Exor. of the Last Will of William Bashaw decd, Probate, proved by Richard Shirley and William Dawson.

Pet. of John Webb and John Boaz, Com. of Adm. to them on the Estate of William Grimsteed.

Pages 764-765 (none)

Page 766

John Turberville vs. Barthol. Shrever as marrying Mary the Exx. of Capt. Wm. Lee, dec'd, to next Court.

John Hartley Att. of Mrs. Anne Brent Relict of Robert Brent, dec'd, vs. Capt. Rodham Kenner to next Court.

Page 767

Thomas Rout vs. Anne Dank Exx. of Thos. Dank, referred.

Court 19 May 1697

Page 769 (no mention made of page 768)

The Last Will of Thomas Salisbury proved by Barthol. Dameron, Thomas Winter and Christo. Garlington.

The Last Will of John Lewis proved by Vincent Garner and Phillip Aherne.

Com. of Adm. to Thomas Webb on the Est. of his dec'd Wife Elizabeth Webb.

John James, aged 12, the 18th of Sept., orphan of John and Mary James dec'd, to serve Mary Paine until 21.

Page 770

Thomas Algrove son of Elizabeth Algrove, aged 8, the 9th of the inst. May with the consent of the Mother, to serve Thomas Hughlett until 21.

Motion of Samuel Smith, a Com. of Adm. with the Will annexed of James Austen dec'd is granted to him during the minority of Rainsford Smith,

Northumberland County Orders

Page 770 cont'd:

son of the said Samuel and legatee mentioned in ye said Will.

    Constables: Samuel Winstead for Matapony; George Groves, Cherry Pt.; George Kesterson, lower ffairfield; Charles Nelms, for middle ffairfield and Thomas Sims for upper ffairfield.

    Charles Dermott and Ann his wife as evidence in behalf of John Webb vs. William Wood.

Page 771

    Pet. of Sarah Span Widow and Relict of John Span, dec'd, Com. of Adm. to her.

Court 20 May 1697

    William Harcum cheifest Cred'r of the Est. of Anne Bee, Com. of Adm., and Anne Bee dyed intestate; Sheriff to summons William Williams who marryed one of the daughters of the said Anne and Sarah Hawkins another Daughter of the said Anne to appear at next Court.

    Motion of Mary Timmons Widow and Relict of Thomas Timmons, Com. of Ad. to her.

Pages 772-775 (none)

Page 776

    Col. Wm. Fitzhugh vs. John Pope heire of James Pope.

Page 777 (none)

Court 21 May 1697

Page 778

    Wm. Man and Elizabeth his wife vs. Dorcus Higgenson, Cont'd.

Page 779 (none)

Court 21 July 1697

Page 780

    John Dudly and Elizabeth his wife ack. a deed of Indenture to Thomas Curtis.

    Sarah Salisbury Widow and Relict of Thomas Salisbury ack. a deed of Indenture to Isaac Gaskins.

    Pet. of Nicholas Morrica and Elinor his wife Relict of John Thomas, dec'd, Com. of Adm. to them.

Court 22 July 1697

Page 781

    John Sharpe and Thomas Hughlett sworne subsheriffs.

    The Last Will of John Hanye Sen. proved by Richard Robinson and John Hanye Jun.

    The N. C. Will of Thomas Ashton proved by Ignatius Olliver and Cath. Mackdonnell.

    Motion of William Williams and Elizabeth his wife, daughter of John

Northumberland County Orders

Page 781 cont'd:

Bee, dec'd, Com. of Adm. to them.

 Katherine Austen Widow and Relict of Thomas Austen, dec'd, allowed bed and furniture. Katherine relinquishes Adm. and it is given to Chas. Austen and Est. to be App.

Page 782

 Motion of William Sanders and Elizabeth his wife Exx. of the Last Will of Richard Eaton, dec'd, ordered that John Webb, Thomas Rout, Richard Rice, John Bryant and Richard Rout, sen. and any 4 App. the Est.

 Ignatius Oliver and Cath. MacDonnell, Attended the Court in proofs of the N. C. Will of Tho. Austen.

Court 18 Aug. 1697

 Motion of Thomas Hayes, Probate to him of the Last Will of Elinor Coles dec'd, proved by Cuthbert Span and Henry Lane.

 Motion of Mary Nutt, Probate of the Last Will of her dec'd husband William Nutt, proved by Cuthbert Span and Christpher Mayes.

 Motion of Jane Harding Widow and Relict of Henry Harding, Com. of Adm. to her.

Page 783

 Motion of Jane Greensteed Widow and Admx. of John Greensteed dec'd, App. of Est. ordered.

 Motion of Mrs. Jane Rogers and Thomas Bankes Exors. of Richard Rogers, dec'd, Probate to them of the Last Will on the oaths of Capt. Rodham Kenner, Ellinor Greene and Jane Muckantion, and the Est. to be App.

Pages 784-788 (none)

Court 15 Sept. 1697

Page 789

 Motion of Wm. Parker, Com. of Adm. on Est. of Lawrence White, dec'd.

Pages 790-793 (none)

Court 16 Sept. 1697

Page 794

 Thomas Webb Adm. of Elizabeth Webb his wife dec'd vs. Samuel Smith adm. with the Will annexed during the minority of his son Rainsford Smith a minor Legatee of James Austen.

Page 795 (none)

Court 20 Oct. 1697

Page 796

 Motion of Ruth Ross Exx., Probate to her of the Last Will of John Ross, dec'd, proved by Christopher Garlington and Patrick Pollick.

 Motion of Elizabeth Gaskins Exx. of the Last Will of Henry Gaskins, dec'd, Probate to her, proved by Thomas Maize and Thomas Hobson.

Northumberland County Orders

Page 796 cont'd:

Thomas Brereton ack. Indenture of Lease for life to Capt. Thomas Winder and Elizabeth his wife.

Andrew Salisbury and Mary his wife ack. a deed of sale to George Berratt.

Pet. of Hannah ffeilding Relict of Edward ffeilding, Com. of Adm. to her and Estate to be App. and Com. of Adm. of the Est. of Thomas Jones also to her.

Court 17 Nov. 1697

Page 797

Motion of Jam. Yarrett Exor. of Wm. Yarrett dec'd, Probate of the Last Will to him, proved by Richard Hanye and James Oldham and Thomas Petty.

Motion of Ruth Parker, Exx., Probate to her of the Last Will of William Parker dec'd, proved by Ignatius Oliver and James Genn.

Court 18 Nov. 1697

Motion of Henry Rosse on Behalf of Mrs. Elizabeth Bankes, a Probate to her on the Last Will of her dec'd husband, proved by Henry Rosse, Jane Harris and Katherine Talbut.

Upon petition of Ruth Parker, Com. of Adm. to her on the Estate of Lawrence White, dec'd.

Page 798

Motion of Thomas Lee and Elizabeth his wife Relict of John Wornom, a Com. of Adm. to them and App. of the Estate.

Court 19 Nov. 1697

Josias Gaskins moved this Court for Adm. of the Est. of James Hawkins, dec'd, as greatest creditor.

Page 799

Motion of Jane Hanks Widow and Relict of George Hanks, dec'd, Com. of Adm. to her and App. of the Estate.

Upon motion of Richard Hanye and Charles Harris Att. of Ester Sanders Widow that William Harvie doth deteyne her Son from her and all or most of her Estate.

Court ffeb. 1697/8

Motion of Margarett Mary Relict of Henry Mary, dec'd, Com. of Adm. to her and App. of the Estate.

Motion of John Nickless Exor., a Probate to him of the Last Will of his dec'd ffather John Nickless, proved by Tho. Chilton and James Ginnis.

Page 800

Motion of Henry Rosse Exor., Probate of the Last Will of Jane Linton, dec'd, proved by George Leasure and David Gill and App. of the Estate.

Motion of John Huske and Susannah his wife Relict of John ffeilding, dec'd, Com. of Adm. to them and App. of the Estate.

Motion of Mrs. Anne Elliott, Exx., Probate of the last Will of her

Northumberland County Orders

Page 800 cont'd:

dec'd Husband William Elliott, proved by David Straughan and Henry Boggas.

Motion of Sarah More Relict of James Moore dec'd, Probate to her of the Last Will, proved by George Hutton and Alice Watson.

Motion of John Cralle, Probate to him of the N. C. Will of James Perry, dec'd, proved by Sarah Bashaw and William Maxteed.

Page 801

Motion of Margarett Beane Exx., Probate to her of the Last Will of her dec'd Husband Wm. Beane, proved by George Allen and Morris Deron.

Motion of Bartholomew and George Leazure Exors., Probate to them of the Last Will of John Leazure, proved by Vincent Cox and Ann Dankes.

Motion of Mrs. Anne Elliott, Com. of Adm. with will annexed on the Estate of Cath. MacDonnell, proved by Tho. Bushrod and Teige Allen.

Motion of Henry Dawson Exor., Probate to him of the Last Will of Tho. Millard, dec'd, proved by Teige Allen, Rich. Hughs, and Mary Browne.

Page 802

Motion of Richard Tulles Exor., Probate to him of the Last Will of Thomas Adams, Dec'd, proved by Tho. Bushrod, Ruth Proverb and Samuell Browne.

Robert Jones and Sarah his wife ack. a Bond to Thomas Ferne.

Court 16 ffeb. 1697/8

John Way and Eliza. his wife by her Att. Tho. Hobson ack. a Deed of Sale to John Gralis.

Rawl. Travers and John Cralle to take pos. of the Est. of William Harvey, dec'd, and dispose of the land at outcry.

Samuell Blackwell orphan of Sam'l Blackwell, dec'd, chose John Moore guardian.

Motion of Mary Woodland, Com. of Adm. on the Est. of Joyce Trape, decd and Est. to be App.

Motion of David Straughan and Ruth his wife Admx. of Lawrence White, dec'd, Est. to be sold at outcry.

Motion of Robt. Clifford a Probate to him of the N. C. Will of Jno. Staton, proved by James Rogers and Andrew Cockrell.

Page 803

Motion of Henry Dawson, Probate to him of the Last Will N. C. of Lucy Mallard, proved by Dennis Cornwell and Susannah West.

Court 17 ffeb. 1697/8

Com. of Adm. to Phillip and Jane Bussle and Rebecca Mallard, petition for the same by Symon Robins their Att. on the Est. of Thomas Mallard, dec'd.

Pet. of Sarah Span, Com. of Adm. to her on the Est. of her dec'd dau. Elizabeth Span.

Northumberland County Orders

Page 804

William Harvy, orphan of William Harvy dec'd, to serve James Johnson until 21. James Harvy, ditto, to serve Rawl. Travers until 21. Allen Harvy, ditto, to serve Capt. Rodham Kenner until 21. Charles Harvy, ditto, to serve Wm. Knott until 21. Mary Harvy, ditto, to serve Rawl. Travers until 18. Margarett Harvy, ditto, to serve Peter Coutanceau until 18.

Page 805

Thomas Rout and Henry ffranklin to take the Estate of Jno. Crawford into their possession and account for it.

Court 18 ffeb. 1697/8

Page 806

John Cralle and David Straughan to take the Est. of Mary Barnes into their possession and exhibit an inventory.

Page 807

Elizabeth Algroves vs. Mary Woodland: whereas Thomas Trape dec'd father of the said Mary dyed possessed of a personal Estate and Mary dau. of the sd. Thomas, dec'd by his late wife two thirds of which Estate the said Elizabeth conceives to be rightfully belonging to her by the Law of the Country being the only child of the said Thomas.

Page 808 (none)

Page 809

Attachment to Eliza Sharpe Widow and Relict of John Sharpe dec'd vs. William Allen Adm'r of the sd. dec'd.

Richard Robinson and ffrances his wife vs. Edward Watkins and Anne his wife Exx. of Ralph Warrington for a third part or filiall portion of the sd. dec'd. She, the sd. ffrances, being daughter of the sd. Warrington.

Page 810 (none)

Page 811

Cuthbert Span brother of John Span, dec'd vs. Sarah his Admx.

Page 812

John Hughlett vs. Joseph ffranklin and Susannah his wife late Susannah Hughlett, Co-Ex. of the Last Will of John Hughlett.

Page 813 (none)

Court 19 ffeb. 1697/8

Page 814

Motion of Charles Ashton and Jane his wife, Com. of Adm. to them on the Est. of William Harding, dec'd.

Motion of Henry Dawson, Com. of Adm. to him with the Will annexed on the Est. of Lucy Mallard, dec'd.

Rawl. Travers vs. Christopher Neale and Jane his wife Exor. of Rich'd Rogers, dec'd.

Court 20 Apr. 1698

Northumberland County Orders

Page 815

Present: Lt. Col. Sam. Griffin, Capt. Geo. Cooper, Capt. Rodham Kenner and Capt. Peter Hack.

Page 816

Motion of Henry Rosse Exor., App. of the Est. of Mr. Linton's.

Motion of John Bushrod, Exor., Probate to him of the Last Will of Tho. Bushrod, dec'd, by oaths of Wm. Knott, Vincent Garner and Rich'd Pryce.

Charles and Edward Lewis sons of Edward and Mary Lewis with the consent of their Mother to serve James John until 21.

Robert Rowland aged 4 the 31st of Jan. last by the consent of his Mother Mary Rowland to serve Edward Woodridge until 21.

Motion of John Eustace Exor., Probate of the Last Will of his dec'd ffather Jno. Eustace, proved by the oaths of Tho. Pinckard and James Ginnes.

Page 817

Motion of Martha Haynes Relict of Edward Haynes, Com. of Adm.

Edward Watkins and Anne his wife assign 50 Acres to Tho. Sims.

Motion of ffrances Nickless Relict of John Nickless, dec'd, Com. of Adm. to her.

Page 818

Thomas Williams and Allice his wife by their Att. Thomas Hobson ack. an Indenture for 40 acres to Richard Lattimore.

Motion of Robert Munkin, Com. of Adm. on the Est. of Martha Barnes.

Page 819 (none)

Court 21 Apr. 1698

Page 820

John Purney and Katherine his wife serv't to Tho. Hughlett for evidence in Court.

Motion of Valentine Munslow, Com. of Adm. on the Est. of Tobert Robinson, dec'd.

Page 821 (none)

Court 18 May 1698

Page 822

Motion of Richard Lattemore, Probate of the Last Will of Clement Lattemore, dec'd, proved by Capt. Peter Knight and Elizabeth Bowen.

Philip Tignor appointed Constable for lower St. Stephen's and William Cornish for Newman's Neck.

Motion of Dorothy Tillett Exx., a Probate to her of the Last Will of Tho. Tillett, dec'd, proved by Rich'd Lattimore.

Motion of John Linne, Probate to him of the Last Will of Alexander Griffin, dec'd, proved by Elizabeth Bowen.

Northumberland County Orders

Page 822 cont'd:

Motion of Mary Betts Exx. of her husband, Probate to her of the Last Will of Mary Royston dec'd, proved by Alex'r Mulraine and Jno. Gater.

Page 823

Charles Ashton appointed Constable for Cherry Poynt.

Motion of Thomas Hayden, Com. of Adm. on the Est. of ffrancis Cursone, dec'd,

Motion of Elizabeth Downing Exx. of John Downing, dec'd, Probate to her of the Last Will, proved by David Spens, John Limkin and Thomas Hobson.

George Gerratt appointed Constable for upper Wiccocomoco.

Motion of Eliza Curtis, Com. of Adm. to her on the Est. of her dec'd husband Henry Curtis.

Thomas Webb Adm. of his late wife Elizabeth Webb complains vs. Samuel Smith, whereas James Austen late dec'd father to the said Eliza. dec'd, possessed of considerable personal Estate and Eliz. daughter and Co-heir with her sister Alice the said Samuel, his wife and James Austen bequeathed all his Estate Personall to Rainsford Smith.

Pages 824-825 (none)

Court 13 June 1698

Chris. Garlington and Margaret his wife convey land to Hancock Lee, 200 acres.

Motion of Elizabeth Lee, Exx., Probate to her of the Last Will of her dec'd husband Thomas Lee, proved by Richard Robinson, Jno. Chapman and Tho. Gill.

Motion of David Straughan, Com. of Adm. to him on the Est. of Ruth Straughan his wife dec'd.

Motion of Susanna Littrell, Com. of Adm. to her on the Est. of her dec'd husband James Littrell.

Page 827

John Claughton moved the Court for Adm. on the Est. of James Claughton his dec'd father and there being others the daughters of the sd. dec'd in whom the Court are of the opinion equal right of Adm. and unless they join with him, Adm. to him.

Upon the motion of Thomas Crowder, Com. of Adm. on the Est. of James Edney dec'd, he being next of kin and Est. to be App.

Court 20 July 1698

Page 828

John Rodes, aged 13, the 5th of Dec. next and Eliz. Rodes, aged 6, son and daughter of Hannah Rodes, dec'd, and she left them to Tho. Everard to serve him and her Est. to be App.

Page 829

Motion of David Straughan who marryed the Exx. of Wm. Parker, dec'd, Com. of Adm. on his Estate.

Motion of Capt. William Jones, Com. of Adm. to him on the Est. of his

Northumberland County Orders

Page 829 cont'd:

dec'd brother Mr. Samuel Jones.

Motion of Matthew Myer who marryed Mary Palmer Exx. of Thomas Keen, dec'd, Probate of the Last Will of Thomas Keen, proved by Edward Williams and Cloud Tullos.

Motion of Esther Hickman, Exx., Probate of the Last Will of her dec'd husband Tho. Hickman, proved by Geo. Berratt and Ann Dermott.

Motion of James Ginnes and John Craven Exors., Probate to them of the Last Will of ffrancis Nickless, proved by Thomas English and John English.

Page 830

Motion of John Claughton, William Lambert and Edward Smyth on behalfe of their wives and Middleton Claughton by her brother the aforesaid Jno. Claughton, Com. of Adm. to them on the Estate of James Claughton, their dec'd ffather.

Motion of Hannah ffuker Relict of David ffuker, Com. of Adm.

Pages 831-832 (none)

Court 21 July 1698

Page 833

Anne Hull Admx. of John Hull vs. Capt. Peter Hack and Charles Harris surviving overseers of the Estate of Richard Hull.

Pages 834-835 (none)

Court 17 Aug. 1698

Page 836

Motion of William Sanders, Com. of Adm. on the Est. of Elizabeth Sanders, his dec'd wife.

Motion of Josias Gaskins, Com. of Adm. on the Est. of James Hawkins.

Court 25 Sept. 1698

Page 837

Motion of Anne Hobson, Exx., Probate on the Last Will of Wm. Hobson, her dec'd husband, proved by Capt. Geo. Cooper and Richard Hilliard.

Motion of Elizabeth Pinley, Widdow and Relict of Thomas Pinley, dec'd Com. of Adm. to her.

Court 22 Sept. 1698

Page 838

Motion of Capt. Peter Hack, Peter Coutanceau, Exors, of the Last Will of Capt. Spencer Mottrom, dec'd, Probate to them, proved by Barbara Cazar and Mary Robins and Codical proved by Charles Harris and Dennis Conway.

Motion of William Hill, Com. of Adm. to him on the Estate of John Hill, dec'd.

Pages 839-840 (none)

Northumberland County Orders

Court 16 Nov. 1698

Page 841

Richard Cundiff ack. a Deed of Gift to his son Richard Cundiff.

Page 842

Motion of Charles Lee Legatee, a Com. of Adm. with the Will annexed to him of the Last Will of Walter Jenkins, proved by John Lewis and Geor. Powell.

Page 843

Walter Grady orphan of Walter Grady dec'd, 15 years old last March chose Cloud Tullos guardian.

Court 17 Nov. 1698

Motion of Bartholomew Dameron, Com. of Adm. on behalf of the orphans of George Dameron, dec'd.

Page 844

ffrancis Vanlandegham, petitions the Court that his sisters son Phillip Clowes without father or mother, aged 8 or 9, John Wallers to be guardian, at 17.

Page 845 (none)

Court 21 Dec. 1698

Page 846

Com. of Adm. of the Est. of John Eason, dec'd, to James Johnson the greatest cred'r.

Page 847 (none)

Page 848

John Webb and Elizabeth his wife ack. Deed for 100 acres of land to William Bundle.

End of #4

Section II

#5   Northumberland County Orders

Page 1 (none)

Court 19 Jan. 1698/9

Page 2

Stephen Coleman and Katherine his wife ack. Deed of Sale of Land to Henry Mayre.

Page 3

Motion of Winifred Hughlett, Com. of Adm. to her on the Estate of Allice fferne.

Motion of Margery Lunseford, a Com. of Adm. to her of the Last Will of William Reeves, dec'd.

Motion of Elizabeth Aldridge, Exx., a Probate to her of the Last Will of Clem't Aldridge, proved by David Straughan and Mary Tullos.

Cuthbert Span to be a Justice of the Peace.

Mary fferne orphan of Thomas fferne dec'd chose Charles Harris guardian. Motion of Mary fferne, Com. of Adm. granted her on the Est. of Tho. fferne, dec'd.

Court 19 Apr. 1699

Page 4

Wm. Howson sworne Justice of the Peace.

Page 5 (none)

Page 6

Motion of Patrick Pollick Exor., a Probate to him of the Last Will of John Cranstone, dec'd, proved by James Cox and Dennis ffallon.

Motion of Alexander Newman, Exor., a Probate of the Last Will of Walter Dun, dec'd, proved by John Dalton and Jonathan Dabinett.

Motion of Elizabeth Sheere Relict of Abraham Sheare, Com. of Adm. to her with the Will annexed on the Est. of her dec'd husband, and the Will proved by Barthol. Dameron and Chris. Garlington.

Page 7

Peter Watkins son of Henry Watkins, aged 6 the 24th of Oct. Next, and with the consent of the Mother, to serve Richard Smith and Elizabeth his wife until 21.

Motion of Margaret Chapman Sister of John ffarragon dec'd, nine mon's being expired since his death, Com. of Adm. to her.

Court 20 Apr. 1699

Page 8

George Knott ack. a Deed of Guift for an acre to ffrancis Voyer.

Page 9 (none)

Page 10

John ffarnefold vs. Robert Jones as marrying Sarah Relict of Thomas Salisbury.

Northumberland County Orders

Page 12

Mrs. Elizabeth Downing guardian of her son John Downing vs. Susannah ffranklin and John Hughlett, Exors. of John Hughlett ..cont'd.

Pages 13-14 (none)

Page 15

William Parker and Jane his wife vs. the Estate of Richard Pearce.

Court 21 June 1699

Page 16

Capt. Rodham Kenner sworne High Sheriffe.

Pages 17-18 (none)

Page 19

Motion of Phillip Bussle Exor. a Probate to him of the Last Will of Phill. Drake, dec'd, proved by Richard fflynt and Thomas fflynt and Richard Booth.

Motion of George Curtis (his son), a Probat of the Last Will of Thos. Curtis, dec'd, proved by William Simpson and John Dudley.

Page 20

Mrs. Mary fferne made choice of Capt. William Howson to be her guardian.

Mrs. Elizabeth Newman Ex. (blotted out ---) ---r Dun, dec'd, vs. John Graham att. of Richard S(mith by Thomas Hobson. (Note: the latter part of the name appears later; more suits, pp. 21-23)

Pages 21-23 (none)

Page 24

Motion of John Williams who marryed Sarah the Daughter of Thomas Towers, Towers land to be surveyed.

Estate of Charles Harris to be inspected.

Court 22 June 1699

Page 25

James Rogers vs. John Hurst and Susannah his wife Admx. of John ffeilding.

Page 26

James Atkins and Mary his wife vs. Richard Pritchard Exor. of William Ward.

Edward Watkins appointed Constable for Wiccocomoco; Daniel Swillivant for Matapony; John Daily for Newman's Neck.

Dorcas Tillett Admx. of Thomas Tillett dec'd by her son Richard Hartney sued by John Edwards.

Page 27

John Ingee gave evidence in behalf of William Man vs. James Lockman.

Northumberland County Orders

Page 28 (none)

Page 29

Richard Hughs appointed Constable for Cherry Poynt.

Pages 30-33 (none)

Court 23 June 1699

Page 34

Elizabeth Gregory Exx. of William Thornbury vs. John Jones.

Mrs. Elizabeth Downing Exx. of John Downing vs. John Champion Exor. of John Champion.

Page 35 (none)

Court 19 July 1699

Page 36

Pet. of John Eustace, a Com. of Adm. to him on the Est. of his dec'd Brother William Eustace.

Page 37

Motion of Phillip Shapleigh cheifest cred'r, a Com. of Adm. on the Est. of John Walkinsha.

Court 20 July 1699

Page 38

John White orphan son of Lawrence White aged 12 to serve David Straughan and his wife until 21.

William Mary aged 10 and Ann Mary aged 7 orphans of Henry Mary, dec'd to serve John Lawrence and his wife until the sd. William is 20 and sd. Ann 18.

Pages 39-46 (none)

Court 21 July 1699

Page 47

Motion of Hannah fflucker Admx. of David fflucker nonsuit to her vs. William Man.

Court 22 July 1699

Page 48

Motion of Capt. Peter Hack, an Inv. on the Est. of Charles Harris.

Pages 49-50 (none)

Court 16 Aug. 1699

Page 51

Cuthbert Spann and Capt. Thomas Winder sworne Justices of the Peace.

Page 52

Motion of William Algood, a Com. of Adm. to him on the Estate of John Algood, dec'd.

Northumberland County Orders

Page 52 cont'd:

Estate of Edward Williams to be App. N. C. Will of Edward Williams proved by Henry Dawson. The Estate to his wife Katherine Williams and her two children, and a Probate of the said will to William Howard and Ruth his wife.

Motion of John Pope, a Com. of Adm. to him on the Est. of Dorcas Higginson.

Page 53

Motion of Mrs. Mary Brereton Exx., a Probate to her of the Last Will of Capt. Thomas Brereton, dec'd, proved by the oaths of Capt. George Cooper and Edward Bennett.

Court 17 Aug. 1699

Page 54

Thomas Webb, Adm. of Elizabeth Webb his wife vs. Samuel Smith, Adm. of James Austen: James Austen dec'd left only 2 daughters (Viz:t) the said Elizabeth and the said Samuel's wife and Samuel Smith refuses to give to Thomas Webb half of the Est., and a nonsuit is granted the def't vs. the pl't. with damages and Court charges. Pl't appeals to the General Court.

Pages 55-63 (none)

Court 20 Sept. 1699

Page 64

Thomas Sheere, orphan of Abraham Sheere, chose Barthol. Sheere guardian.

James Southorne, poor and decrepid, freed from Levy.

Sarah Eaton orphan of Richard Eaton made choice of William Sanders to be her guardian.

Page 65

Cert. to Major Rodham Kenner for 500 Acres, trans. of 10 persons: Thomas Stott, Thomas Smith, Mathew Jackman, Philip Sennett, Richard Burk, Daniell Howland, David Poore, Richard Cushion, Robert fferne and Elizabeth Wilcox.

Cert. to Dan'll Swillivant for 300 Acres, trans. of 6 persons: George Armstronge, John Chambers, John ffegan, Richard Vaxon, John Camady and John Smith.

Cert. to Rawl. Travers for 300 Acres, trans. of 6 persons: Lawrence ffox, Edward Peters, Robert McGregory, Gowen Steward, Elizabeth Dobson and James Letherborough.

Court 21 Sept. 1699

Page 66

Motion of Clem't Arlege, Probate to him of the Last Will of Eliz. Arlege his wife, proved by Edw'd Barnes and Hugh Stathen.

Cert. to Peter Coutanceau for 550 Acres, trans. of 11 persons: James Mortemore, John Aro, Denie Mc carty, Edwd. ffolio, Margt. Chapman, John Bryan, Tho. Walters, Henry Hutson, William Parker, Mary Day and John Hayes.

Cert. to John Cralle for 1050 Acres, trans. of 21 persons: John Cralle

Northumberland County Orders

Page 66 cont'd:

Dn;1 Neale, Ignatius Oliver, John Mast, James Carne, Ralph Holmes, Sarah Hutchins, Elinor Browne, Wm. Batting, John Lindsey, Mary Williams, Tho. ffitzgerrard, Cornelius Allen, Patrick Codd, William Wool, Allice Evans, Dan'l Dane, Phill. Welsh, Thomas Phillips, Robert Phillips and John Owen.

Pages 67-69 (none

Court 23 Sept. 1699

Page 70

David Spens and Sarah his wife legatee of John Downing vs. Mrs. Eliza Downing Exx. of John Downing.

Pages 71-72 (none)

Court 25 Sept. 1699

Page 73

John Tarpley and Elizabeth his wife Exx. of Walter Dunne vs. John Reason Dismissed.

Martha Haynes Admx. of Edw. Haynes vs. John Nickless as marrying Elizabeth Exx. of Henry Curtis, dec'd.

Motion of Capt. Wm. Jones Assignee of Coll. Wm. ffitzhugh as cheifest cred'r, a Com. of Adm. on the Est. of Anthony Lynton, dec'd.

Court 18 Oct. 1699

Page 75

Henry Durckin and Dorothy his wife ack. a Deed of Indenture to Vincent Garner.

Motion of Nathaniel Tingcomb, a Com. of Adm. on the Est. of John Stott.

Court 19 Oct. 1699

Judgement granted John Pope admr. of Dorcas Higginson dec'd vs. the said Higginson Estate.

Page 76

Judgement granted Dorcas Pope by her brother John Pope vs. Estate of Dorcas Higginson dec'd.

Page 77

Barthol. Dameron adm. of George Dameron to pay unto Philip Tigner and Sarah his wife late Sarah Dennis daughter and sole heire of John Dennis dec'd and her Estate in the possession of the sd. George Dameron who marryed the sd. Sarah's Mother and widow of the sd. John Dennis.

Pages 78-81 (none)

Court 15 Nov. 1699

Henry Mayze and Litia his wife ack. a Deed of Sale to Thomas Gill.

William Metcalfe made choice of Benjamin Boggasse to be his guardian.

Motion of William Metcalfe the N. C. Will of Phil. Metcalfe dec'd was proved by Ignatius Olliver and John Conway.

Northumberland County Orders

Page 82 con'td:

Motion of Mary Brereton Exx. of William Nutt dec'd, an Inv. ordered.

Motion of William West who marryed the Relict of Richard Orland dec'd a Com. of Adm. to him.

Page 83

John West orphan son of John West chose Henry Dawson guardian.

Court 16 Nov. 1699

Page 84

Motion of Capt. Wm. Jones Admr. of Sam. Jones, App. of Estate.

Page 85

David Jones and Diana his wife Deed of Sale to John Claughton.

Winifred Hughlett Adm. of Allice fferne vs. Mary fferne Adm. of Thos. fferne: Thomas fferne by his Last Will gave half of all and singular goods and chattle said Thomas dyed in possession of, received in marriage by then wife sd. Allice from John Hughlett her ffather and left her by her father's will and the def't has lately Adm. her father's estate and Allice dyed as Exx. of the sd. will and before the will was proved or division made and after Allice's death Letters of Adm. with the will annexed granted to the one of the said Allice her sisters and also Adm. with the will annexed; the Court believes the negroes were vested in the def't.

Page 86 (none)

Court Nov. 1699

Motion of Bartholl. Schreever guardian of Thomas Sheere orphan of Abraham Sheere, dec'd, a division of the Estate and James Richardson and Elizabeth his wife Exx. of the sd. Sheere has possession of the Estate.

Page 88

Henry Dawson Adm. of Lucy Mallard vs. Phill. Bussell and Jane his wife and Rebecca Mallard, and Lucy's 4th part of Thomas Mallard's estate, and Thomas the Lawful husband to Lucy and Thomas dying left said wife and three children and 4th part rightfully belonging by Thomas' Will to Lucy.

Court 20:Xber:1699/1700

Page 89

William Sheere Orphan of Abraham Sheere has chosen Major Rodham Kenner guardian.

Page 90

Elizabeth Parker orphan of William Parker chose Capt. Thomas Winder guardian.

Court 21 ffeb. 1699/1700

William Barber and Joyce his wife ack. Deed of Indenture of 100 acres to William Colston.

Page 91

Mary Brewer Relict of Thomas Brewer, Com. of Adm. to her and App. of the Est. ordered.

Northumberland County Orders

Page 92

John Blentone chose John Middleton guardian.

John Selfe on behalfe of himselfe and Susannah his wife Daughter of James Blentone, a Com. of Adm. to him.

ffenly Morrison on behalfe of himselfe and Ann his wife next of kin to Thomas fflatman and Elizabeth his wife Sister to the sd. Ann, a Com. of Adm. to the sd. ffenly during the minority of Anne the daughter of sd. Thomas and Elizabeth fflatman and the Estate to be App. of Tho. fflatman.

Court 17 Apr. 1700

Page 93

Henry Metcalfe sone of Henry Metcalfe chose William Keene guardian.

Motion of James Nipper Exor., a Probate to him of the Last Will of Jane Nipper dec'd, proved by John ffarnefold and for a codical by Rich'd Smith.

Motion of Sarah Bird Widow and Relict of John Bird, Com. of Adm. to her and App. of his Estate.

Page 94

Katherine Swillivant on her owne and her Brother Owen Swillivant complained that Capt. William Thornton whose shipp they arrived here in did deteyne their indentures and a report to be made at the next Court.

Pages 95-97 (none)

Court 19 Apr. 1700

Page 98

John Million excused from paying Levy; also Henry Proverb.

Elizabeth Middleton wife of John Middleton Relinquishes her right of Dower of 50 Acres of Land sold by her sd. husband to Ignatius Oliver.

Charles Lee sworn High Sheriff.

Motion of Sarah Tullos, a Probate of the Last Will of Cloud Tullos, dec'd, proved by Vincent Garner and John Walter.

George Knott ack. a Deed of Sale of Land to Rawley Travers.

Stephen Coleman excused from paying Levy this year.

Tho. Williams appointed Constable for Wiccocomoco.

Page 99

John Corbell appointed Constable for Chickacone; John Dawson, lower Mattapony; and John Hadwell, lower St. Stephen's.

Motion of Mary Baker, a Com. of Adm. to her on the Est. of her dec'd husband Thomas Baker and Est. to be App.

Motion of Winifred Hughlett, a Com. of Adm. to her on the Estate of Thomas fferne.

Peter Hack, Peter Coutanceau and Rodham Kenner Gentl'n, Exors. of the Last Will of Capt. Spencer Mottrom dec'd vs. William Howson Gentl'n, as

78

Northumberland County Orders

Page 99 cont'd:

marrying with Sarah the Widdow of the said Mottrom.

Richard Staplee excused from Levy this year.

Capt. Wm. Jones and Margaret his wife ack. a Deed of Sale of 250 acs. to Major Wm. Lister.

Page 100 (none)

Court 20 June 1700

Page 101

William Howard and Ruth his wife Admx. of Edward Williams dec'd, App. of the Estate.

Motion of Elizabeth Baily Exx. of the Last Will of her dec'd Husband John Baily, Probate, proved by Peter Coutanceau, John Evans and Ann Grady.

John Turberville vs. John Claughton, William Lambert, Edward Smith, Richard Smith and Middleton his wife Admrs. of James Claughton dec'd.

Page 102

Richard Pemberton vs. David Jones as marrying the Relict of David Depue, dec'd, dismissed.

Page 103

William Man Adm. of Elizabeth Spencer vs. Joannah ffluker Admx. of David ffluker dec'd, dismissed.

Page 104 (none)

Court 17 July 1700

Page 105

Motion of Margaret Berry Exx. of Thomas Berry, a Probate of the Last Will, proved by William Harcum and Christopher Newton.

Henry Dawson appointed Overseer of highways; also Henry ffranklin and Nicholas Edwards and Christopher Newton and David Speens, Richard Nutt, Arthur Mayhaze, John Bryan, Richard Swanson, Thomas Miller and John Graham.

Barthol. Screiver in behalfe of his sonne Dennis Screiver pet's the Court that Mary fferne being sole dyed intestate (as ms.), and the said Dennis next of blood and kin of the sd. Mary, and Winifred Hughlett claimed greater right to the Est.; from which Mr. Screiver appeals to the General Court.

Page 106

Capt. Peter Hack surviving Exor. of Richard Hull, dec'd, a Com, of Adm to on on the Est. of Charles Harris, dec'd.

Court 18 July 1700

Page 107

John Rotherom excused from Levy this year.

Page 108   James Norris vs. John Thomas

Northumberland County Orders

Page 109

John Creel attended Court in evidence of Jas. Norris vs. Jno. Thomas.

Pages 110-116 (none)

Court 19 July 1700

Page 117

John Selfe and Susanna his wife Adm. of James Blinko vs. Matthew Myer.

Page 118

Peter Hack Surviving Admr. of Richard Hull petitioning the Court for Adm. of the Estate of Charles Harris dec'd and Mrs. Anne Chowning on the behalf of Jane Harris Daughter of Anne Harris dec'd, granddaughter of sd Anne Chowning petitioning also on the above sd. Estate and the Court considered the right was of the above sd. Hack.

Richard fflynt appointed overseer of highways.

Court 16 Aug. 1700

Page 119

Elizabeth Wildey wife of William Wildey complains that they have been married many years, that he mistreated her, and that she is living now with her Mother, and that she seeks to compel her husband, and that he being absent should be brought to the next Court.

Page 120 (none)

Court 22 Aug. 1700

Page 121

John Tarpley and Eliz. his wife, Adm. of William Bruce vs. Capt. Wm. Jones Admr. of Sam'l Jones.

John Richardson vs. Edward Watkins and Elizabeth Porter Widow of this County.

Page 122 (none)

Page 123

James Rogers vs. Henry Durkin who marryed Dorothy Maclanchan.

Page 124 (none)

Court 23 Aug. 1700

Page 125

Henry Sutton and Margaret his wife for Slander vs. James White.

Thomas Hewlett vs. Winifred Hughlett Admx. of Tho. fferne.

Page 126

Leonard Howson and Mary his wife late widow and Exx. of Capt. Thomas Brereton, dec'd, vs. Col. Geor. Cooper cont'd.

Pitts Curtis as marrying Hannah Fluker Admx. of David Fluker sued by Wm. Man, Admr. of Elizabeth Man.

Northumberland County Orders

Page 126 cont'd:

Hannah Manley wife of Edmund Manley gave evidence on behalf of Jno. Stott vs. James White.

David Spens and Sarah his wife late Sarah Span Widdow vs. Thomas Winder dismissed.

Page 127

Barthol. Shreever vs. Tho. Ball and Elizabeth Widdow and Admx. of Tho. Brewer dismissed.

Page 128 (none)

Court 18 Sept. 1700

Page 129

Motion of William Coppage Exor., a Probate granted him of the Last Will of William Coppage dec'd, proved by John Howson and William Browne.

Capt. John Tarpley and Elizabeth his wife Exx. of Walter Dun vs. John Reason.

Page 130

Motion of Thomas Downing, the N. C. Will of Marmaduke Thompson was proved by John Merryfeild and William Broughby.

Thomas Ball and Elizabeth his wife Admx. of Thomas Brewer sued by George Violett.

Page 131

Difference between ffrancis Jones and Thomas Couth and Barthol. Schrever and Mary his wife late Mary Heath, Exx. of Capt. William Lee, dec'd.

Court 19 Sept. 1700

Page 131 cont'd:

Motion of Peter Presly, Jr., Com. of Adm. on the Estate of Peter Presly his dec'd father.

Page 132

Winifred Hughlett Admx. of Thomas fferne vs. Capt. William Howson: def't damaged the Estate of Tho. fferne in her custody and def't admitted guardian of Mary fferne dec'd daughter and Admx. of Thomas fferne, dec'd and Court divided 4 vs. 4, and the case sent to the General Court.

Page 133 (none)

Court 16 Oct. 1700

Page 134

Motion of Thomas Miller Exor., a Probate is granted him of the Last Will of Hugh Stathen, proved by Jonathan Palefrey, Sarah Bashaw, Teige Allen and Teige Canady.

Motion of Dan'l Neale, Exor., a Probate to him of the Last Will of his dec'd ffather Dan'l Neale, proved by John Corbell and Thomas Hobson.

Page 135 (following page)

Northumberland County Orders

Page 135

Motion of Jane Coppage late Jane fforest a Com. of Adm. to her on the Estate of Alexander fforest dec'd, and a division of the Est. ordered, with Inventory.

Motion of William Percifull Exor., a Probate to him of the Last Will of John Webb dec'd proved by Richard Robinson and Roger Jones.

Motion of Mary Simpson Relict of Wm. Simpson, a Com. of Adm. to her.

Pages 136-137 (none)

Court 17 Oct. 1700

Page 138

William Medcalfe to choose another guardian at next Court.

Page 139

Mrs. Elizabeth Downing vs. Phillip. Clarke as marrying ffrances Relict and Exx. in her own wrong(?) of George Page dec'd.

Court 15 Jan. 1700/1

Page 140

Motion of Isabella Linton, a Probate to her of the Last Will of John Linton, dec'd, proved by ffra. Dawson, James Crean, James Crean, Jr. and David Gill.

The Last Will of Charles Ashton proved by Trigue Allen and Charles Carpenter.

Motion of Capt. John Cralle, a Com. of Adm. on the Estate of John Long, dec'd.

Thomas Gaines to take the estate of Samuel Bashaw into his custody & return an inventory.

John Oldham ack. Deed of Guift to his son James Oldham.

Page 141

Tho. Williams and Alice his wife by her Att. John Sharpe ack. a conveyance to Jno. Champion.

The Last Will of William Howson proved by Leonard Howson and John Howson.

Probate of the Last Will of Cuthbert Span granted to Mrs. Dorothy Span by Thomas Hobson on her behalfe who produced her noate to that effect.

Page 142 (none)

Court 19 ffeb. 1700/1

Page 143

Motion of William Neale, A Com. of Adm. with the Will annexed of Dan. Neale, dec'd, and the will proved by James Rogers and Eliz. Annoy.

Richard Ruth and Eliz. his wife Relict of John Brewer, dec'd, that John Brewer made a will but nominated noe exor. therein and prayed Adm. on the sd. Estate.

Northumberland County Orders

Page 143 cont'd:

Motion of Hannah Trimlett, a Com. of Adm. on the Estate of John Trimlett, dec'd to her.

Motion of John Langsdon and Arthur March, a Com. of Adm. to them with the Will annexed proved by Tho. Hobson and Jno. Bundle of Richard Bannister, dec'd.

Motion of Thomas Robinson, a Probate of the Will of Jno. Robinson, dec'd, proved by Thomas Hobson and John Blundle.

Motion of William Bolster a(nd-blotted out) John Reason, a Com. of Adm. to them on the Est. of John Gralose.

Court 20 ffeb. 1700/1

Page 144

Charles Ashton aged 13 chose William Cornish guardian.

Motion of William Neale, Com. of Adm. on the Est. of Edward Neale,

Page 145

Motion of Stephen Smith who marryed Elizabeth Exx. of John Baily,decd to divide the Estate.

Court 21 ffeb. 1700

Page 146

Motion of Hannah ffranklin Exx. a Probate to her of the Last Will of Henry ffranklin, dec'd, proved by the oaths of John Langdell and Anne Langdell.

Peter Coutanceau appointed guardian for John Baily orphan of John Baily.

Pages 147-149 (none)

Court 22 ffeb. 1700

Page 150

Motion of David Straughan and William Cornish Exors. of the Last Will of Charles Austen dec'd, the sd. dec'd Est. to outcry.

Page 151

John Howson guardian of John Coppage vs. William Coppage Exor. of his father William Coppage.

Page 152

William Coppage Exor. of William Coppage vs. Jane Coppage Relict of William Coppage dec'd in Chancery Court cont'd.

Page 153 (none)

Court 19 Mar. 1700

Page 154

Jacob Baily sone of John Baily dec'd chose Peter Coutanceau guardian in advance.

Northumberland County Orders

Court 20 Mar. 1700/1

Page 154 cont'd:

Motion of Thomas Williams and Elizabeth his wife next of kin, a Com. of Adm. with the Will annexed to them on the Estate of John Browne, decd.

Motion of Peter Coutanceau, a Com. of Adm. to him on the Estate of his dec'd wife Mary Coutanceau.

Page 155

Thomas Webb, Joseph Hoult, Edward Sanders, George Crosby, Thomas Kesterton to App. the Estate of Thomas Berry dec'd being sworn by the Next Justice and ordered that Margaret Gill late Margaret Berry Exx. of sd. dec'd Exhibit an Inventory.

Matthew Myers and Jane his wife late Jane fflint daughter of Thomas fflint dec'd vs. Anne fflint Admx. of Thomas fflint dec'd referred at the def'ts motion.

Pages 156=158 (none)

Court 16 Apr. 1701

Page 159

Motion of Jane ffallon Exx. of the Last Will of Charles ffallon decd. a Probate, proved by Benjamin Browne and John Hogan.

Page 160

Mary Eyes Widdow and Relict of Dennis Eyes Petitions for Adm. on her dec'd husband's estate.

Motion of Martha Robinson, widdow and Relict of John Robinson, dec'd, Com. of Adm. to her.

Page 161 (none)

Court 21 May 1701

Page 162

John Howing (as it is written) ack. Deed of Gift to his kinswoman Elizabeth Howson.

Motion of John Steptoe, a Probate to him of the Last Will of Arthur Steptoe, dec'd, proved by John Eustace and George Anderson.

Page 163

Rawl. Travers Gent. and Sarah his wife by her Att. Thomas Hobson ack. a Deed of Sale of Land to Colston. (Mr.)

Motion of Dennis Conway, John Conway and Dennis Conway, Jr., Exors. a Probate to them of the Last Will of Dennis Eyes dec'd, proved by Rich. Rice, Dennis Conway, Jr. and Patrick Conner.

Pet. of Mary Eyes, Com. of Adm. on the Estate of Dennis Eyes, dec'd, denied, for a Probate already granted on the Will.

John Champion appointed Constable.

Page 164 (none)

Court 22 May 1701

Northumberland County Orders

Page 165

Mrs. Elizabeth Bankes on behalf as next ffriend to her sone John Keen vs. Matthew Myer.

Court 18 June 1701

Page 166

Motion of Martha fflint, Thomas fflint and Xper Dawson Exors., a Probate of the Last Will of Richard fflint, proved by Manly Browne, Susannah Browne, Charles Richardson and Isaac Utine.

Motion of Mrs. Berratt Exx., a Probate to her of the Last Will of Geo. Berratt, proved by Vallentine Munsloo, ffra. Roberts and Sarah Burrut.

Page 167

James Oldham appointed Constable of Lower Cone, and Nicholas Listone for Newman's Neck.

Court 16 July 1701

Jeremiah Bell, poor, aged and impotent, freed from Levy.

Peter Coutanceau, Coronor, letter to the Sheriff dated 12th day of this instant, July, produced the body of one Evan Robertt, serv't of Capt. John Cralle for a Jury of Inquest.

Page 168

Edward Watkin Constable for Lower St. Stephen's.

William Grady orphan of Walter Grady chose John Tullos guardian.

Motion of Thomas Gaines, a Com. of Adm. on the Est. of Sarah Bashaw, dec'd.

Page 169 (none)

Court 17 July 1701

Page 170

Henry Sutton and Margarett his wife late Margarett Key vs. Barthol. Shepheard Dismissed.

Page 171

Wm. Percifull Sen'r, and Wm. Percifull, Jun'r, Exors. of the Will of John Webb vs. William Bundle dismissed.

Richard fflynt petitions that Peter fflynt dec'd by Will bequeathed to Richard fflynt the Elder Exor. of the sd. Will and he is dec'd, and Martha fflynt his widdow with his son Thomas fflynt and Christ. Lawson his Exors. and they refuse to act.

Pages 172-175 (none)

Court 15 Oct. 1701

Page 176

Motion of Mary Hornsby Relict and Widdow of John Hornsby, a Probate of the Will of her dec'd husband John Hornsby, proved by Leonard Knight and Elizabeth Knight.

Northumberland County Orders

Page 176 cont'd:

John West orphan son of John West, dec'd, formerly chose Capt. Henry Dawson, but petitions for another guardian.

Richard Smith ack. a deed of guift for 200 acres of Land in Rich. Co. to his two sons Richard and John Smith.

Court 16 Oct. 1701

Page 177

Motion of Richard Lattemore Exor. a Probate is granted him of the Last Will of John Evans, de'cd, proved by William Nelms and Nicholas Lehngh and the estate to be App.

John Baily by his next ffreind or Prothonamie Mr. Peter Coutanceau vs. Stephen Smith.

Page 178

Motion of Richard Pemberton, a Com. of Adm. on the Estate of Morris Dorron, dec'd.

Page 179 (none)

Court 19 Nov. 1701

Page 180

Mary Rout ack. Deed of gift to her children.

Motion of Henry ffleet, Exor., a Probate of the Last Will of James Wildy, proved by John Ross and Mary his wife late Blackerby.

Page 181

Motion of Mrs. Anne Keene Widdow of Mr. William Keene dec'd, Com. of Adm. James Ginn, Henry Dawson, Henry Bogasse, Richard fflynt and John Lawrence any 4 to App. the Estate.

Henry Metcalfe chose William Metcalfe guardian.

Page 182 (none)

Court 17:Xber:1701

Page 183

Motion of Mrs. Eliza. Lee Exor. of Capt. Charles Lee, dec'd, by John Turberville, a Probate to her of the Will not proved by witnesses, but appears to the Court to be his Will.

Pages 184-186 (none)

Court 18:Xber:1701

Page 187

Mary Ingee Exor. of Jno. Ingee vs. John Hill.

Court 21 Jan. 1701/2

Page 188

Motion of Thomas Holly, Com. of Adm. on the Estate of Abraham Knott, dec'd, and Est. to be App.

Northumberland County Orders

Page 188 cont'd:

James Jones ack. Deed of Sale together with George Eskridge, att. of Eliza. wife of the sd. James Jones unto Henry Hutson.

Pages 189-194 (none)

Court 23 Jan. 1701/2

Page 195

Cert. to Thomas Hobson for 500 acres, trans. of 10 persons: John Topping, John Thompson, Dorothy Thompson, Richard Dobles, Margaret Lawson, William Gay, Susanna Read, Anne ffryer, Henry Parry and Andrew Armsley.

Court 15 Apr. 1702

Page 196

Motion of Alice and John Taylor Exors. of the Last Will of John Taylor, a Probate, proved by John Howson and Michael Keady.

Motion of James Innis, John Steptoe, and Tho. Pinkard, a Probate to them of the Last Will of John Eustace, dec'd, proved by John Steptoe, George Wale and John Hurst.

Motion of Elizabeth Ball Widdow and Relict of Thomas Ball, dec'd, Com. of Adm. to her and App. of the Estate.

Page 197

Motion of Anne Tignor, Exx., a Probate to her of the Last Will of her dec'd husband William Tignor.

Motion of Charles Ingram by his petition for division of the Estate of George Dameron dec'd into 4 Equal parts and possession of the said Charles Ingram who marryed one of the sd. Dameron Daughters with her part.

Page 198

William Cornish petitions that his Brother Richard Key who dyed two years since, leaving an estate, a wife and daughter and the wife married one Henry Sutton and dyeing and the estate is in the possession of the sd. Sutton, and he to be admitted guardian of Key's daughter.

Court 16 Apr. 1702

Page 199

Jno. Adams and Katherine his wife ack. a conveyance of 60 acres of Land unto John Shirley.

Henry Mayze Jun'r Att. of his ffather Henry Mayze, Sen'r and Lydia Mayze wife of the sd. Henry Mayze, ack. deed of Sale of land to James Innis.

William Dawson on behalfe of John Blencone a minor orphan of James Blencone dec'd that John Middleton sent the orphan to the Easterne shore under pretence of giveing him learning and damaged the orphan's land, prayed security for the land.

Pages 200=203 (none)

Court 17 April 1702

Page 204

John Arnett vs. Phill. Rogers and Isabella his wife Exx. of John Lin-

Northumberland County Orders

Page 204 cont'd:

ton (Linton), dec'd.

Nicholas Spencer and John Spencer surviving Exors. of Nicholas Spencer Esq. dec'd, vs. Peter Hack, Gent.

Page 205 (none)

Court 17 June 1702

Page 206

Thomas Day, aged and poor, freed from Levy.

Constables: Richard Price, Cherry Poynt; Enock Hill, Middle St.Stephen's; John Tullos, Jerrico; John Ross, Newman's Neck.

Motion of Jane Crean late Jane Weatherstone Exx. of Alexander Weatherstone, a Probate to her of the Last will of the dec'd, proved by Chris. Newton and John Johnson.

Thomas Percifull and Katherine his wife ack. Deed of Sale of 100 acrs. of Land unto Charles Moorehead.

Page 207

John Coleman, orphan child of John Coleman, with the consent of his mother Mrs. Dorothy Coleman (the orphan being 4 years old) to serve Tho. Smith and Margery his wife until 21.

Rebecca Hutton orphan daughter of George Hutton to serve Phil. Rogers and Isabella his wife until 17.

Page 208

Motion of Elizabeth Eustace, Com. of Adm. to her on the Estate of Mr. William Eustace.

Court 18 June 1702

Overseers of the Highways: Capt. Chris. Neale and John Howson.

Motion of Ann Ryder, a Com. of Adm. to her on the Estate of Henry Ryder, dec'd.

Page 209

Motion of Lydia Mayes Exx., a Probate to her of the Last Will of her dec'd husband Henry Mayze.

Lucy ffurned orphan daughter of Edward and Lucy ffurned, aged 12, chose Phillip Bussell.

John Graham and Patience his wife to issue in Chancery a bill to Wm. Neale.

Page 210

James Haynes and ffrances his wife ack. an Indenture for 1000 acres and 186 acres marsh to Major Wm. Lister.

Page 211

Cert. to Thomas Hobson for 1500 acres, trans of 30 persons: John Mackdonnell, Mary Mackdonnell, Elizabeth Wilkes, John Scott, William Gluge, Andrew Peacock, and John Scott and assigned by Col. George Cooper, Dan-

Northumberland County Orders

Page 211 cont'd:

iell Smith, Hugh Broughton, Alice Argile, Alexander Cammell, Phill Pitts, Mary Evans, Joseph Bland, Thomas Shorthouse, James Allen, James James, James Mackbeth, Margaret ----, Elinor Coat, and Arthur Thomas assigned by Capt. Peter Hack, Hugh Cannon, Peter Platt, Mary Plodwell, Joseph Hould, ffrancis Ward, Thomas James, William Clay, Mary Swetman and Henry Sanders.

Court 15 July 1702

Motion of Edmund Baisie Exor. of the Last Will of John Merryfeild, proved by John Hill, Isaac Basie and Edmund Baisie, Jun.

Richard Robinson ack. Deed of guift of 50 acres of land to his bro:r Samll Robinson.

George Dameron orphan son of George Dameron chose Chris. Garlington guardian.

Page 212 (none)

Court 16 July 1702

Page 213

James Waddy sworne High Sheriff.

Richard Russell vs. William Davis and Mary his wife late Mary Berratt Exx. in her own wrong of George Berratt dec'd.

Page 214

David Spens and Sarah his wife Admx. of John Span vs. John Reason.

Pages 215-216 (none)

Court 17 July 1702

Page 217

Motion of Wiliam Cornish next of kin to Mary Key, a minor, a Com. of Adm. to him on the Est. of Mary of the Est. of Richard Key dec'd.

Pages 218=219 (none)

Court 16 Sept. 1702

Page 220

James Longhman and Margaret his wife ack. Deed of Sale of 50 acres to John Scott.

Cert. to Major Rodham Kenner, 1700 acres, trans. of 34 persons: Hugh Williams, Evan Hill, Ann Price, Joseph Parris, John Marquant, Margarett Lawrence, Anthony Jackson, Jone Murphew, Thomas Sadler, Jane Mackfassion, Owen Jones, Thomas Williams, John Poope, John ----, William Dunnawan, Wm. Price, Sarah Richardson, Henry Gallion, Evan Rann, Timothy Higgins, Robert Mitchell, Richard Dowgell, Dawland Berry, William Wilkins, John Skeles, Thomas Knight, Hannah Anderson, Richard Colphen, Andrew fflanagon, Thomas Lock, Richard Bently, George Screech and Elinor Christopher.

Motion of Thomas Hobson and Richard Wright during the minority of the orphans of Thomas Webb, dec'd, a Probate to them of the last will, proved by Thomas Hobson and John Spry.

Probate to Maj. Rodham Kenner, Capt. Peter Hack, Chris. Neale, John

Northumberland County Orders

Page 220 cont'd:

Haynie and Thomas Hobson of the Last Will of John ffarnefold, proved by Charles Nelms and Symon Robinson.

Pages 221-223 (none)

Court 17 Sept. 1702

Page 224

Charles Betts and Mary his wife devisee and sole Heire of Mary Royston dec'd, vs. Davis Spans cont'd.

Court 21 Oct. 1702

Page 225

John Hawkes aged 8 last August an orphan child Sone of George Hawkes and Jane his wife late Jane Barecroft dec'd to serve Thomas Barecroft, until 21.

Thomas Wheeler and ffrances his wife ack. a Deed of Land to Thomas Crowder.

Mary Everett Daughter of Alice Taylor dec'd late widdow of John Taylor answers claim to her sd. Mother's estate.

Page 226

John Short legatee of John Roach vs. Estate of William Sheares in the hands of David Straughan who married Ruth the Exx. of William Parker.

Motion of Anne fflynt Exx. of the Last Will of Richard fflint, by Chs. Dermott, a Probate, proved by Robt. Bradly, James Claughton and Charles Dermott.

Pages 227-229 (none)

Court 23 Oct. 1702

Page 230

Peter Coutanceau informed the Court that Stephen Smyth who married the Relict and Widdow of John Baily dec'd is a Roman Catholic and has custody of Thomas Baily orphan sone of the sd. John Baily by a former wife & Thomas Hughlett moved that he (being Godfather to the said orphan) to bring him up until 21 and to be his guardian.

Court 18 Nov. 1702

Page 231

Christtopher Kirk and Anne his wife by her Att. Thomas Taylor ack. a Deed of Sale of Land to Thomas Walters.

Thomas Allerton ack. Deed of indenture for Land in Lankeshire in K'm (Kingdom?) of England unto Henry Williams.

Page 232

Jacob Baily orphan Son of John Baily aged 15 the 11th of June last to serve Capt. Chris. Neale.

Page 233 (none)

Court 20 Nov. 1702

Northumberland County Orders

Page 234

Motion of Sarah Dawson Widdow and Relict of John Dawson, a Probate to her of the Last Will of the dec'd, proved by Capt. Chris. Neale and ffrancis Dawson.

Motion of Capt. Thomas Winder guardian and Procheimaine*to Eliza. Winder, ordered that Col. George Cooper, Capt. Peter Hack and Thomas Hobson surviving Exors. of Capt. Thomas Brereton dec'd, appear at next Court. (* prochein ami: nearest/next friend)

Page 235 (none)

Court 18 Dec. 1702

Page 236

Capt. Henry Brereton Prochemaine to his Sonne Thomas Brereton by his Att. Daniell McCarty, to cite Capt. Peter Hack, Thomas Hobson and Coll. George Cooper surv'rs of the Exors. in trust of Capt. Thomas Brereton, dec'd, for Thomas' part of the sd. Estate.

Court 17 ffeb. 1702/3

Page 237

Thomas Winder guardian to his daughter Elizabeth Winder Legatee of Capt. Thomas Brereton , dec'd.

Motion of Henry Brereton to be guardian of his sone Thomas Brereton a minor Legatee of Capt. Brereton.

Motion of Joseph, Sarah and Elizabeth Churchill Exors. of the Last Will of Sam'll Churchill, a Probate.

Page 238

John Scott and Anne his wife ack. assignment of 50 acres to John Ross.

Court 18 ffeb. 1702/3

Motion of Ann Dawson late Ann Tignor Exx. of William Tignor, dec'd & the App. of his Estate.

Page 239 (none)

Court 19 ffeb. 1702/3

Motion of Anne Sutton Exx., a Probate to her of the Last Will of Richard Sutton, proved by Thomas English and Dennis Conway.

Page 241

Motion of Ellinor Lewis Exx., a Probate to her of the Last Will of her dec'd husband John Lewis, proved by Tho. Hayden, Daniell ffeilding and Edward Weston.

Motion of Mary Clerke Exx., a Probate to her of the Last Will of her dec'd husband Thomas Clerke, proved by John Gator.

N. C. Will of Jane Stathen proved by Mary Browne and John Hartly.

Court 18 Mar. 1702/3

Ester Sanders, a poor woman, compl't vs. Robt. Reeves and he being absent, to be summoned to the next Court.

Capt. Peter Presly pet. that he is aged 20 and chose the Hon. Coll.

Northumberland County Orders

Page 241 cont'd:

Edmund Jennings, Esq. guardian.

William Mary orphan Sone of Henry Mary decd Serv't to John Lawrence to come to next court to choose a guardian.

Page 242 (none)

Page 243

Major Rodham Kenner, Capt. Peter Hack and Mr. Peter Coutanceau Exors. of Capt. Spencer Mottrom, dec'd, vs. Capt. Richard Ball and Sarah his wife late Sarah Howson, Exx. of Capt. Wm. Howson.

Clement Arlege and Mary his wife vs. John Conway.

Wm. Neale vs. John Graham and Patience his wife, late wife and Relict of Dan'll Neale, dec'd, continued.

Abraham Bletsoe and Catherine his wife for a child's part of the Est. of her ffather Thomas Ball, dec'd.

Page 244

Alexander Mulraine vs. Eliza. Webb Exx. of Tho. Lee, Dec'd.

Page 245 (none)

Court 19 May 1703

Page 246

Wm. Arlege and Alice his wife ack. a Deed for 50 Acres to Hannah Neale and Mrs. Hannah Neale ack. Deed of 50 acres to Rodham Neale.

John Adams and Katherine his wife ack. Deed for 240 acres to Robt. Harrison.

William Howard, an ancient, poor and indigent, excused from Levy.

Motion of Maurice Jones Exor., a Probate to him of the Last Will of Robert Jones, dec'd, proved by John Ashford, Susannah Ashford and William Wederiffe.

Motion of Anne Dermott Exx., a Probate of the Last Will of Charles Dermott, proved by Elizabeth Lambert and Elizabeth Wooldridge and David Straughan.

Page 247

James Palmer Excused from Levy; also Thomas Evans.

Constables: Richard Oldham, Jerrico; George Dawkins, Jun., head of Wiccocomoco and Richard Hudnall, Lower Wiccocomoco.

Page 248

William Mary, orphan Sone of Henry Mary, serv't of Jno. Lawrence chose Edward Wooldridge guardian.

Mr. John Harris sworne High Sheriff.

Court 20 May 1703

Page 249

Charles Betts and Mary his wife sole heir of Mary Royston vs. David

Northumberland County Orders

Page 249 cont'd:

Spens, trespass of 100 acres of Land in Newman's Neck of a Patent of 800 acres to Daniell Holland and William Cornish dated 9 December 1662 and confirmed with addition of 150 acres to William Cornish and from sd. Cornish to Jonathan Royston who devised 10 acres to his wife Mary Royston who devised it to her daughter Mary Betts, yet def't 1 March 1701 entered upon it.

    Motion of Chris. Neale and Jane his wife, a Com. of Adm. of the Est. of Richard, John and Hannah Rogers the said Jane's children.

Page 250

    Laughly Conaly and Sarah his wife ack. an Indenture of 80 acres to Sennour Moore. Seymour Moore ack. the Bond.

    Thomas Barnes vs. Nich. Listone continued: the Pl't by his Att.Rich. Haynie and George Eskridge affirming that Ralph Hughs by his procheinmaine could and the Def't by Daniell McCarty his Att. that he could not make a Lease in which the Court were divided on their opinion Maf'r Rodham Kenner, Capt. Chris. Neale and Capt. Leon'd Howson being of the opinion that he could and Lt. Col. George Cooper, Capt. Peter Hack and Capt. Tho. Winder that he could not by his Procheimaine make a Lease to the Pl't.

    William Harcum vs. David Williams and Rachel his wife and she was late Rachel Reason before her marriage to the said David in 1701.

Page 251

    Elizabeth Bennett wife of Edward Bennett attended the Court in behalf of Harcum vs. Williams.

Court 21 May 1703

    Richard Russell and Hannah his wife late Hannah ffranklin Exx. of Henry ffranklin vs. Thomas Downing Exor. of Marmaduke Thompson.

Pages 252-253 (none)

Court 21 July 1703

Page 254

    John Nipper ack. Deed of Sale to Samuell Lunseford. Samuell Lunseford and Rebecca his wife by ffenly Morrison her Att. ack. the Deed of Sale to John Nipper.

Page 255

    Motion of John Davis and Isabella his wife Relict of Edward Smithee, dec'd, a Com. of Adm. to them.

    Motion of Diana ffletcher, a Com. of Adm. to her on the Est. of William ffletcher, dec'd.

    Motion of Malachi Burburough dec'd, proved by John Pope and Henry Williams.

Page 256

    Thomas Taylor the Sone of Rebecca Taylor with the consent of his Mother to serve Mrs. Hannah ffeilding until 21.

Court 18 Aug. 1703

Page 257

Northumberland County Orders

Page 257

Thomas Gaskins Sone of Henry Gaskins to be bound to William ffletcher to the trade of a Joyner and taught to read, and William dyeing, and Diana ffletcher the Relict of sd. William offered Security to teach the trade to sd. Thomas.

Clement Arledge and Mary his wife Relict of Dennis Eyes who bequeathed in his Last Will a plantation to John Conway and Mary entitle to her thirds of Dower and Conway to be summoned to the next Court.

Page 258 (none)

Court 19 Aug. 1703

Page 259

Jane Yarrett pet. that her late husband Wm. Yarrett had a seat of Land at the head of Coane River which he gave by will to John Webb and his then wife the Remainder to Peter Russell who hath since sold his right thereof to the sd. Webb who denyeth to her her Thirds.

Henry Dawson ack. a Deed for a Plantation and Land to his granddaughter Elizabeth Dawson.

Court 15 Sept. 1703

Mr. Samuel Smith and Alice his wife ack. 50 acs. of Land and she by her Att. John Webb to Tho. Sims.

Motion of Samuel Mahens and Dorothy his wife Relict of Joseph Gaskins and Com. of Adm.

Page 260

Cert. to Mr. John Carnegie, 2400 acres, trans. of 48 persons: William Godnell, Xpher King, John Mason, William Ollibo, William Seward, John Duke, John Mare, Robert Crouch, William Keene, William Langsdon, Anthony Hogherd, Benjamin Coleman, Mary Newell, Mary Crouch, Hannah Staynie, Elizabeth Hobson, Dennis Mahonny, Margt. Cowland, William Pritchett, Wm. McKinall, Joseph Taylor, John Parsons, Daniell Clerke, Rebecca Clerke, ffrancis Williard, William Nellagon, Elizabeth Wilcox, Robert Reeves, Mathew Benthan, Lawrence Oneale, Catherine Langsdon, Stephen Clanckerett, Humphrey Veale, Danniel Olegney, Evan Jones, Solomon Jones, David Murray, Henry Mathare, Edward Rainsford, Mary Gridly, Mary Savey, Isaac Mordam, John Gill, Patience Gridly, Elizabeth Wollham, John Phipp, Michael Gill and James White. The above named 1st named by John Way, the next 2 by Thomas Hughlett, next 2 by John Reason, next 19 by Samuel Smith, the following by Robert Reeves and the remaining 20 by Capt. Phill. Shapleigh.

Motion of Hannah Shapleigh Widdow and Relict of Thomas Shapleigh, dec'd, a Com. of Adm. to her.

Page 261 (none)

Court 16 Sept. 1703

Page 262

Capt. John Bushrod and Hannah his wife ack. an assignment for Land to Mrs. Elizabeth Bankes.

Pages 263-271 (none)

Court 17 Nov. 1703

Page 272 (following page)

Northumberland County Orders

Page 272

Motion of Ester Webb, a Com. of Adm. to her on the Estate of Samuel Webb and App. of the Estate.

Motion of James Harrold Exor., a Probate of the Last Will of Gilbert Harrold, proved by ffrancis Dawson and Mary Chapman.

William Roberts sone of John Roberts aged 2 the 6th of June by his father bound to serve James Gaymore until 21.

Court 17 Nov. 1703

Page 273

Whereas Col. Samuel Griffin by Deed of Guift did five unto Jane Wilkins now Jane Barnes one red cow and tht Thomas Barnes deliver and pay Thomas Wilkins Sone of the sd. Jane a Heifer and Calfe and Two year old Heffer and two year old Steer.

Dennis Conway Jun. ack. Deed of Sale of Land to Stephen Chankerett.

Pages 274-275 (none)

Court 16 ffeb. 1703/4

Page 276

Mary Nutt orphan Daughter of Mr. William Nutt chose Capt. Leonard Howson guardian.
Motion of Mary Sanders Exx. of William Sanders, a Probate of the Last Will, proved by Thomas Rout, David Spens and Edward Lawrence.

Motion of Benjamin Vanlandeghan and Mary his wife, a Com. of Adm. on the Estate of William Taylor and App. of the Est.

Page 277

Motion of Partin Hudnall Exor., a Probate of the Last Will of Partin Hudnall, dec'd, proved by the oaths of Hugh Callam and Richard Smith.

Motion of John Lancaster and ffrances his wife, a Com. of Adm. to them on the Est. of Ralph Warrington.

Patrick Quille and Jane his wife ack. the condition of a Bond made by Jane Walker the said wife late Widow of Joseph Walker, dec'd, unto Mr. Peter Coutanceau.

Elizabeth Porter, poor, with small children, and the small Estate to be sold at outcry.

Pages 278-279 (none)

Court 15 Mar. 1703/4

Page 280

Charles Lee, dec'd, had considerable Estate and Constituted Elizabeth his wife sole Exx., who is also dec'd, Intestate, since that three of the sd. Testator's children Thomas, Elizabeth and Charles are minors and the said Elizabeth chose Hancock Lee guardian and Thomas and Charles also under his guardianship, motion of Hancock Lee, gent., adm. with Will annexed to Mr. Charles Lee, dec'd, with Mr. John Harris, Mr. James Waddy, and Capt. Maurice Jones to make an Inv.

Court 16 Mch. 1703/4

Northumberland County Orders

Page 281

John Porter orphan sone of Thomas and Elizabeth Porter, aged 9, to serve Thomas Whitehead and Mary his wife until 21. William Porter, ditto and aged 11, to serve John Lawrence and ffrances his wife until 21.

Page 282 (none)

Page 283

Richard Ruth and Elizabeth hs wife late Elizabeth Bowen guardian to her son Edward Bowen, also to her son John Bowen. Both cases dismissed.

Court 17 Mar. 1703/4

Page 284

Parish Garner and Elizabeth his wife vs. David Straughan: Plt' complains that William Parker late of this County by his Will (inter alia) did give to his Daughter Eliza Parker now Garner certain goods.

Pages 285-286 (none)

Court 17 May 1704

Page 287

Constables: Tho. Gill, William Coppage, James Badger, Robert Reeves and Nicholas Morrica.

Mrs. Leanna Lee chose Capt. Tho. Pinkard guardian.

Page 288

Sm'll Timons aged 10 the 11th of June next with the Mother Mary Roberts her consent to serve Geo. Dawkins until 19.

John Howell with his Mother Diana Britt's consent to serve Mr. John Carnegie for 5 years.

John and William Nelms ack. a Division of Land to each other.

Motion of John Claughton and Anne his wife and Eliz. Pemberton a Com. of Adm. to them on the estate of Richard Pemberton.

Page 289

Elizabeth Porter aged 10 the last of April to serve Thomas Tolson and Mary his wife until 18. Ann Porter orphan daughter of Tho. and Elizabeth Porter dec'd, aged 11 last March, to serve John Million and his now wife until,18.

Estate of John Dawson to be Appraised.

Court 18 May 1704

Page 290

Motion of Richard Wright, Robert Palmer and Thomas Downing Exors., a Probate to them of the Last Will of Joseph Palmer, proved by Dennis Conway and Henry Mayze.

Page 291

Barthol. Dameron, Barthol. Shrever, Thomas Gaskins, Thomas Knight and Maurice Jones, any 4 to app. Estate of Tho. Winter.

Northumberland County Orders

Page 291 cont'd:

Jane, Allice and Sarah Hutton pet. the Court vs. Phill. Rogers and Isabella his wife to summons to the next Court, to show why they render not the Petitioner's Legacies of Jane Linten, dec'd.

Page 292 (none)

Court 22 June 1704

Page 293

George Graves and Eliz. his wife vs. James Cream and Daniel Sullivant cont'd.

Page 294

John Bridgeman and Christian his wife, daughter and Legatee of Joseph Long vs. Alexander Mulraine Exor. of Josias Long.

Page 295 (none)

Page 296

Susannah Opie Exx. of the Last Will of Tho. Opie dec'd returned non est Inventory at the suit of William Planner.

Page 297

Anne fflynt Exx. of the Last Will of Richard fflynt, Jun. vs. Daniel Swillivant.

Pitts Curtis and Joanna his wife late Joanna ffloker, Admx. of David ffloker sued by Wm. Whittangton Adm. of Mr. Wm. Monteeth merch't.

Wm. Davis and Mary his wife late Mary Berratt Exx. of George Berratt vs. Lady Culpeper, Thomas ffairefax and Katherine his wife Proprietors of the Northern Neck.

Page 298

Samuel Mahen and Dorothy his wife late Dorothy Gaskins Admx. of Josias Gaskins sued by Nicholas Seabourne.

Page 299 (none)

Page 300

Xpher Robinson and Judith his wife one of the Exors. of the last Will of Corbin Griffin, Peter Presly and Winifred his wife and Thomas Griffin the other Exors. vs. Henry Dawson.

John Carnegie and Winifred his wife late Winifred hewlett vs. Capt. Maurice Jones Exor. of Robert Jones cont'd.

Court 19 July 1704

Page 301

Richard Smith Deed of gift to his son Jno. Smith.

Page 302

James Innis and Kath. his wife ack. Deed of Indenture for a parcel of land by Henry Mayze to Capt. Leonard Howson.

Pages 303-305 (none)

Northumberland County Orders

Page 306 (Court was 25 July 1704)

Anne Smyth aged 4 years with the consent of her Mother to serve Phill. Bussell.

Page 307

Jane Allice and Sarah Hutton vs. Phill. Rogers and Isabella his wife Relict of and Exx. of John Linton referred to next Court.

Pages 308-309 (none)

Court 20 Sept. 1704

Page 310

Thomas Williams and Alice his wife by her Att. Thomas Hobson ack. a Deed for Land to Mr. Thomas Gaskins.

Capt. Wm. Jones and Margt. his wife by her Att. Wm. Jones Jun. ack. a Deed for Land to Mr. Hancock Lee Att. of Hon'ble Robt. Carter.

Page 311

John Berry orphan of Thomas Berry to serve Thomas Gill until 21.

Mrs. Elizabeth Winter Exx. of Mr. Tho. Winter presents an Inventory of his Estate.

Court 25 Sept. 1704

Motion of Thomas Harrison and Mary his wife late Mary Sanders Exx. of Wm. Sanders, de'd, App. of his Estate.

Page 312

Lazarus Dameron Sone of George Dameron chose Barthol. Dameron guardian.

Cert. to James Waddy for 500 acres, trans. of: George Violett, Anne Violett, Charles Colgin, Simon Holland, William Harsell, John Birke, Jno. Cambell, ffrancis Brookes, Gillian Stallin and Mary Parson.s

Cert. to Rich. Haynie for 250 acres, trans. of: Jno. Butler, James ffleming, Robt. Hughs, Patrick ffisher, and Eliza Sheppard.

Cert. to John Lawrence for 100 acres, trans. of: John Williams and Jane McDonnell.

Cert. to George Eskridge for 1000 acres, for trans. of: Matthew Kelly, Nich. hutchinson, John Poor, Alexander Salmon, Mary Bullery, How. ffrankling, Robert Teigne, Shahanna Shaw, Alex'r Browne, Tho. Burnett, William Browne, Wm. Rennelds, Mary Caseley, Eliza Wooll, Archebald Shirsly, John Howson, Wm. Henley, Kate Carty, Wm. Henderson and Margt. Murfy. The 1st by Mrs. Anne Coutanceau, the next 3 by John Burne, next 5 by Rich. Howe and the rest by Thomas Rout.

Court 22 Sept. 1704

Page 313

Pet. of John Bridgeman and Christian his wife one of the Daughters of Joseph Long dec'd and the Sheriff to cite Alex. Mulraine Exor. of the sd dec'd to answer sd. petition.

Page 314

Cert. to Hugh Callan for 200 acres, trans. of: Hugh Callan, Margaret

Northumberland County Orders

Page 314 cont'd:

Callan, Eliza Consedy and Kath. Chalan.

Page 315 (none)

Page 316

Rich'd Russell and Hannah his wife Exx. of Henry ffranklin dec'd vs. Thomas Downing Exor. of Marmaduke Thompson.

John Bashford aged 11 and Rebecca Bashford aged 5, orphans of Simon Bashford to serve Barth. Dameron, the boy until 21 and the girl until 18.

John Williams and Sarah his wife ack. Deed of Lease and Release of 300 acres to Vincent Garner.

Edward Paul and Elizabeth his wife ack. Deed to John Curtis.

Court 15 Nov. 1704

Page 317

Motion of Jane Pollick, a Probate to her of the Last Will of Patrick Pollick, proved by Onesephorus Harvey and Anthony Haynie.

Motion of John Cockrell, a Probate to him of the Last Will of John Cockrell, dec'd, although the witnesses are dead.

Josias Gaskins chose Anthony Haynie guardian.

Robt. Warington chose Phill. Shapleigh guardian.

Motion of John and Jane Bowes, a Probate to them of the Last will of John Bowes, dec'd., proved by Richard Cross and Adam Grinsteed.

Motion of Rebecca Carpenter, Com. of Adm. to her on the Est. of Chas. Carpenter.

Court 17 Jan. 1704/5

Page 318

Edward Sanders pet. the Court to choose a new guardian, and to summon John Cockrell who marryed the Mother of the said Edw. to the Next Court. Mr. Edward Sanders sworne Justice of the peace.

Court 21 ffeb. 1704/5

Page 319

Motion of Capt. John Howson and Richard Wright, a Probate of the Last Will of Capt. Leonard Howson, dec'd, proved by Richard Cockrell, Edward Cockrell and David Williams.

Page 320

Mary Nutt orphan of William Nutt her late guardian Capt. Leonard Howson chose Edward Cole Guardian.

Thomas Crowder and ffearnot his wife ack. by her att. a Deed of Sale of Land to Christopher Thelkeld.

Thomas Williams and Elizabeth his wife by her Att. Thomas Hobson ack. an Indenture to Capt. Maurice Jones.

Motion of Kath. Dawson, Henry Dawson and John Conway, App. the Estate of Henry Dawson.

Northumberland County Orders

Page 321

Motion of Thomas Leethman for an in behalfe of his Brother in Law, John Gralie a minor, and John Reason to be cited to the Next Court for mistreatment of the minor.

Court 22 ffeb. 1704/5

Motion of Phill. Rogers and Vincent Cox, a Probate to them of the Last Will of Daniell Swillivant, proved by John Cream and Joseph Willgrass.

Page 322

Cert. to George Eskridge, 2950 acres, trans. of: Thomas Miller, John Ashton, Jonathan Palfry, Edmond Bowes, Mary Westerby, Mary ffrankling, Mary Canalan, Mary Price, James Jones, Elizabeth Jones, Thomas Oxe, John Joyne, Thomas Seddon, Joane Seddon, Evan Morgan, Richard Price, John Davis, David Savige, Wm. Janeway, John Skinage, George Groves, Patrick Quisse, David Straughan, Robert Smith, Sarah Anderson, Mary Barnes, Tho. Moore, Henry Comons, Henry Brabin, John Croshit, Abraham Proctor, John Dowly, Christopher Petty, John Conner, Phillip Antrobus, Marg't ffitzmorris, Henry Pinckney, John Thomas, Susanna Nutbank, William Lanbert, Wm. Jones, Wm. Probie, Joseph Atkins, Thomas Sims, George Dodson, Anne Dodson, James Neele, Thomas Lane, Wm. Stephenson, James Genn, Thomas Genn, Mary Genn, John Cofflin, Arthur Bell, John Laland, Wm. Thompson, David Thomas and John Arshell.

Page 323

Thomas Grinsteed orphan of Wm. Grinsteed chose his brother William Grinsteed guardian.

Court 23 ffeb. 1704/5

Page 324

Jane, Alice and Sarah Hutton Legatees of Mrs. Jane Linton by her Last Will left in the hands of John Linton by Henry Ross Exor. of the said Will which sd. Linton being since dec'd and the legacy as come unto the hands of Phillips Rogers by marrying with Isabell the Relict and Exx. of the said John Linton and sd. Rogers to be summoned to Court.

Pages 325-327 (none)

Page 328

Richard Lee, Esq., and Lettice his wife vs. David Straughan Exor. of John Arnott dec'd.

Anne fflynt, Exx. of the Last Will of Richard fflynt, the Younger, dec'd, vs. Martha fflynt, Thomas fflynt and Christopher Dawson Exors. of the Last Will of Richard fflynt the Elder.

Page 329

Wm. Medcalfe vs. Thomas Barecroft late husband of Mary Barecroft formerly Mary Medcalfe, Ex. in his own wrong of the said Mary Medcalfe the Exx. of Henry Medcalfe dec'd.

Page 330

John Claughton and Anne his wife and Elizabeth Pemberton Admx. of Richard Pemberton vs. Phill. Shapleigh.

Page 331 (none)

Court 21 Mar. 1704/5

Northumberland County Orders

Page 332

Motion of Mary fflynt Exx. of the Last Will of her husband Thomas fflynt, a Probate proved by ffrancis Dawson, James Genn and Richard Booth.

Motion of Robert Banks, Exor., a Probate to him of the Last Will of Martha fflynt, dec'd, proved by David Straughan and Edward Barnes.

Court 16 May 1705

Page 333

Constables: Christopher Dawson, lower St. Stephen's; Mr. Phill. Rogers, Mattapony; Jno. Pope, upper Wiccocomoco; John Turner for Cupid's Creek; Patrick Quille, Cone Neck; ffrancis Dawson, upper Mattapony.

Hannah Conner (orphan of Turle Conner) pet. that John Spry might be her guardian.

Elizabeth Lewis orphan of John Lewis chose Tho. Byram to be her guardian.

Page 334

Capt. Rich'd Hewes by the Court Appointed Guardian of Robert Beane orphan of William Beane dec'd until he arrive at the age of 14.

Court 17 May 1705

John Ingram appointed Constable of Lower Wiccocomoco. James Jones appointed overseer of the highways.

Pages 335-336 (none)

Court 18 May 1705

Page 337

Overseers of highways: John Hill, Capt. Rich. Haynie and John Conway.

Pet. of Josias Gaskins and Dorothy Gaskins, Sone and Daughter of Mr. Josias Gaskins, for equal portions of their father's Estate.

Page 338 (none)

Court 9 June 1705

Page 339

Col. Rodham Kenner sworne High Sheriff.

Court 18 July 1705

Page 340

Thomas Gill, poor, aged and impotent, freed from Levy.

Richard Lattimore and Anne his wife ack. a deed of Indenture of Land to Robert Carter Esq.

John Thomas and Sarah Brewer orphans of Thomas Brewer complain that John Burne and his wife who was widow and Relict of their sd. father abused them and cite Burne and his wife to court.

Thomas Bridgeman ack. a Deed of guift to his granddaughter a cow (the name of the granddaughter not specified.)

Motion of William Moorehead and Charles Moorehead, a Probate to them

Northumberland County Orders

Page 340 cont'd:

of the Last Will of their dec'd ffather Charles Moorehead, proved by Jno. Hughlett and Andrew fflanagan.

Motion of Richard Kenner in behalfe of his Mother and Wife Joynt Exx. of the Last Will of Mr. Thomas Winder, a Probate, prv'd by Joseph Tipton, Thomas Hobson, William Winder, and Thomas Leechman.

Page 341

Motion of James Knight, Exor., a Probate to him of the Last Will of his dec'd ffather Mr. Peter Knight, proved by Patrick Maley and Robert Marsh.

Nicholas Bager, poor, impotent and aged, freed from Levy.

Pages 342-343 (none)

Court 15 Aug. 1705

Page 344

Anne Churchill, wife of Samuel Churchill, relinquishes her Dower rights by her Att. Thomas Hobson of land sold by her husband.

Mary Mottrom, daughter of Spencer Mottrom, Gent., pet. for Capt. Rich. Ball for her guardian.

Mary Hill late Mary fflynt, presents an Inventory of her dec'd husband Thomas fflynt's estate.

Page 345

David Browne and Manly Browne Sons of David Browne Pet. the Court that George Hill and Mary his wife hold them illegally as servants and the Court ruled they were to return to their Master.

Pages 346-348 (none)

Court 16 Aug. 1705

Leonard Knight and Anne his wife Ack. a Deed of Indenture of Land to William Short of Lancaster County.

Pages 350-361 (none)

Court 19 Sept. 1705

Page 362

ffrancis Lastly an orphan child to serve Elizabeth Nelms the daughter of Charles Nelms until 21.

Page 363

Peter Coutanceau Gent. petitions the Court that Mrs. Eliza. Bankes, widdow of Mr. Thomas Bankes late of his Co., dec'd, is possessed of all the Lands, etc., that her ffirst husband Mr. William Keene dyed possessed of and she has right of Dower, and the said Coutanceau hath intermarryed with Anne Keene Late Widdow of William Keene Sone and Heire of the sd. Keene dec'd and Eliz. Banks who hath right in behalfe of her Dower and in behalfe of her Sone William Keene to two thirds of the sd. land etc., and William Metcalfe likewise making oath to the Court that the sd. Coutanceau had offered to assigne her the sd. Elizabeth her Right of Dower which she refused to accept and the Court orders the Dower to be laid out and a report to the next Court.

102

Northumberland County Orders

Court 20 Sept. 1705

Sarah Dawson Widdow in behalf of her children Elizabeth, Margaret and Sarah children of John Dawson dec'd vs. Katherine Wilshire, Henry Dawson, and John Conway Adm. of Henry Dawson.

Page 364

Capt. Wm. Jones, vs. Mrs. Elizabeth Winder Capt. Rich. Kenner and Elizabeth his wife Exors. of the Last Will of Maj. Thomas Winder.

Page 365

Ralph Waddington by his Procheinany John Lancaster Action of Trespass vs. John Nelson.

Page 366

Ignatius Oliver and Ellen his wife vs. William Hill and Ellis his wife and George Hill and Mary his wife.

Page 367 (none)

Court 16 Jan. 1705/6

Page 368

Motion of Mary Baker Widdow and Relict of Thomas Baker, Com. of Adm. to her.

Court 17 Jan. 1705/6

William Wiltshire and Katherine his wife late wife of Henry Dawson, dec'd, vs. Sarah Dawson, Widdow and Relict of John Dawson, dec'd, for her right of Dower.

Mary Boaz for her proportion of the estate of her dec'd ffather John Boaz.

Page 369 (none)

Court 19 Jan. 1705/6

Page 370

John Bales ack. D/S of 150 acres to Thomas Gill as alsoe Angell his wife Relinquishes her Right of Dower.

James Gayner assignment of D/S to William More as alsoe Diana his wife relinquishes her Right of Dower.

Probate of the Last Will of John Hughlett dec'd to Mary hughlett Exx. proved by Robt. Christopher and John Stanley and Anne Christopher.

Page 371

Robert Harrisin ack. a deed of guift two parcells of Land to his two daughters Mary and Alice Harrison.

Pet. of John Haynie on behalfe of his two children Thomas and Thompson for their proportional pte. of the Est. of Thomas and Richard Sadler, dec'd.

Court 20 Mar. 1705/6

Col. Peter Presly and John Steptoe sworn Justices of the Peace.

Northumberland County Orders

Page 371 cont'd:

Probate of the Last Will of John Moore dec'd to Mr. Richard Hull, Ex-'or., proved by Thomas Hobson.

Mr. John Webb, D/S to Patrick Quille as alsoe Katherine his wife relinquishes Right of Dower.

Page 372

Pet. of Mrs. Judith Smith, Widow, Com. of Adm. to her the Estate of her dec'd husband, Mr. James Smith.

Pet. of Mary Arledge, a Com. of Adm. to her on the Est. of her de'cd husband Clement Arledge, with will annexed.

Court 21 Mar. 1705/6

Page 373

Cert. to Capt. George Eskridge for 450 acres, trans. of: Jane Harrison, William Thompson, Matthew Cheltwood, William Dyetfeild, John Williams, Thomas Cabernett, Rachell Newton, Uriah Bryant and Kath. Talbott.

Edmond Manly ack. Deed of Guift to John Turner in Trust for his wife Mary Manly.

Elizabeth Way wife of John Way by her Att. Mr. George Eskridge relinquishes her right of Dower in land sold by her husband to Capt. Richard Haynie.

Parish Garner and Elizabeth his wife vs. David Straughan.

Edward Coles guardian to Mary Nutt the daughter of William and Mary Nutt dec'd, vs. George Cooper, Peter Hack and Thomas Hobson surviving Exors. of Thomas Brereton.

George Groves and Elizabeth his wife one of the Daughters of George Hutton dec'd vs. Phill. Rogers and Vincent Cox Exors. of the Last Will of Daniel Swillivant.

Pet. of Dennis Vallen, Com. of Adm. to him on the Est. of his dec'd wife Elizabeth Vallen.

Page 374 (none)

Page 375

Cert. to Capt. George Eskridge, 1050 acres, trans. of: John Langhee, George Jackson, Arthur Kaufelaugh, Thomas Rock, John Roach, Dennis Roarke, Patrick Earne, James Theary, Anthony Delany, John Connell, John Poore, Katherine ffling, Margarett Bryan, Issabell Davis, Elinor Hunt, Mary Olliver, Edward Kelly, Allice White, Katherine Keaton, Mary Lane and Mary Wheeler.

Thomas Dameron Jr. D/S of Land to James Waddy Att. of Barthol. Dameron as alsoe Katherine Dameron wife of the sd. Thomas Relinquishes her Right of Dower.

Page 376

Cert. to George Eskridge, 1050 acres, trans. of: Robert Reeves, Chas. Moorehead, Thomas fflatman, Thomas Price, Anthony Bateman, Mary Lilley, Jane Shirly, Richard Booth, John Poore, John Wilkins, James Russell, Tho. Ryder, Sam'l Ball, John Walker, Turlur Conner, Solomon Mason, Thomas Jackson, Robt. Harrisin, Jms. Stanly, John ffloyd, and ffrancis Wheeler.
The Last Will of John Moore proved by John Scott.

Northumberland County Orders

Page 376 cont'd:

Mr. Daniel McCarty guardian to Francis Spencer vs. Peter Hack, Gent.

Cert. to George Eskridge for 300 acres, of land for trans. of: Patrick Quill, John Medly, Margaret Medly, Andrew ffisher, Margery Merritt and John Cleren. Also to him 200 acres for John Lyon, John Hay, Humphrey Dunaby and Mary Milbanks.

Page 377

Cert. to Capt. George Eskridge for 250 acres, trans. of: Henry Harding, Lawrence Gamwell, Thomas Dickenson, Phebe Whitter and Edward Plea. Also, 100 acres, for John Jameson and Hugh Price; also 150 acres for John Davis, David Savige and Morris Braseele.

Court 17 April 1706

Page 377 cont'd:

Susanna Spens, Daughter of William Spens to serve Bartholomew Leasure until 21.

Page 378

Cert. to Capt. George Eskridge, 2350 acres, trans. of: David Kenner, Hugh McDevmil, Will Kalleron, Thomas Heale, James Loope, Owen Doyle, Tho. Redish, Lawrence Trea, Lawrence fferne, George Baskerville, Nora Higgins, Tagor King, Margaret Hand, Hannah Wills, Toby Kelly, Michael Kelly, Margaret Morris, Henry Hanbrooke, Patrick Sarchfeild, Thomas Burke, Teague Kelly, Patrick Naster, Alice Mealy, Ellinor Cannon, Margaret Mullens, Tho. Lolly, Edward Butler, Ellinor Holbert, John McLanna, William Liddon, Ellinor Phillips, Ellinor Morris, Roger Dey, Thomas Corne, Patrick Anninner, Edmund Kendall, Sary Carty, Susanna Polenest, Sam;l Mitchell, Elizabeth Patton, Sam'l Short, John James, William James, Jeremiah Grantham, George Newton, Anne Monarth, and Tomson Gayer.

John Gouthe ack. Deed of Indenture to Richrd Neale as also Mary Gouth wife of the sd. John by her Att. Robt. Nash relinquishes Right of Dower to the land.

Page 379 (none)

Court 15 May 1706

Page 380

Constables: Hugh Callan, Lower St. Stephen's; John Warrington, Middle St. Stephen's; James Richardson, Lower Wiccocomoco; and James ffulkes, Cone.

John Garrett chose Capt. ffrancis Kenner guardian.

Court 19 June 1706

Vincent Garner and Martha his wife ack. D/S of Land to Robert Reeves.

Court 17 July 1706

Page 381

Pet. of James Richardson and Eliz. his wife Admx. of Abraham Sheare vs. Thomas Gaskins.

Page 382

John Dunaway and Margaret his wife by her Att. James Hill ack. D/S to

Northumberland County Orders

Page 382 cont'd:

Edmond Denne.

Thomas Hughlett and Margaret his wife ack. a Deed of Guift to Thomas Dameron Jun'r and Katherine his wife for 100 acres.

Christopher Garlington and Margaret his wife ack. a D/S to Capt. Maurice Jones.

Pages 383-384 (none)

Page 385

John Cole one year old Christmas Next with the consent of his Mother Alice White to serve Mr. John Carnegie until 21.

Pages 386-393 (none)

Court 21 Aug. 1706

Page 394

Motion of Capt. ffrancis Kenner and Capt. Chris. Neale Exors., a Probate to them of the Last Will of Rodham Kenner, proved by Eliz. Kenner, Daniel McCarty and Mrs. Hannah Neale.

Pet. of Priscilla Higginson in behalfe of herselfe and others Legatees mentioned in the Will of Peter Russell, John Conway and John Hill, Exors., of the sd. Will.

Page 395 (none)

Court 18 Sept. 1706

Page 396

Mutton Lewis with the consent of his brother in Law John Nickless being aged 16 to serve Richard Swanson until 21.

Court 19 Sept. 1706

Page 397

Hannah Kenner Relict of Rodham Kenner to have wearing apparell.

Probate of the Last Will of Peter Russell to John Conway, Exor., and proved by the sd. Conway and Susanna Conway.

John Conway and Susannah his wife ack. D/S to Arthur Bridgeman.

Pages 398-400 (none)

Court 19 Nov. 1706

Page 401

William Trussell, orphan sone of John Trussell chose Henry Hudson guardian.

Page 402

William Wildy Ack. Deed of Indenture for 385 acres to Daniel McCarty Att'y of Richr'd Christopher Esq. and P/A from Elizabeth Wildey to Geo. Eskridge to ack. her right of dower sold by her husband.

Page 403 (following page)

Northumberland County Orders

Page 403

Motion of Anne Belcher Exx. a Probate to her of the Last Will of her dec'd husband William Belcher, proved by Mrs. Elizabeth Winder.

Motion of Mary Graham Exx., a Probate to her of the Last Will of John Graham, proved by John Carnegie and Thomas Hobson.

Pages 404-405 (none)

Court 22 Nov. 1706

Page 406

Philip Shapleigh sued by John Haynie and Hannah his wife Relict of Thomas Shapleigh dec'd, detayned a female child Elizabeth, aged 4, lawfully the child of Thos. and Hannah Shapleigh, and nonsuit granted the def't.

Page 407 (none)

Page 408

William Sax and Hannah his wife, evidence of 10 days in the above suit

Pages 409-412 (none)

VOLUME 2

Page 413 (none)

Court 23 Nov. 1706

Page 414

Edward Barnes vs. Anne Oldham Admx. of John Oldham late of Richmond County, dec'd, dismissed.

Pages 415-418 (none)

Page 419

Capt. John Cralle vs. Jonathan Palfrey and Mary his wife late Mary Arlege Admx. of Clement Arlege dec'd, dismissed.

Pages 420-421 (none)

Court 18 Dec. 1706

Page 422

Pet. of John Garrett and Eliza. his wife, Com. of Adm. on the Estate of Robert Shepherd.

Nicholas Edward petitions to keep an ordinary.

James ffernot petitions that William Wiltshire be his guardian.

Henry Brereton and Sarah his wife vs. Richard Hull.

Thomas Sims ack. Deed of Indenture and Anne his wife relinquished her Right of Dower to Nicholas Robinson.

Pages 423-428 (none)

Court 19 Dec. 1706

Page 429 (on following page)

Northumberland County Orders

Page 429

Petition of John Haynie in behalfe of his children Thomas and Thomasin who were the children of Mary Haynie late wife of the sd. John and one of the Daughters of Thomas Sadler, dec'd, vs. John Corbell for deteyning from them their portion of the Est. of Richard and Thomas Sadler.

Daniel McCarty guardian to ffrances Spencer of Westmoreland County: the late ffrances Spencer the late Widow and Relict of Nicholas Spencer, Esq., gave her a perle neckless value of 80 pounds and in custody of Mm. Mary wife of Peter Hack to be kept for sd. ffrances and both ffrances and Mary now departed and the Neckless in the hands of sd. Hack and it belongs to ffrances who has reached the age of descretion (Note: there are two ffrances Spencers.)

Page 430 (none)

Court 19 Mar. 1706/7

Page 431

Richard and John Marshall orphan sons of George Marshall (ages 14 and 9) to serve Thomas Gaskins until 21.

Hannah Page orphan daughter of George Page aged 9 th 10 June next to serve Alexander Love until 18.

Motion of Elizabeth Winder, Exx., a Probate to her of the Last Will of John Biswick, proved by Thomas Hayes and Joseph Tipton and Timothy Swillivant.

Pet. of ffrances Wheeler, Com. of Adm. to her on the Est. of her decd husband Thomas Wheeler.

Page 432

Probate of the Last Will of William Neale, dec'd, to Ebenezer Neale, Exor., proved by James Rogers and Sam. Blackwell.

Page 433

Pet. of Joseph Ball and Mary his wife Daughter of Spencer Mottrom,Ge't dec'd, vs. Col. Peter Hack and Peter Coutanceau, Gent., Exors. of the Last Will of the sd. Mottrom for rateable part of deceased's Estate.

Court 20 Mar. 1706/7

Page 434

Motion of Richard Nelms, Com. of Adm. to him on the Est. of Lovie Bee, dec'd.

Pages 435-436 (none)

Page 437

John Neale, orphan sone of Daniel Neale aged 10 to serve John Conaway until 21.

Court 21 Mar. 1706/7

Page 438

Peter Coutanceau and Anne his wife ack. Deed to their two daughters Elizabeth Keene and Anne Coutanceau.

Pages 439-445 (none)

Northumberland County Orders

Court 21 May 1707

Page 446

Motion of Allice Williams Adm. with the Will annexed to her on the Estate of her dec'd husband, Thomas Williams, proved by John Price, Robert Gordon and John Taylor.

Page 447

Motion of John Ingram, Exor., a Probate to him on the Last Will of Thomas Ingram, proved by John Harris, and Barth. Dameron and Anthony Haynie.

Page 448

James Moore and Agnes his wife, Deed of Indenture to Henry Hudson.

P/A from Clement Spelman to his wife Mrs. Hannah Spelman.

Capt. Richard Haynie High Sheriff and Richard Haynie, Jun. undersheriff. Richard Algood, a poor man, excluded from Levy.

Page 449

Thomas Hobson by P/A from Eliza. Webb ack. an instrument of writing to John Wornom.

Court 22 May 1707

Wm. Howard, a poor ancient man, excluded from Levy.

Page 450

Phillip Norgate, a Poore anceint man, excluded from Levy.

John Bridgeman moveing this Court for a Probate of the Last Will of John Gaines dec'd and he not producing security and Mary Gaines Widdow and Relict of the sd. dec'd renouncing Adm., Estate to be divided into 3 parts and Mary to get her thirds.

Page 451 (none)

Page 452

Henry Brereton and Sarah his wife one of the Daughters and Legatees of Richard Hull, dec'd, vs. Richard Hull, ref. to the Next Court.

Pages 453-455 (none)

Court 23 May 1707

Page 456

Dennis ffallen adm. of Elizabeth his wife late Elizabeth Tignor vs. Rich. Robinson.

Pages 457-459 (none)

Court 16 July 1707

Page 460

Motion of Ann Bales, Exx. of the Last Will of William ffeilding, a Probate to her, proved by Simon White, Theophilus Settswerell and Rich'd Hull.

Northumberland County Orders

Page 460 cont'd:

Pet. of William Browne and Eliz. his wife, adm. to them on the Estate of John Garter.

Page 461

Attachment to Wm. Nelms vs. Estate of Timothy Higgins.

James Cowe, ancient descript man, excluded from Levy.

Page 462

Thomas Kingwell Pet. that Thomas Hobson and John Webb deteyne from him his part of his dec'd ffather Nicholas Kingwell Estate and they to appear at the Next Court.

Page 463

Richard Nutt ack. Deed of Guift of two negroes to his children being Benfa. and farnefold.

Pages 464-474 (none)

Court 18 July 1707

Page 475

Richard Smith and Elizabeth his wife vs. Anthony Haynie.

Court 20 Aug. 1707

Page 476

ffrancis and Richard Vanlandegham Exor. of Ben. Vanlandegham dec'd, App. of the Estate.

Page 477

James Jones ack. D/S of Land to Phillip Rogers as alsoe Eliza. Jones his wife of sd. James Relinquishes her Right of Dower.

John Gaynes orphan sone of John Gaynes to serve Capt. John Hawson until 21. Daniel, ditto, to serve Capt. ffrancis Kenner until 21.

Pages 478-479 (none)

Page 480

Pet. of Mr. John Carnegie who marryed Winifred Hughlett Adm. of Thomas fferne dec'd which sd. Winifred is since dec'd, Com. of Adm. to him of that part of the sd. ffernes Estate not yett administered on.

Pages 481-485 (none)

Court 17 Sept. 1707

Page 486

John Wright, ack. Deed of Indenture for Land to John Crump.

Page 487

William Moore, ack. Deed of Indenture for Land to Timothy Kenady. Hannah Moore P/A to George Murdock to Relinquish Right of Dower.

Cuthbert Sharpless, Richard Gilbert and Tho. Mason all of the Towne

Northumberland County Orders

Page 487 cont'd:

of Leverpoole in Ye Co. of Lancaster and Kingdom of England and Mariner and John Lancaster of the same towne county and kingdom mariner pl't and Wm. Mason Shipwright late of the said Town of Leverpoole and now of ye Parish of St. Stephen's in ye County of Northumberland def't, an arbritration.

Pages 488-490 (none)

Court 19 Nov. 1707

Page 491

Motion of James Waddy Gent. Exor., a Probate to him of the last Will of John Washi dec'd, proved by William Jones, Thomas Browne and John Taylor.

Edward Cockrell deed of Indenture for Land unto his brother John Cockrell.

Page 492

Deed of Indenture concerning bounds of Land between John and Charles Ingram. Deed of Indenture concerning ye bounds of Lands between John Ingram and ye orphans of Mr. Thomas Winter, dec'd.

John Gralie orphan Sone of John Gralie aged 17 the 24th of may to serve William Edwards until 21.

John and Daniel Gaines orphans of John Gaines to serve Capt. John Howson and Capt. ffrancis Kenner as in Aug. Court.

Pages 493-494 (none)

Court 30 Nov. 1707

Page 495

Mary Nutt by her procein annie John Tarpley vs. Chris. Newton.

Pages 496-498 (none)

Court 17 Dec. 1707

Page 499

William Lambert and Anne his wife ack. a Deed of Indenture for Land unto Matthew Myere.

Jeoffrey Johnson ack. Deed of Indenture for Land to Capt. John Howson and Elizabeth ye wife of Jeoffrey Johnson by her Att'y Thomas Hobson ack her Right of Dower in the Land sold by her sd. husband.

John Waters Pet. this court that he is grandfather and nearest kinn to Phebe William Mary Elizabeth and John Taylor who are orphans of William Taylor dec'd who dyed possessed of a small Est. and that Benjamin Valandegham since marryed with the widdow and Relict of the sd. Wm. decd and before his death made his Last Will and therein appointed his Bro's ffrancis and Richard Vanlandegham Exors. and the Court is prayed to cite them for an accounty.

Page 500

Anne Davis daughter of Elizabeth Davis by her Mother's consent to serve William Read and Elizabeth his wife until 18. Mary Davis, ditto, to serve Jos. Holt and Mary his wife until 18.

Northumberland County Orders

Page 501 (none)

Court 21 Jan. 1707/8

Page 502

Jhn. West, Sen. ack. Deed of Lease and Release of Land to his halfe Brother John West, Jr.

Mary Nutt, orphan of William Nutt, chose Capt. John Tarpley guardian.

Court 18 ffeb. 1707/8

Page 503

P/A from Richard Lee Esq. to Thomas Stretton for the ack. of Deeds of Lease and Release for Lands to his Brother Hancock Lee, Gent. and Charles Lee Youngest Son of Chas. Lee.

Thomas Berry Ack. Deed of Indenture for Land, Patience his wife by her Att'y Richard Lattimore relinquishes her Right of Dower, to Thomas Gill.

John Rice Pet. the Court vs. Sam'll Poole who had the care of the sd. Rice his Estate during his minority.

Page 504

Charles Austen orphan of Thomas Austen chose Capt. John Cralle guardian.

Court 19 ffeb. 1707/8

Page 505

ffrancis Dawson and Elizabeth his wife D/S of Land to Vincent Garner.

Pages 506=507 (none)

Court 17 Mar. 1707/8

Page 508

Pet. of Jane Holly widow and Relict of Thomas Holly, dec'd, Com. of Adm. to her.

James fferned aged 14 chose Wm. Wiltshire his guardian.

William Taylor orphan son of William Taylor to choose a guardian and his grandfather John Waters to show reason vs. it.

The N. C. Will of Richard Hilliard, upon the Motion of James Bryant, proved by Nicholas Morrica and John Huske.

Page 509

John Rice pet. the Court vs. Richard Rice for personal estate.

Court 18 Mar. 1707/8

Page 510

Parish Garner and Elizabeth his wife Bill in Chancery vs. David Straughan for legacies by the Last Will of William Parker the dec'd father of the sd. Elizabeth and an App. of the Estate.

Pages 511-514
. (see following page)

Northumberland County Orders

Pages 511-514

    Henry Brereton and Sarah his wife daughter and Legatee of Richard Hull, by his Last Will dated 11 Oct. 1693 and Richard Hull his Sone sole Exor. and Peter Presly Capt. Hack and Charles Harris overseers during minority of his daughters with the codical dated 11 Jan. 1693/4, bequeathed to his Daughter Sarah one young Indian Slave named James; Richard Hull disputes that there is a will of his father and the giving of the Slave; The orator petitions the Court to settle the matter.

Page 514 (dated Court 19 May 1708)

    Constables: John Reason for Lower St. Stephen's; Thomas Dameronie in room for John Haynie; David spence for Newman's Neck in roome of William Nelms; Bartholl Leasure for Mattopany; Thomas Downing for upper Wiccocomoco; James Symons for lower Wiccocomoco and James Oldham for Jerrico.

Page 515

    John Claughton and Anne his wife ack. a Deed of Lease and Release to their Sone Pemberton Claughton.

    Thomas Algrove orphan Sone of Nicholas Algrove to chose a guardian, as his ffather dying in South Carolina, and Thomas Barnes to be his guardian.

Page 516

    Thomas Bryam and Sarah his wife ack. a Deed of Indenture for Land to John Champion.

    Marjery Palmer ack. Deed of Guift to Grace Bridgeman, Daughter of Arthur Bridgeman.

    Laughly Conoly and Sarah his wife ack. a Deed of Indenture for Land to Henry Hudson.

                              Court 20 May 1708

Page 517

    William Clay pl't vs. John Day def't for ousting the Def't from two Messuages, Lands, etc., now in possession of William Davis which John Huske prochemamie of Rachel feilding devised to him the sd. William for a term not yet expired.

Page 518

    Mary Baker and Lucy Baker daughters and coheirs of Thomas Baker, decd. by their nearest ffriend Henry Hopkins complains that Thomas Baker dyed seized of 425 acres and that Richard Smith undersheriff to Col. Rodham Kenner entered into 100 acres of Land part of ye aforesaid 425 acres and that he cease any further use of the Land of the sd. Mary and Lucy.

Page 519

    Pet. of Henry Harding and Anne his wife, Com. of Adm. to them on the Estate of William Beltcher, Jun'r, dec'd.

Page 520

    Edward Woldridge vs. James Jones for trespass; cites that when one Thomas Bonam and Rebecca his wife the 1st of Jan. 1706 devised to the sd. Edward three messages for three years and on 5th of Jan. 1706 James Jones forcibly trespassed on the land, and he seeks a settlement.

Northumberland County Orders

Pages 521-526 (none)

Court 21 May 1708

Page 527

ffrancis Kenner and Chris. Neale, Gent. Exors. of Rodham Kenner decd. vs. Clement Spellman and Hannah his wife late Hannah Kenner dismissed.

Court 21 July 1708

Page 528

John Corbell ack. an Indenture of Lands and alsoe Margaret Corbell wife of the sd. John relinquished Right of Dower.

Motion of William Nelms and Elizabeth his wife, a Probate of the Last Will of Elizabeth Bledsoe to them, proved by Alexander Mulrane, Richard Smith and Daniel Dunaway.

Motion of Jervase Gamar and Mary Ellistone Exors., a Probate to them of the Last Will of their dec'd ffather Jervase Ellistone, proved by William Payne, Robert Davis and Sarah Clerke.

Page 529

John Bledsoe and John Ingram ack. an Indenture of Division of Land.

Page 530

Mary Hughlett, ack a Deed of Indenture for Land to her son John Hughlett.

Pages 531-532 (none)

Court 22 July 1708

Page 533

Motion of Mr. Phillip Shapleigh that Edward Watkins who marryed the Widdow and Relict of Ralph Waddington who left behind him a daughter Hannah and her portion in sd. Watkins lands; Sheriff to take sd. Watkins into custody and at next Court to make her rights appear to sd. Shapleigh of nearest ffriend to the said Hannah.

Richard Bushrod and Elizabeth his wife one of ye daughters of Col. Rodham Kenner, dec'd, vs. ffrancis Kenner and Chris. Neale Exors. of the dec'ds Last Will.

Pages 534-539 (none)

Court 19 Aug. 1708

John Bushrod orphan Sone of Symon Bushrod and Grace his wife dec'd, chose Christopher Dameron guardian.

Page 541

Record of the Probate of the Last Will of Elisha Mayes to Thomas and Henry Mayes Exors., proved by Richard Wright and James Badger.

Page 542

Thomas Suggett and Rebecca his wife vs. Richard Hull Exor.

Page 543

Northumberland County Orders

Page 543

Thomas Stretton P/A from Patience Graham widow confesses judgement to the Royal African Company.

Pages 544-548 (none)

Page 549

Mary Nutt daughter of William and Mary Nutt late of this County, decd. by her guardian Edward Cole a Bill in Chancery vs. John Howson and Richard Wright Exors. of the Last Will of Leonard Howson late dec'd setting forth that Mary her late Mother dec'd did before her Intermarryage with Thomas Brereton dec'd, gave her all of Mary ye Mother's part of household stuffe that was left her by the Last Will of her dec'd husband during her Intermarryage with the sd. Brereton and the sd. Mary ye Mother againe Intermarryed with the sd. Leonard Howson and ye sd. Mary ye Mother dyed and shortly after the sd. Leonard Howson also dec'd leaving ye aforsaid Def't Exors. and Mary ye daughter to have her Est.

Court 17 Nov. 1708

Page 550

Probate of the Last Will of Bartholl Dameron dec'd to Eliza. Dameron Exx., proved by Bartholl Shreever, Thomas Gaskins and John Ingram.

Benja. Browne and Anne his wife ack. a Deed of Indenture for Land to George Murdock and Mary his wife.

John Dunaway ack. a Deed of Indenture for Land to Stephen Chilton.

Page 551

Margaret Dunaway Relinquishes her Right of Dower for the sale of land by her husband.

Thomas Cammell and Elizabeth his wife, Adm. to them on the Estate of William Angell, dec'd.

Probate of the Last Will of Nicholas Badger to James Badger, Exor., proved by Mary Scofill.

Page 552

Pet. of Henry Boggess, Adm. to him on the Estate of Katherine Oblin.

John Brewer chose Wm. Chilton guardian.

ffelix Oconoly and Margaret his wife, Edw. Gallington and Margaret Ester, Elizabeth Chilton, Mary Wornom, John Kent, Alice Williams, Elias Lowry, Hancock Nicholls, George Hill, Ellinor att Capt. Cralles James Guttridge, Andrew Danielson, William Blundall and the overseers of the highways from Lazarus Taylors unto fflints Mill presented to Grandjury.

Court 19 Nov. 1708

Page 553

Probate of the Last Will of John Sutherland dec'd, to Alice Sutherland Exx., proved by Thomas Hughlett and Thomas Bridgeman.

Pages 554-557 (none)

Court 19 Jan. 1708/9

Page 558 (on following page)

Northumberland County Orders

Page 558

Andrew Peacock and Anne his wife ack. a Deed of Indenture for Land unto John Corbell.

Motion of Elizabeth Banks to be admitted guardian to her two grandchildren Wm. and Elizabeth Keene orphans of Wm. Keene.

James Atkins vs Thomas Trueman (the case covers pp. 558-560) for trespass of two dwellings, which William Jones devised to the said Thomas; Robert Jones late of this County decd, by will dated 14 Jan. 1675 devised unto his son Samuel Jones land adj. "my Cozen Robert Hews" and my Sone Maurice Jones to have a seat of Land and Sone Maurice and his older brothers William, Samuel and Robert; will proved 1 March 1675 and Samuel Jones dyed in the month of October 1697; suit dismissed and pl't to pay costs, which he appealed to the next General Court.

Page 560

James Pugh and Diana Gill ack. an Indenture to Capt. George Eskridge.

Page 561

Thomas Evans orphan son of John and Margaret Evans, aged 6 last May, to serve William Warwick until 21. John Evans, ditto, aged 5 the 15th of Oct. last, to serve Tho. Ashburne until 21.

Dennis McCarty orphan Son of Daniel and ffrances McCarty, aged 14 in Oct. last, with the consent of his mother to serve John Hill and Hannah his wife until 21.

Mrs. Anne fflint to take unto her care and custody James fflint Son of Thomas and ye sd. Anne fflint.

Court 20 Jan. 1708/9

Page 562

Pet. of William Browne and Elizabeth his wife, Adm. to them on the Est. of Sarah Gater dec'd.

Probate of the Last Will of Richard Nelms to Sarah Nelms, Exx., proved by Dorothy Templer and Hannah Thrapp.

Pet. of Mr. Thomas Palmer and Katherine his wife Sister and nearest kin to Peter Coutanceau dec'd, Adm. to them.

Pet. of James and Richard Oldham, Adm. to them on the Est. of John Oldham, dec'd. James Oldham moveing for a Probate of the Will of Abigal Oldam, dec'd, and Capt. George Eskridge in behalfe of Richard Oldam making exception vs. the granting thereof until next Court and so to be settled.

Pages 563-567 (none)

Court 21 Jan. 1708/9

Psge 568

Richard Smith as marryed to Mary the Widow and Relict of ffuder Baker and as nearest friend to William Baker eldest Sone and heir apparent of the sd. ffuder Baker in his life time purchased of his brother Thomas Baker dec'd 100 acres and Thomas Baker's heir Thomas Baker being underage one Henry Hopkins who marryed Mary the Widdow of the sd. Thomas Baker dec'd hath lately caused declaration in the name of one Thomas Sheares who claims by Demise from and under Mary Baker and Lucy Baker vs. James Cunningham, and petitions the Court that the suit be stopped and the

Northumberland County Orders

Page 568 cont'd:

whole matter to be heard and determined in chancery.

Pages 569-570 (none)

Court 16 Mar. 1708/9

Page 571

The N. C. Will of Elizabeth Maise by Cornelius Swillivant and Kather- his wife.

The Last Will of Robert Nash proved by Richard Nutt, Lazarus Taylor and Thomas Waters.

Court 20 Apr. 1709

Page 572

Pet. of Joseph Ball, Adm. to him on the Est. of Mr. John Carnagie, deceased.

Probate of the Last Will of M'm Elizabeth Kenner, dec'd, to Matthew Kenner, Exor., proved by Richard Rice and Mary Rice.

Probate of the Last will of Richard Prichard, dec'd, to Daniell Hall, Exor., proved by Richard Wright and David Moore.

Probate of the Last Will of James Jones to Elizabeth Jones, Exx.., proved by Vincent Cox and Robert Phillips and Bartholl Leasure.

Last Will of James Genn, but no witness for proof, and Court granted probate to Thomas and James Genn, Exors.

Probate of the Last Will of George Leazure to Hannah Leazure, Exx., proved by George Eskridge and Sam'll Damonile.

Page 573

Probate of the Last Will of Hugh Callan to John and Anne Callan, Exor's, proved by Alexander Mulraine, John Lewis, and Thomas Hobson.

Last Will of Peter Coutanceau, proved by Thomas Hobson, David Straughan and Mary Price.

Pet. of Anne Edwards, Widow and Relict of Nicholas Edwards, Adm. to her.

Katherine Palmer surviving Admx. of Peter Coutanceau, Gent., dec'd, Thomas Palmer husband of ye sd. Katherine ye other adm'r being lately dec'd and the Est. to be App. and sold at outcry.

Pages 573-577 (Settling of Coutanceau's Estate.)

Court 15 June 1709

Page 578

Pet. of Andrew Jackson and Dorothy his wife and John Grisham, Exors. of the Last Will of Wm. Lester late of Lancaster County, Gent., Dec'd, to App. Est. of dec'd, in this county.

Richard Hudnall and Mary his wife ack. a Deed of Indenture for Land to Richard Neale.

Probate of the Last Will of Dennis Conway to John and Christ. Conway,

Northumberland County Orders

Page 578 cont'd:

Exors., proved by Daniel McCarty and Tho. Thackrell.

Probate of the Last Will of Thomas Hall to Thomas Hall and James Claughton, Exors., proved by Phill. Rogers and David Straughan.

Probate of the Last Will of Thomas Waters to Elithie Waters and Chris. Maile, Exors., proved by Edmd. Baisie and Lazarus Taylor.

Court 15 June 1709

Page 579

Probate of the Last Will of Henry Mayse to Susannah Mayse, Exx., and proved by Isaac Basie and Joseph Hughs.

Probate of the Last Will of Thomas Palmer to Katherine Palmer, proved by Matthew Mason.

Page 580 (none)

Court 20 July 1709

Page 581

Probat of the Last Will of Dennis Conway to Thomas Berry and John Gouthe, Exors., proved by Robert Duat, the other witness being dead.

Probat of the Last Will of John Bryan to Mary Bryan, Exx., proved by Richard Swanson and Elizabeth Swanson.

Probat of the Last Will of John Webb to Edward Sanders and Thomas Webb and Sarah Dickenson, Exors., proved by John Allen and Jno. Hartey.

Motion of Mr. John Howson, Probate of the Last Will of Hancock Lee, Gent., to Robert Carter, Esq., Richard Lee, Esq., and John Howson, Gent. Trustees and Guardians therein named, proved by Thomas Knight, Mary Hughs Daniell ffeilding, Robert Spencer, John Harris and William Jones, JR.

Page 582

Pet. of Richard Dougle, Adm. to him on the Est. of William Dougle.

Thomas Leechman and Elizabeth his wife ack. a deed of Indenture for the Land to Thomas Smith.

Pet. of Joseph Holt, Adm. as Greatest Creditor on the Est. of Richard Archer..

Pet. of Susannah Rogers, Widow and Relick of James Rogers, Adm. to her.

Page 583

Probate of the Last Will of Ignatius Olliver to Elizabeth Olliver,Exx. and proved by ffrancis Kenner and David Straughan.

Probate of the N. C. Will of Thomas Kingwell to Isaac Basie and Thomas Everett, proved by George Everett and Thomas Earth.

Page 584

Probate of the Will of Robert Roebuck to Robt. Robuck, Exor., proved by John Gaylor and Margt. Browne.

Probate of the Last Will of Alice Southland to Symon Thomson, Exr.,

Northumberland County Orders

Page 584 cont'd:

proved by Thomas and Mary Hughlett.

Probate of the Last Will of George Cooper, Gent. to Elizabeth Robinson, Exx., proved by Thomas Harte and Wm. Due and Charles David.

Probate of the Last Will of Isaac Hester to Margt. Hester, Exx., and proved by Pitts Curtis and Charles Davis.

John Nicholls and John Bently pet. the Court for Adm. of the Estate of Thomas Crowder dec'd, and George Eskridge pet. for the orphans to be brought to the next Court.

Pages 585-586 (none)

Court 21 July 1709

Page 587

Enock Hill and Frances his wife ack. Deed of Indenture for Land to Jno. Dunaway.

Pet. of ffrancis Vanlandeghan on ye behalfe of the Orphans of John Taylor, dec'd vs. John Walters.

Pet. of Richard Smith a poore distempered man, Excused from Levy.

Page 588

Acc't of the Est. of William Keene dec'd and Peter Coutanceau who marryed the said William Keene's Widow and Mrs. Elizabeth Banks Guardian of the sd. orphans and Mrs. Katherine Palmer surviving Adm.r of Peter Coutanceau to deliver Est.

Pages 589-596 (none)

Court 17 Aug. 1709

Page 597

Probat of the Last Will of Valentine Munsloe to John Gouthe, Exor., proved by Onesep:h Harvey and John Browne.

Pages 597-599

John Day to answer William Clay for Trespass on two Messuages, etc; whereas John Huske Prochein Amie the 2nd of July 1707 demised (?) to aforesd. William the Messuaged, etc.; for 3 years but John Day on the 1st of Aug. 1707 trespassed on the sd. Messuages and tried by Jury, with the following verdict: Joseph ffeilding the Elder dec'd by his Last Will devised his Est. in these words (vix:t) "In the Name of God Amen I Joseph ffeilding --- I give to my two sons Joseph ffeilding and William ffeilding my Land which is comonly called Scotland to be equally divided between them ---Son William ---Son John ---Son Joseph ---rest of my moveable to be equally divided between My Son John and My daughter Rachel & if either of them die to be equally divided between the rest of the children --- Wife Elizabeth ffeilding --- and witness ----". The sd. Will was not signed by the Testator but on 18 Aug. 1675 the same was proved to be the Last Will and Joseph the eldest Son by his Last Will gave the Land to his Daughter Sarah who is since dec'd without Issue after whose death William the Second Son of the aforesd. Joseph the ffirst Testator became possessed of all the Lands called Scotland and John the Youngest Son dyed in the life time of his Brother William leaving Issue a daughter named Rachell now Lessor of the Plt. also that the sd. William is lately dec'd without Issue who by will gave ye sd. Land to Anne now wife of Ralph Pearce deft; the Sheriff to give William Clay the possession

Northumberland County Orders

Pages 597-599 cont'd:

of the Messuages.

Pages 599-602

Richard Day to answer Robert Clay for trespass of Sixteen Messuages, etc.,; Thomas Gaskins Guardian and nearest friend to Elizabeth Brereton demised to sd. Robert for a Term which is not yett expired, and Richard trespassed on the Sixteen Messuages; by verdict of Jury: a copy of William Claybourne the Elder and William Clayborne the Younger their deed to Thomas Brereton (late Coll. Thomas Brereton, dec'd), copy proved as the sd. Coll. Brereton's Will, a copy of the clause of a Deed of Thomas Brereton the Younger to John Downing dated 12 June 1688, a copy of the Will of Thomas Brereton the Younger and viva voce evidence in Court; the verdict of the Jury that the Pat. of Wm. Clayborne dated 5 Jan. 1651 and land vested in Thomas Brereton the Elder and William Clayborne the Younger dated 16 Oct. 1665; Capt. Hobson being sworne said that his ffather told him that Thomas Brereton the Elder when he was going to Susquehannah ffort he delivered his will to him and after Brereton the elder's decease he knows not whether it was carried to Court, and a clause of a deed of Thomas Brereton the Younger to John Downing dated 12 June 1688 which mentions a Will bearing equal date with the said Will; Mary ye Widdow Brereton marryed and dyed and she was marryed to Leonard Howson and is dead and by Will Brereton the Younger the disputed Land is in possession of Coll. George Cooper and Thomas Hobson the trustees and Brereton the Younger died about nine or ten years old(?) and he died before his Mother in Law and the said Hobson and Cooper relinquished possession to Capt. Winder and Henry Brereton in their Children's behalfe and Mrs. Winder is the Sister in the whole blood to Thomas Brereton ye Younger and Aunt to ye whole blood to Brereton; said Land after Intermarriage of Howson was divided by consent and the Court further judged the Right of the said Land to be vested in the sd. Elizabeth Brereton ye Lessor to the Plt., as heir of her ffather and not in Elizabeth Winder as Aunt of the whole blood to him the sd. Thomas Brereton the Youngest; several reasons for error given and Sheriff to give to Robert Clay the Messuages.

Court 18 Aug. 1709

Page 602

Motion of John Moone, Adm. to him on the Est. of James Edes, dec'd.

Page 603

Mr. Charles Lee orphan of Mr. Charles Lee, dec'd, chose Hancock Lee guardian.

Mary Ellistone orphan Daughter of Jervis Ellistone chose John Thomas guardian.

Page 604

Probate of the Last Will of Joseph Hudnall to Margery Hudnall, proved by Richard Nutt, Ephraim Hughlett and James Mitchell.

ffernott Crowder orphan Daughter of Thomas Crowder to serve Charles Ingram until 18.

Probate of the Last Will of Mrs. Martha Robinson to Samuel Robinon, Exor., proved by John Wornom and Richard Robinson.

Pet. of John Nicholls and John Bently, Adm. on the Est. of Thomas Crowder dec'd and they being securities for the sd. Crowders due admistration on the Estate of James Edny, dec'd.

Northumberland County Orders

Page 605 (none)

Page 606

Richard Robinson moveing for Probate of his Bro:r John Robinson's NC Will and Anthony Robinson coming into Court and seeks invallidation; referred to next Court.

Page 607

Probate of the Last Will of Jane Robinson Widow to Richard and Thomas Robinson Exor., proved by Anthony Haynie and Henry Maise.

Motion of Mr. Ebenezer Neale, a letter from Capt. Tho, Pretty John in England to his late Brother Mr. William Neale.

Pages 608-609

Thomas Suggett and Rebecca his wife one of the Daughters of Richard Hull dec'd, that sd. Richard Hull by Will dated 11 Oct. 1693 bequeathed to his daughter Rebecca personal property and an Indian Slave and nominated Mr. Peter Presly, Capt. Hack and Charles Harris overseers and Richard Hull the Son and Exor. sd. his father never made a Will and there was no slave born of a slave and the Court orders the negro to be given them and sd. Richard Hull to pay costs and the Deft. appeals to the General Court.

Court 18 Aug. 1709

Page 610

James Mortimore orphan Son of James Mortimore aged 5 the 25th of Mar. last by consent of his mother to serve Thomas Gill.

Court 19 Aug. 1709

Page 610 cont'd:

Robert Crowder orphan Son of Thomas Crowder to serve Thomas Dameron and his wife until 21.

Page 611

Thomas Crowder, ditto, to serve Henry Hopkins until 21.

Page 612 (none)

Page 613

John Saby pet. this Court for his ffiliall portion of his dec'd Grandfather John Oldham's Estate and James and Richard Oldham adm'rs possess Est. and they to appear at next Court.

Pages 614-615 (none)

Court 21 Sept. 1709

Page 616

Probat of the Last Will of Isaac Edwards to Eliza. Edwards, proved by Simon Bowly and John Nelms.

Pages 617-618 (none)

Court 22 Sept. 1709

Page 619 (on following page)

121

Northumberland County Orders

Page 619

Clem't Corbell and Mary his Wife ack. a Lease for There Lives unto Charles Creele. Clem't Corbell and Mary his wife ack. a Lease for There Lives unto John Baily.

Page 620

John Carnegie Adm'r of Thomas ffernes vs. Maurice Jones, Exor. of Robert Jones.

Page 621

Mutton Lewis by his nearest ffriend Richard Swanson vs. John Nickless.

Pages 622-625 (none)

Page 626

Anne Webb by her Att. Thomas Stretton ack. a Deed of Indenture for Land to Thomas Hobson.

Page 627 (none)

Court 23 Sept. 1709

Page 628

William Lambert of the Parish of South ffarnham in the County of Richmond Planter vs. Matthew Myers of the Parish of White Chappell in ye Co. of Lancaster Cordwinder.

Page 629 (none)

Court 16 Nov. 1709

Page 630

Timothy Kenady ack. a Deed of Indenture for Land unto Dennis Conaway.

Pet. of Robert Boyd and Anne his wife and John Pope, Adm. to them of the Estate of Simon Thomson, dec'd.

Page 631 (none)

Court 21 Dec. 1709

Page 632

Probate of the Last Will of Christopher Garlington to Mary Garlington proved by William Galway and Thomas Hill.

Josias Gaskins ack. a Deed of Indenture for 250 acres unto Thomas Gaskins; Elizabeth Gaskins by her att. Thomas Stretton ack. her relinquishment of Dower in the Land sold by her husband; Thomas Gaskins ack. Deed of Indenture for 100 acres to Josias Gaskins; Martha Gaskins by her att. Thomas Stretton ack. her Relinquishment of Dower in Land sold by her husband.

Margery Hudnall Widow ack. a Deed of Indenture for Land to Samuell Blackwell in trust for her children John, Joseph, Anne and Mary Hudnall.

Court 15 ffeb. 1709/10

Page 633

Probat of the Last Will of Thomas Knight, dec'd to Mary Knight, Exx. proved by John Burne.

Northumberland County Orders

Page 633 cont'd:

Motion of Robert Huffe in behalfe of his grandchildren orphans of William Short, dec'd and a Probate to him on the Last Will, proved by Rich. Nutt and William Hoult.

Court 15 ffeb. 1709/10

Motion of Giles Kelly a Probate to him of a N.C. Will of James Glover, proved by John Shaw and Thomas Crane.

Probate of the Last Will of James Simons, dec'd, to Richard and John Marsh, Exors., proved by Wm. Haslass and Wm. Parlar.

Probat of the Last Will of John Linsey, dec'd to Mary Linsey, Exx.,& proved by David Straughan and Andrew Peacock.

Probat of the Last Will of Richard Price, decd to Mary Price, Exx.,& proved by Richard Thomson and David Straughan.

Clem't Corbell and his wife ack. an Indenture of Lease for 100 acres to Thomas Rout.

John Champion ack. a Deed of Indenture for Land unto Pitts Curtis;P/A from Josian Champion to Thomas Hobson for Ack. her Right of Dower of the Land sold by her husband.

Pet. of Anne Dunaway, a Com. of Adm. to her on the Est. of her dec'd husband Samuel Dunaway.

Pet. of Hannah Russell, Com. of Adm. to her on the Est. of her dec'd husband Richard Russell.

Page 634

Jane Northen, Orphan aged 12 to serve Mr. John Ingram until 18. Samuel Northen orphan aged 8 to serve Mr. Thomas Waddy.

Christ. Mortemore orphan of James Mortemore, dec'd, aged 9 the 16th of Aug. next to serve Mr. Thomas Gill until 21.

Elizabeth Arlege chose Capt. ffrancis Kenner guardian. ffrancis Kenner and William Medcalfe bond for it.

Jno. Baily orphan chose William Medcalfe Guardian.

Page 635

William Medcalfe and Capt. ffrancis Kenner bond for it.

Mr. Samuell Smith ack. a Deed of Indenture for 100 Acs. to William Nelms.

Mr. Henry Linton pet. for Adm. on the Est. of Mr. Richard Bushrod, dec'd and the Sheriff to summons Mrs. Elizabeth Bushrod to the next court to see that Adm. may not be granted to him.

Pet. of Elinor Turner, Adm. to her on the Est. of her dec'd husband John Turner.

Court 16 ffeb. 1709/10

Page 636

Capt. George Eskridge with consent of Eliza. Bushrod Wid. and Relict of Richd. Bushrod decd. admitted guardian to her infant son Richd. Bushrod.

Northumberland County Orders

Page 636 cont'd:

Pet. of Richard Howe, Com. of Adm. to him on the Est. of James Southerne, dec'd.

Page 637

Motion of Capt. John Tarpley and Mr. Richard Nutt, Com. of Adm. to them on Est. of Mary Nutt, dec'd.

Motion of Rebecca Pue Wid. and Relict of John Pue, decd, Com. of Adm. to her.

Page 638

Motion of Richard Robinson, Com. of Adm. to him on the Est. of John Robinson, dec'd.

Pet. of Charles Moorehead on behalfe of Elizabeth Anne Mary John and Winifred Moorehead the younger children of Charles Moorehead, dec'd; Est. divided between children and Mother.

Court 17 ffeb. 1709/10

Page 639

Edward ffeilding and Winfred his wife Bill in Chancery vs. John Conway and Chris. Conway, Exors. of Dennis Conway.

Ellinor Hawkins vs. Samll. Blackwell and Margery his wife Relict of Joseph Hudnall.

Hannah Warrington orphan Daughter of Ralph Warrington dec'd vs. Edward Watkins for deteyning from her her proportional part of her dec'd ffather's Estate.

Page 640 (none)

Pages 641-642

Susannah and Isaac Atkins children of James Atkins the sd. Susannah being aged 8 in March next and Isaac a year old next April to serve Edward Atkins. John, ditto, aged 11, Sept. next to serve John Blundell until 21.

Motion of Patience Neale in behalfe of Nathan Neale her son by her former husband Mr. Daniell Neale, dec'd that Capt. Danll. McCarty or Cpt. George Eskridge have Liberty to bring a Bill in Chancery in the sd. Nathan's behalfe.

Motion of Mrs. Katherine Palmer the Sister and Surviving Admx. of Peter Coutanceau dec'd she is admitted Guardian to Peter and Anne Coutanceau the Orphans of the sd. Peter.

John Spry and Mary his wife pet. for Adm. on Edward Nesbitt's Estate.

Page 643

Thomas Stretton att. of Thomas, John and Elizabeth Webb orphans of Thomas Webb, dec'd, ack. a General Release to Thomas Hobson and Richard Wright (Exors. of the Last Will of their dec'd father) for their several proportions of his Estate.

Court 15 Mar. 1709/10

Probat of the Last Will of Pemberton Claughton dec;d to Mary Claughton Exx., proved by Jno. Douglas and David Straughan.

Northumberland County Orders

Page 644

Anne Edny chose Mr. George Ball guardian.

James Moulder to be keeper of ordinary.

Pet. of Anne Kilpatrick Adm. to her on Est. of her dec'd husband Edward Kilpatrick.

Pet. of Thomas Mahone and Elinor his wife Adm. to them of the Estate of Nicholas Merrica.

Page 645

Pet. of Wm. Jones Adm. to him on the Est. of his dec'd ffather William Jones his Mother Marg'tt Jones del. the same.

Page 646 (none)

Court 16 Mar. 1709/10

Page 647

Probat of the Last Will of Mrs. Hannah Neale to Capt. Christ. Neale, Mr. Daniell Neale, Mr. Richard Neale and Mr. Rodham Neale Exors., proved by Capt. ffrancis Kenner and William Medcalfe.

Pet. of Jacob Baily Adm. on the Est. of Anne Alliday.

Pages 648-650 (none)

Court 17 Mar. 1709/10

Page 651

Probat of the Last Will of Isaac Gaskins to Elizabeth Gaskins Exx., proved by George Dameron and Charles Ingram.

Pages 652-654 (none)

Page 655

William Young guardian in Soccage to John Coutanceau minor and Orphan of Peter Coutanceau to appear at next Court.

Court 17 May 1710

Page 656

Probat of the Last Will of William Howard to Sarah Howard, Exx., proved by Isaac Basie and John Basie.

Page 657

Probat of the Last Will of William Percifull to Elizabeth Percifull, proved by John Taylor and Michaell Keady.

Probat of the Last Will of Charles Betts to Mary Betts Exx., proved by Richard Wright, Edward Coles and Wm. Tolson.

Motion of Elizabeth Boaz Adm. to her on the Est. of her dec'd husband John Boaz.

Motion of Capt. john Tarpley, Tho. Rout and Jno. Conaway, Dennis Conaway, Rich. Oldam and James Oldam any 4, to App. a Negro Slave belonging to the Est. of Mary Nutt, dec'd.

Page 658 (on following page)

Northumberland County Orders

Page 658

William Murrow, poor and ancient, excused from Levy.

Constables: William Payne in roome of David Spence of Cone, Henry Bryan of Middle Wiccocomoco in Roome of James Oldam and John Burne of lower Wiccocomoco the other being dead.

Mary Hester orphan Daughter of Isaac Hester chose Richard Lattimore guardian.

Court 18 May 1710

Page 659

Commission for Surveyor of this County to John Coppage.

Page 660

John Coppage Surveyor to lay out Land in dispute between Charles Coppage and his Brother Wm. Coppage.

John fforest an orphan chose Robert Roebuck Guardian.

Page 661

Pet. of William Betts, Guardian of Mary Cassady, Com. of Adm. on Est. of William Cassady.

Page 662 (none)

Court 21 June 1710

Page 663

Capt. Maurice Jones sworne High Sheriff.

Page 664

Probate of the Last Will of Anthony Haynie to Sarah Haynie and Grace Ball Exors., proved by Richard Ball and Hancock Nicholls.

Samuell Downing, Eliza. his wife Pet. for Surveying and Laying out ffour hundred acs. of Land left by her dec'd ffather's Will.

Page 665 (none)

Page 666

Hannah Wadding daughter and Legatee of Ralph Waddington Pet. Court vs. Edward Watkins who married the Widdow and Relict of the sd. Dec'd for her ffiliall portion of Dec'ds Est.

Margaret Nowland wife of Richard Nowland in great want because her husband carryed away with him all his substance and Richard Talbot who is in possession thereof (as alsoe the palce of abode) and the Sheriff to take him in custody.

Pages 667-674 (none)

Court 19 July 1710

Page 675

John Hill ack. a Deed of Indenture to Wm. Dare; Anne Hill wife of sd. John Hill Relinquished her Right of Dower.

Northumberland County Orders

Page 676 (none)

Page 677

Pet. of Samuel Downing and Elizabeth his wife Daughter and one of the Legatees of Ebenezer Sanders, to lay out the Land of the Legatees of the Will.

Thomas Thompson as being brother and nearest kin to Simon Thompson, dec'd pet. for Adm. and John Pope, Robert Boyd and Anne his wife by their att. Wm. Dare alledging that Adm. in Right of Philip Thompson orphan son of the sd. dec'd (during his minority) and by order of the Court formerly granted unto them which Tho. Thompson by his att. Danll. McCarty alledged they out not to have done. John Pope, Robert Boyd and Anne his wife appeal to the General Court.

Court 20 July 1710

Page 678

Motion of Samll. Robinson Exor. of the Last Will of Martha Robinson, dec'd, App. of her Estate.

Pages 679-680 (none)

Page 681

Francis Webb by his nearest ffriend Edwd. Sanders vs. John Dunaway.

Page 682

Judgement granted to Philip Howell vs. the Estate of John Graham, deceased, in the hands of William Coppage and Patience his wife Exx. of the Last Will of the said dec'd.

Pages 683-700 (none)

Court 20 Sept. 1710

Page 701

Richard Lattimore assignee of William Nelmes and Eliza. his wife assignee of Eliza. Lattimore dec'd vs. Thomas Berry and Jno. Gouthe, Exors. of the Last Will of Dennis Conway dismissed.

Pages 702-704 (none)

Court 5 Oct. 1710

Page 705

N. C. Will of Mr. William Winder, dec'd, proved by Mr. Tho. Hobson & Clark Hobson his Wife and Thomas Stretton.

Court 22 ffeb. 1710/11

Pages 706-709

(Note: "--- the book of Records in which they have been recorded burned with the office the 25th day of October Domini one thousand Seven hundred and ten." Bk. 17, unpaged.)

The Records being burned, Records re-recorded.

Motion of Sarah Lee, Wid. and Relict of Mr. Hancock Lee for a division of the Est. of her late husband.

Northumberland County Orders

Pages 706-709 cont'd:

Thomas Stretton named in Re-recorded Records deputy Clerke.

Probat of the Will of Vincent Garner dec'd to Martha Garner, Parish James and Benj. Garner Exors., proved by David Straughan, Wm. Lewis and Wm. Grinsteed.

Court 21 Mar. 1710/11

Page 710

Elizabeth Hughlett orphan Daughter of John Hughlett chose Richard Nutt her guardian. Yarrett Hughlett, ditto, chose Ephraim Hughlett his guardian.

Page 711 (none)

Court 22 Mar. 1710/11

Page 712

Motion of John Hughlett with the Will annexed Adm. to him of the Est. of Jno. Hughlett, and App. of his Est.

Pet. of Richard Howe that Clement Corbell hath illegally possessed the Estate of Robert Bartlett (who dyed Intestate).

Pet. of Ralph Bickly Adm. as greatest Creditor to him on the Estate of James Allen, dec'd.

Page 713

Pet. of Richard Vanlandegham att. of Anne Norgate Adm. to him on the Est. of Phillip Norgate dec'd.

Motion of Susanna Smith Wid. and Relict of Richard Smith, Adm. to her.

Motion of Sarah Nelms Wid. and Relict of Richard Nelms; Thomas Stretton and Alexander Rogers were sworne to the truth of a Copy of her dec'd husbands Will.

Page 714

Edward ffeilding and Winifred his wife one of the Daughters and Legatees of Dennis Conway, dec'd, Bill in Chancery vs. John and Christopher Conway Exors. of the Last Will.

Court 16 May 1711

Pages 715,716,717 Re-record.

Last Will of Robert Boyd presented by Anne Boyd his Exx., proved by John and Mary Murdock.

Page 718

John Hall orphan Sone of Thomas Hall aged 3 the 18th of Sept. last, to serve George Harrison and Anne his wife.

John Hayes Son of John Hayes (who departed this County and took no care of him) to serve Joseph Holt and Anne his wife.

Court 17 May 1711

Pages 719, 720, 721 Re-Recorded.

Northumberland County Orders

Page 721

Motion of Capt. Thomas Hobson Adm. with the Will annexed of William Winder, dec'd, Adm. to him during the minority of his son John Hobson.

John Grinsteed 7 years old the 11th April last and William Grinsteed 9 years old the 4th of Dec. last Orphan Sons of John Grinsteed, dec'd, by the desire of their Mother to serve Danll. McCarty of Westmoreland County until 21.

Pet. of George Hopkins and Elizabeth his wife one of the Daughters of Thomas Porter, dec'd, to have a 4th part of the Estate.

Page 722

Christopher Conway pet. the Court as Greatest Creditor on the Estate of Arthur Bridgeman, dec'd, and the Sheriff to summons Mary Bridgeman, Widdow and Relict to the Next Court.

(Note: Re-recorded Records)

Pet. of Daniel Dunaway and Jane his wife Late Jane Wall Wid. and Relict of John Wall, dec'd, Adm. to them.

Page 723

Pet. of Ephraim Hughlett and Elizabeth his wife Daughter of Thomas Winter dec'd that Hancock Nicholls who marryed the Wid. and Relict of sd. dec'd Winter to pay sd. Hughlett for his sd. Wife's filliall part of the ffather's estate.

Mary Hamlett orphan Daughter of John Hamlett to serve Lawrence Dameron.

Edward Sanders ack. an Identure of Land to Alexander Love and also P/A from Eliza. wife of the sd. Edward Sanders to Tho. Stratton for Relinquishment of her Dower.

Page 724

Pet. of Richard Howe Adm. to him as greatest Creditor on the Estate of Robert Barton.

Henry Curtis and George Curtis chose Robt. Gordon guardian.

Pages 725-730 (none)

Court 20 June 1711

Page 731

Pet. of William Payne and Susannah his wife late Susannah Husk, Adm. of Est. of John Husk to them.

Edward Algood orphan Son of William Algood chose James Palmer Guardian. William Algood, orphan son of William Algood to serve James Palmer and his wife until 21.

App. of the Est. of John Hurst and that Wm. Payne and Susannah his wife late Susannah Hurst (as recorded).

Page 732

John Lawrence, a poor Iddiott, excluded from the Levy.

Page 733

Motion of Thomas Gill, Adm. to him as greatest Creditor on the Estate

Northumberland County Orders

Page 733 cont'd:

of William Dewe, dec'd.

Page 734

Pet. of Clement Corbell, John Corbell and Wm. Browne next of kin to John Corbell, dec'd, Adm. to them of Jno. Corbell's Estate.

Richard Harrold, Jr. and Margaret his wife one of the Daughters of Thomas Ball, dec'd, vs. John Burne who marryed the Widdow and Relict of sd Ball for Margaret's ffiliall portion of Estate.

Court 18 July 1711

Page 735

Motion of Thomas Lee, Navall officer of the Potomack District, Capt. John Howson his deputy.

Elizabeth Richardson orphan Daughter of Charles Richardson age 12 to serve Thomas Webb and Charity his wife until 18.

Rainsford Smith ack. a Deed of Land to Thomas Gill.

Pages 736-738 (none)

Court 19 July 1711

Page 739

Robert Vaulx and Elizabeth his wife one of the Daughters of Rodham Kenner, Gent., dec'd. Bill in Chancery vs. Chris. Neale and ffrancis Kenner, Gent. Exors. of the dec'ds Will.

Daniel McCarty on behalfe of Richard Eaton orphan Son of Richard Eaton now in the possession of Daniell Dunaway, complains that he is not well used.

Page 740

Motion of David Spence who married the Relict of Nicholas Edwards decd, App. of Dec'ds Estate.

Court 20 July 1711

Page 741

Phillip Shapleigh ack. a Deed of Guift unto Elizabeth Hobson Daughter of Thomas Hobson. Thomas Hobson ack. a Deed of Guift to his Sone John Hobson.

Page 742 (none)

Page 743

John Lyons and Anne his wife late Anne Callam and John Callam the Exors. of the will of Hugh Callam vs. Richard Haynie.

Pages 744-746 (none)

Court 15 Aug. 1711

Page 747

Clement and Mary Arlege a Deed of Sale to Patrick Malery.

Northumberland County Orders

Page 748

Pet. of John Cralle, Com. of Adm. on the Estate of Arthur Bridgeman.

Joseph Ball Son of Coll. Joseph Ball presented an Inventory of the Estate of Mr. John Carnegie.

Mary Mayes orphan Daughter of Henry Mayes, dec'd, aged past 12 chose Jno. Coppage.

Timothy Sachiverall and Elizabeth his wife late Relict and Widdow of Jno. Dawson, Com. of Adm. to them.

Page 749

Frances Wigginton orphan Daughter of Geo. Wigginton to serve Daniell Webb.

Court 19 Sept. 1711

John Nelmes to keep an ordinary.

Pages 750-753

Suit in Chancery of George Eskridge Guardian to Richard Bushrod an infant son of Richard Bushrod, dec'd who was the Son of Tho. Bushrod, decd vs. John Bushrod, Gent., that Thomas Bushrod did by his last Will desire Negro and English servants to be kept and divided betwixt his son Richard and Daughter Ann, and his Brother Jno. Bushrod be sole Exor. of his sd. will, and Richard the Elder after his father's death before he attained the age of 21 by and with the consent of his Uncle Jno. Bushrod intermarryed with one Eliza. Bushrod, Daughter of Rodham Kenner, Gent., and the sd Ann also after her father's death before aged 18 intermarryed with one Griffin ffantleroy of the County of Richmond, Gent. and John Bushrod gave both children their rateable portion of the Estate and offered security to John Bushrod in Westmoreland County Court and Richard departed this life soon afterwards leaving his young wife with child and the Court under comon law to decide how the small Estate is to support the child, and decreed that the negroes be divided, and Eskridge to have them for his pupil and Jno. Bushrod appeals the case to the General Court.

Page 753 (none)

Court 20 Sept. 1711

Page 754

Anne Coutanceau daughter of Peter Coutanceau by Datherine Palmer her Guardian vs. John Coutanceau heir of Peter Coutanceau.

Deed of Jonathan Edwards ack. to Isaac Edwards.

Page 755

Motion of Yarratt Hughlett orphan of Jno. and Mary Hughlett dec'd, chose his brother William, Guardian.

Court 21 Sept. 1711

Page 756

Maurice Jones to be High Sheriff.

Court 21 Nov. 1711

David ffloker orphan Son of David ffuker (as recorded), dec'd, chose Jno. Champion Guardian.

Northumberland County Orders

Page 757

Samuel Blackwell chiefest creditor of Mary Walker, dec'd, Com. of Adm. to him. Ann Walker, orphan Daughter of Emmanuell and Mary Walker to serve Samuel Blackwell.

Thomas Crowder orphan Son of Thomas Crowder pet. the Court 19 Aug.1709 to serve Henry Hopkins and no learning given him by his Master and the Court ordered Hopkins to put the sd. orphan in school and instead of the trade of carpenter to be the trade of weaver.

Motion of Richard Eaton orphan Son of Richard Eaton, dec'd, chose Daniel McCarty guardian.

Court 19 Dec. 1711

Page 758

Richard Walker orphan Son of Emmanuel and Mary Walker dec'd, to serve Samuel Blackwell until 21.

Robert Davis chiefest Creditor of Thomas Stratton dec'd, Com. of Adm. to him.

Deed of Land by Proprietors of the Northern Neck to Charles Betts, deceased and re-recorded.

Jno. Meath and Mabel his wife Relict of Daniell Murphew, dec'd, Com. of Adm. to them.

Page 759

Jno. Cotrell for himselfe and Lucretia his wife and Jno. Haynie for himselfe and Hannah his wife (the sd. Lucretia and Hannah nearest of Kin to Ebenezer Neale, dec'd), Com. of Adm.

Court 16 Jan. 1711/12

Page 760-761

Elinor Moon ye Relict of Tho. Moon, dec'd, entered an original Last Will of Thomas Moon; presented by Elinor the Exx., proved by Ephraim Hughlett, Thomas Smith and Anthony Delawny.

Last Will of Christopher Threlkell, dec'd, presented by Mary Doggett his Exx., proved by Geo. Everitt and motion of Benjamin Doggett and Mary his wife for it.

Tho. Hayden and Anne his wife the late Anne Denny Relict of Edmund Denny dec'd, Com. of Adm. to them.

Page 762

John Hadwell vs. Est. of Elizabeth Porter and George Hopkins who marryed one of the Daughters of the sd. Eliza. and Judgement as to the Est.

Pages 763-764 (none)

Page 765

Motion of Eliz. Hughlet (orphan Daughter of Mary Hughlet, dec'd) her brother Ephraim Hughlet admitted Guardian.

John Trussell and his now Wife ack. a deed of Indenture for Land unto Thomas Barecroft. Thomas Barecroft and Martha his now wife ack. a deed of Indenture for Land unto John Trussell.

Northumberland County Orders

Page 766

Ruth Oldam ye Relict of James Oldam, dec'd to have at next Court Tho. Hobson, Tho. Hughlett and Rich. Oldam.

Court 20 ffeb. 1711/12

Page 766 cont'd:

Last Will of Peter Hammon, dec'd, presented by Charles Hammon, proved by Henry Tapscott and Jno. Marsh.

Page 767

Barthol. Scriever chiefest Cred'r of Tho. Urquahart, Dec'd, Com. of Adm. to him.

Page 768

Robert Gordon who marryed ye Relict of Jno. Nickless, dec'd, Com. of Adm. to him.

Pages 769-770 (none)

Court 19 Mar. 1711/12

Page 771

Last Will of Dorothy Spann, dec'd by Jno. Spann and Samuel Spann her Exors., proved by Edward Jones and Sam. Samford.

Page 772

Mary Bridgeman a poor orphan Daughter of Arthur Bridgeman aged 9 Jan. last past to serve Charles Nelmes and Alice his wife until 18. Grace Bridgeman, ditto, aged 11 in Oct. last past to serve Andrew Dew and Flora his wife until 18.

Thomas Seddon and Joanna his wife ack. a Deed of Lease and release unto William Tyney.

William ffalon presented the Last Will of his dec'd ffather Charles ffalon, and re-recorded.

Thomas White, poor ancient and feeble, free from Levy.

Pages 773-774 (none)

Page 775

Richard Haynie on behalfe of his daughter Catherine Haynie vs. John Way and Elizabeth his wife dismissed.

Pages 776-780 (none)

Court 18 June 1712

Page 781

John Lewis appointed Constable.

Page 782

Mary Davis a poor orphan of James Davis aged 12 ye 15th April last to serve Ann Hoult until 18.

Petition of Mary Everitt Relict of Geo. Everitt dec'd, ordered that

Northumberland County Orders

Page 782 cont'd:

the Sheriff cite the sons of the sd. Mary (to wit: George and Thomas Everitt) to appear at next Court.

Richard Spann ack. a Deed of Indenture for Land called Codd plantation to Jno. Spann.

Richard Oldham appointed Constable for Cone.

Rachel ffeilding orphan of Jno. ffeilding, dec'd, Alexander Mulraine admitted Guardian.

Page 783 (none)

Page 784

Edward Sanders, Jr. ack. a Deed of Indenture to Hugh Edwards.

Ann Hoult Relict of Joseph Hoult, Com. of Adm. to her.

Peter Presly, Gent., sworne Sheriff.

Court 19 June 1712

Page 785

John Hulk a poor orphan son of Jno. Hulk aged 5 to serve Robert Davis until 21.

Spencer Mottrom orphan Son of Spencer Mottrom, Gent., dec'd, chose Joseph Ball guardian.

Jno. Hart and Sarah his wife one of the daughters of Peter Hamond, dec'd, pet. the Court for legacyes devised him by the will of the said Peter.

Jno. Davis, a poor feeble man incapable of labor, excused from Levy.

Page 786

Henry King, a poor feeble ancient, excused from Levy.

Court 16 July 1712

Page 787

Thomas Webb ack. a Deed of Land unto Richard Wright and Charity Webb by her att. Chris. Newton relinquished her right of Dower in the sale of Land by her husband.

Page 788 (none)

Page 789

Letty Wilson wife of Jno. Wilson stole from Charles Ingram.

John Bashford orphan of Simon Bashford, dec'd, and Christopher Dameron his Guardian.

Court 20 Aug. 1712

John Trussell and Jane his wife ack. a Deed of Indenture unto Thomas Miller, Jr.

Page 790

Abner Neale orphan of Dan'l Neale, dec'd,, Tho. Barnes Guardian.

Northumberland County Orders

Page 790 cont'd:

Henry Mayes ye Son of and Att. of his father, Tho. Mayes in March last past ack. a Deed of Land to Tho. Berry, confirmed.

Ruth Oldam Relict of Jam. Oldam, Com. of Adm. to her.

Richard Nutt and Ann his wife, one of ye Daughters of William Downing, Jr. ack. a Deed of Indenture for land to Samuel Blackwell.

Page 791

The Last Will of Wm. Pickering, dec'd presented by Wm. Nelms and Simon Bewley overseers, proved by John Aires and Henry Gaskins.

Pages 792-793 (none)

Court 21 Aug. 1712

Page 794

Richard Haynie complains vs. Wm. Wiltshire that he was ordered to lay out and Assign to the sd. Wm. and Katherine his wife her right of Dower to a mill and several tracts of Land yt Mr. Henry Dawson dyed in right.

Isaac Knight of the Citty of Bristoll, Merch't vs. Maur. Jones, Gent.

Page 795

ffrancis McCormick and Ellinor his wife Adm. of John Turner vs. Clemt. Corbell and Wm. Browne Adm. of Jno. Corbell, dec'd.

Pages 796-800 (none)

Court 17 Sept. 1712

Page 801

Last Will of James Rogers by Susannah Davis late Susannah Rogers, Exx. and Robert Davis her now husband and herself for it.

Ruth Oldam entered Jno. Oldam Deed to Jam. Oldam.

Court 17 Dec. 1712

Page 802

Tho. Mayes P/A to his son Chr. Mayes.

Page 803

Edmund Basie ack. a Deed of Indenture of land unto his Son Edmd. Basie. Lylia Basie ye wife of Edmd. Basie, Jr. relinquishes her Right of Dower in the ack. of Edmd. Basie to his father Edmd. Basie.

Honor Dermott Relict of Hugh Dermott, dec'd, Com. of Adm.

Page 804

N. C. Will of Esther Webb, dec'd presented by Tho. Webb and Samuel Webb her sons, proved by Jno. Burgin a witness.

Last Will of Rebecca Price, dec'd presented by Jacob Bayly her Exor., proved by Chris. Neale, Gent.

Enock Hill and ffrances his wife ack. a Deed of Indenture for Land to Col. Carter.

Northumberland County Orders

Court 18 Dec. 1712

Page 805

Rainsford Smith ack. a Deed of Indenture to Wm. Berry.

Court 18 ffeb. 1712/13

Page 806

Last Will of Hugh Wallis dec'd presented by Henry Boggess his Exor., proved by Parish Garner and Henry Aublin.

Page 807

John Brewer orphan son of Thomas Brewer, dec'd, chose James Richardson Guardian.

Last Will of Edward Singer dec'd presented by Tho. Earth and Jane his wife late Jane Singer relict of the sd. Singer, proved by Jane Bayly and James M'Goon.

Last Will of Tho. Barnes, dec'd presented by Jane Barnes his Relict, proved by Richard Robinson, Jno. Hadock and Pet. Wilkins.

Last Will of Wm. Nutt presented by Hannah Nutt his Exx., proved by Richard Wright and Jno. Harcum.

Page 808

Last Will of Jno. Thomas presented by Eliza. Thomas Exx., proved by Dennis Conway, Jno. Rankin and Bryan Smyth.

Last Will of Geo. Groves presented by Eliza. Groves Exx., proved by Capt. Danl. McCarty and William Crookshank.

Court 19 ffeb. 1712/13

Susanna Lawrence Relict of Jno. Lawrence, dec'd, Com. of Adm.

Pages 809-810 (none)

Court 18 Mar. 1712/13

Page 811

Elizabeth fforeman Relict of Benjamine fforeman, dec'd and Wm. Cornish Cheifest Creditor, Com. of Adm. refused by sd. Elizabeth and Cornish received it.

Page 812

Thomas Burnitt and Anne his wife (late Anne Bell relict of Jeremiah Bell, dec'd), Com. of Adm. to them.

Pages 813-815 (none)

Court 20 May 1713

Page 816

Last Will of Patrick Maley, dec'd presented by Jone Maley his Exx., proved by Rodham Neale, Jno. Tullos and Dav. Straughan.

Edward ffeilding ack. a Deed of Indenture to his Brother Ambrose ffeilding, and Winifred wife of the sd. Edw. ack.

Northumberland County Orders

Page 812 cont'd:

Mary Miller Relict of Tho. Miller, dec'd, Com. of Adm.

Edward Algood orphan Son of William Algood, dec'd, chose Richard Brown Guardian.

Rodham Neale and Anne his wife by her att. David Straughan ack. a Deed of Indenture of lease and Release unto Daniel McCarty, Gent. on ye behalf of the Hon. Robt. Carter for Land.

Page 817 (none)

Court 21 May 1713

Page 818

Samuel Blackwell presented a Deed of Indenture for Land from Richard Smith and Elizabeth his wife, and admitted to record.

Wm. Murrow and Anne his wife ack. a Deed of Indenture for Land unto Matthew Gater.

Wm. Way and Sarah his wife (especially by her means contrivance and procurement) being greatly suspected of harboring entertaining other peoples servants and slaves and concealiing and encouraging their thefts and idleness and other evil practices, to be taken into custody until they enter bond.

Page 819 (none)

Court 17 June 1713

Page 820

John Bashford, orphan son of Simon Bashford and Grace his wife dec'd aged 14 the 19th of Aug. 1708 and chose Chris. Dameron Guardian and John chose the Hon. Robt. Carter Guardian.

Joseph Deek and Catherine his wife ack. a Deed of Lease and Release to John Cralle Gent.

Page 821

William Bundle, poor ancient and infirm, Excused from Levy.

Tho. Gaskins ack. a Deed of Guift to his granddaughter Sarah Hull the Daughter of Mr. Richrd Hull.

Last Will of Richd. Rout decd. presented by ffrances Rout his Exx., proved by Richard Wright and Jno. Bare.

Page 822

Chas. Prichard's Deed of Guift to his son Chas., a cow.

Court 18 June 1713

Peter Hack Gent. Adm'r of James Parker decd. exhibited an Inventory and Appraisal.

Page 823

Mutton Lewis pet. the Court that his decd. father Jno. Lewis left a part of his estate to him by Will which came into possession of Jno. Nickless, decd. whose Relict Robert Gordon intermarryed and legacy remains in his custody and sd. Mutton produced his sd. father's Will whereby it

Northumberland County Orders

Page 823 cont'd:

appears that he gave to his son one short gun and 2 cowes and Gordon denies he had the same, ordered that sd. Gordon deliver the legacy.

Page 824

Last Will of Jno. Harris dec'd presented by Sarah Haynie and George Ball his Exors., proved by Hancock Nickless and Josiah Dameron.

Court 19 June 1713

Page 825

Col. Peter Presly sworn Sheriff.

Page 826 (none)

Court 19 June 1713

Page 827

Eliza Smith Exor. of the Last Will of Richd. Smith to answer Samuel Robinson and Eliz. his wife Exors. of Geo. Cooper.

Pages 828-830 (none)

Court 15 July 1713

Rebecca Husk orphan Daughter of Jno. Husk, dec'd, chose Jno. Thomas Guardian. Rebecca Husk to serve until 18.

Pages 832-833 (none)

Court 19 Aug. 1713

Page 834

Very hott and Rainy and there was no Court.

Court 16 Sept. 1713

Page 835

Motion of Ann ye Mother of Jno. Wiggins the sd. Jno. Wiggins his Indenture to Richd. Tullos.

Page 836

Katherine Boucher Relict of Jno. Boucher, Com. of Adm.

Daniel Murphew aged 7 orphan sone of Danl. Murphew, decd, with the consent of his Mother now Mable Meath the wife of John Meath to serve the sd. John Meath until 21.

Page 837 (none)

END OF BOOK #5

Northumberland co., Vir.

INDEX
Prepared By
Colleen Morse Elliott
Fort Worth, Tex.

Adamough, Tag. 4
Adams, Deborah 13
  Frances 7,31
  John 36,40,87,92
  Katherine 87,92
  Richard 52
  Thomas 3,8,24,66
  William 3,7
Addamson, Jeffery 25
Aherne, Phillip 62
Aires, John 135
Alden, William 38,40,55
Aldridge, Clement 1,13,48,
  50,55,61,72
  Elizabeth 48,61,72
Aldwell, Tho. 58
Alexander, Ann 3,51
  Joan 40,51
  William 51
Algood, Edward 23,26,30,31,
  62,129,137
  Elizabeth 23,30
  -John 30,31,62,74
  Richard 30,31,62,109
  William 30,31,74,129,137
Algrove, Eliza 59
  Elizabeth 42,62
  John 59
  Nicholas 42,59,113
  Thomas 59,62,113
Algroves, Elizabeth 67
Allen, Cornelius 76
  George 59,66
  James 89,128
  John 58,118
  Margaret 61
  Teige/Tigue 66,81,82
  Walter 53
  William 61,67
Allenson, Wm. 31
Allerton, Tho. 90
Alliday, Anne 125
Althorp, John 23
Alverson, Jane 57
  John 57
  Telif 57
Amee, Joseph 48
Anderson, George 84
  Hannah 89
  Sarah 13,100
  Wm. 30
Angell, Wm. 115
Anninner, Patrick 105
Annoy, Elizabeth 82
Antrobus, Phillip 100
Archer, Richard 118
Argile, Allice 6,89
Arledge/Arlege, Alice 92
  Clement 75,92,94,104,107,
  130
  Elizabeth 75,123
  Mary 92,94,104,107,130
  William 92
Armes, Joseph 29
Armsley, Andrew 87
Armstrong, Henry 58
Armstronge, George 75
Arnett/Arnott, John 87,100
Aro, John 75
Arshell, John 100
Ash, Robert 16
Ashburne, Thomas 116
Ashford, John 92
  Susannah 92
Ashton, Charles 67,69,82,
  83

Ashton, Henry 14
  Jane 67
  John 11,100
  Thomas 21,63
Askley, Thomas 20
Atkins, Edward 124
  Isaac 124
  James 73,116,124
  John 2,18,19,48,124
  Joseph 100
  Mary 73
  Susannah 124
Aublin, Henry 136
Austen, Alice 69
  Charles 64,83,112
  Elizabeth 69,75
  James 3,9,26,32,33,37,
  45,52,58,62,64,69,75
  Katherine 64
  Thomas 64,112
Ayry, Richard 46

Badger, James 96,114.115
  Nicholas 115
Bager, Nicholas 102
Bailey, John 50
Baily, Elizabeth 79
  Jacob 83,90,125
  John 79,83,86,90,122,123
  Thomas 90
Baisie, Edmund 89,118
Basie, Isaac 89
Baker. Fuder 116
  John 23,55
  Lucy 113,116
  Mary 78,103,113
  Thomas 33,34,44,78,103,
  113,116
  Wm. 116
Bales, Angell 103
  Ann 109
  John 103
Ball, Catherine 92
  Charles 42
  Elizabeth 81,87
  George 125,138
  Grace 126
  John 42
  Joseph 108,117,131,134
  Margaret 130
  Mary 108
  Richard 92,102,126
  Samuel 104
  Sarah 92
  Thomas 81,87,92,130
Bamford, John 8
Banister, Richard 9
Bankes/Banks, Elizabeth 37,
  57,65,85,94,102,116,119
  Thomas 37,42,43,45,46,
  47,64,102
  Robert 101
Bannister, Richard 83
Barber, Joyce 77
  Thomas 13
  Wm. 77
Bare, John 137
Barecroft, Jane 90
  Martha 132
  Mary 100
  Thomas 90,100,132
Barker, Thomas 13
Barklett, Robert 10
Barnes, Edward 1,13,21,75,
  101,107
  Jane 56,95,136

Barnes, Martha 68
  Mary 13,67,100
  Thomas 15,22,30,31,33,55,
  56,93,95,113,134,136
Barrett, George 8,9,22
  Isabel 9
Barry, Mary 47
  Robert 16
  William 7,9,16,47
Bartlett, Robert 128
Barton, Robert 129
Bashard, Andrew 55
Bashaw, Andrew 60,62
  Samuel 82
  Sarah 66,81,85
  William 17,60,62
Bashford, Grace 137
  John 99,134,137
  Rebecca 99
  Simon 99,134,137
Basie, Edmund 135
  Isaac 118,125
  John 125
  Lylia 135
Baskerville, George 105
Bassett, Ellinor 43
Bassill, Morris 58
Batcheler, John 23
Bateman, Anthony 104
Batesman, Samuel 29
Batson, Samuel 34,59
Batting, Wm. 76
Bayles, Elizabeth 37
  Jesse 60
  John 12,33,34,37,46
  Mary 60
  Sarah (also see Bailes)
  28,46,50
  Thomas 28,50
  Xpher (Christopher) 18
Bayley, Michael 9
Bayly, Jacob 135
  Jane 136
Beane, Margarett 66
  Robert 101
  William 22,33,48,66,101
Bearchamp, Daniel 12
Bearcroft, Thomas 39
Beard, John 58
Bee, Anne 63
  Elizabeth 63,64
  Hannah 61
  John 27,61,64
  Lovie 108
  Sarah 63
Beeton, Joseph 8
Belcher, Anne 107
  Wm. 107
Bell, Anne 136
  Arthur 100
  Jeremiah 85,136
Beltcher, Wm. 113
Bennett, Daniel 57
  Edward 29,75,93
  Eliza 29
  Elizabeth 93
  Mary 57
  Thomas 24
Benthan, Mathew 94
Bently, Elizabeth 50
  Henry 28,50
  John 119,120
  Richard 89
Berkeley, Joan 41
  William 48
Berratt, Geo. 57,65,70,85,

Berratt, Geo. (cont'd), 89,97
  Isabella 57
  Mary 89,97
Berry, Dawland 89
  Israel 23
  John 98
  Margaret 52,79,84
  Patience 112
  Thomas 23,28,52,55,61, 79,84,98,112,118,127,135
  Wm. 136
Betts, Charles 13,25,29, 32,48,59,90,92,125,132
  Elizabeth 32
  Mary 59,69,90,92,93,125
  William 6,13,25,29,32, 126
Bewley, Simon 135
Bickby, Christian 16
  Francis 16
Bickley, Christian 44
  Francis 44
  Ralph 44
Bickly, Ralph 128
Billingham, Francis 58,60
Bird, John 42,78
  Sarah 78
Birke, John 98
Bish, Philip 3
Biswick, John 108
Blackerby, James 23
  Mary 86
Blackley, Peter 4
Blackwell, Charles 4
  Margery 124
  Samuel 66,108,122,124, 132,135,137
Bland, Joseph 33,58,89
Bledsoe, Elizabeth 114
  George 6,13,30,37
  John 114
  William 4
Blencone, James 87
  John 87
Blentone, James 78
  John 78
  Susannah 78
Bletsoe, Abraham 92
  Catherine 92
Blinco, James 14
Blinko, James 80
Bloomfield...7
Blundall, Wm. 115
Blundell, John 124
Blundle, John 83
Boaz, Ann 40
  Elizabeth 30,61,125
  John 30,40,61,62,103,125
  Mary 103
Bogasse, Henry 86
Boggas, Henry 10,14,16,18, 23,35,66
  Ruth 23
Boggasse, Benjamin 76
Boggess, Henry 115,136
Boggis, Benjamin 29
Bolster, Wm 83
Bonam, Rebecca 113
  Thomas 113
Bonas, Anne 22
  Elizabeth 22
  Robert 22
  Wolthian 22
Bonoway, William 21
Bonus, Robert 18
Boon, Francis 26
Booth, Adam 2,6,49,51
  Anne 51
  John 51
  Richard 51,73,101,104
Boreland, John 51
Boucher, John 138

Boucher, Katherine 138
Bowe, John 60
Bowen, Edward 96
  Elizabeth 68,96
  John 96
Bowes, Edmond 100
  Jane 99
  John 99
Bowller, Elizabeth 33
  John 33
Bowly, Simon 121
Bowsham, William 8
Boy, John 9
Boyd, Anne 122,127,128
  Robert 122,127,128
Boyer, Andrew 28
Brabin, Henry 100
Bradley, Owen 12
  Richard 4,18
Bradly, Ann 40,42
  James 40
  Robert 37,40,42,90
Bradshaw, Anne 25
  Robert 21,25
  Temperance 25
Brady, Owen 29
Braseele, Morris 105
Brent, Anne 62
  Robert 62
Brereton...16,18
  Elizabeth 120
  Henry 91,107,109,113,120
  Mary 75,77,80,120
  Thomas 1,2,3,4,5,7,9,15, 22,24,25,35,43,45,56,65, 75,80,91,104,115,120
  Sarah 107,109,113
Brewer, Elizabeth 16,81
  John 82,115,136
  Mary 77
  Sarah 101
  Thomas 16,23,33,58,77, 81,101,136
Bridgeman, Arthur 106,113, 129,131,133
  Christian 97,98
  Grace 113,133
  Hannah 1
  John 50,97,98,109
  Mary 129,133
  Thomas 101,115
Briffin, William 3
Britt, Diana 96
Brittain, Fran. 14
Brittaine...15
  Eliza 29
  Elizabeth 14
  Frances 14,29
  Francis 14,27,29
Brodie, Alexander 11,28
Brooke, Ann 4
Brookes, Francis 98
Brooks, Wm. 53.54
Broughby, Wm. 81
Broughton, Hugh 6,89
  Thomas 13
Brown, Ben. 24
  Richard 137
Browne, Alex. 98
  Anne 115
  Benjamin 84,115
  Charles 38
  David 43,102
  Elinor 76
  Eliz. 56,110,116
  John 84,119
  Manly, 85,102
  Margaret 118
  Mary 66,91
  Samuel 66
  Susannah 85
  Thomas 43,111
  Wm. 56,81,98,110,116,130, 135

Bruce, Henry 38,39,49
  Mary 38,39
  Wm. 80
Bryam, Peter 22
  Sarah 113
  Thomas 113
Bryan, Henry 126
  John 34,75,79,118
  Margaret 104
  Mary 118
Bryant, Anne 14
  James 112
  Jath. 23
  John 14,64
  Uriah 104
Bryerly, Fran. 24
  Robert 24
Bryery, Fran. 15
  Robert 17
Buckley, Samuel 22
Bullery, Mary 98
Bundle, John 83
  William 71,85,137
Burburough, Malachi 93
Burdett, Henry 4
  William 11
Burgess, Richard 19
Burgesse, Richard 58
Burgin, John 135
Burk, Henry 8
  Richard 75
Burke, Thomas 105
Burne, John 98,101,122,126, 130
Burnett, Thomas 98
Burnitt, Anne 136
  Thomas 136
Burrut, Sarah 85
Bushell, Rowland 15,16
Bushrod, Ann 48,131
  Elizabeth 114,123,131
  Grace 114
  Hannah 94
  John 68,94,114,131
  Richard 114,123,131
  Symon 114
  Thomas 37,41,42,48,50,54, 55,58,59,60,66,68,131
Bussell/Bussle, Jane 66,77
  Phillip 66,73,77,78,88, 98
Butler, Edward 105
  Ester 37
  Henry 31,33,44
  John 6,8,37,44,98
  Susan 44
  Susanna 44
Byerly, Xpher (Christopher) 8
Byram, Abr. 15
  Peter 8,26,33,57
  Thomas 46,50,101

Cabernett, Tho. 104
Cadany, Katherine 1
Callam, Anne 130
  Hugh 95,130
  John 130
Callan, Anne 117
  Hugh 98,105,117
  John 117
  Margaret 98,99
Camady, John 75
Cambell, John 98
Camell, Alexander 6
  Samuel 58
Cameron, Dennis 50
  Jane 50
Cammell, Alex. 89
  Anne 14
  Elizabeth 115
  Thomas 115
  William 14

Camplaine, Thomas 16
Canady, Teige 81
Canalan, Mary 100
Cannon, Ellinor 105
  Hugh 7,89
Carbell, John 59
Carew, John 30
Carne, James 76
Carnegie, John 94,96,97,
  106,107,110,117,122,131
  Winifred 97,110
Carpenter, Charles 82,99
  Rebecca 99
  Wm. 61
Carr, Ann 33
  Joseph 33,36
Carter...135
  Dennis 14
  Robert 98,101,118,137
Carty, Dennis 4
  Kate 98
  Sary 105
Caseley, Mary 98
Cask, William 1
Cassady, Mary 126
  Wm. 126
Caton, Richard 11
Caule, Richard 6
Cazar, Barbara 70
Chalan, Katherine 99
Chambers, John 75
Champion, Dorothy 15
  Edyth 16
  John 15,16,74,82,84,113,
  123,131
  Josian 123
Chandler, Thomas 17,28
Chapman, Frances 12
  John 69
  Margaret 72,75
  Mary 60,95
  Will 12
Chankeret/Chankerette,
  Gannah 54
  Elizabeth 56
  Mary 52
  Stephen 54,56,95
Charles, John 35
Chaukerett, Stephen 33
Cheltwood, Matthew 104
Chilcock, Robert 16
Chilton, Elizabeth 115
  Stephen 115
  Thomas 65
  Wm. 115
Chin, Michael 18
Chowning, Anne 80
Christopher, Anne 54,103
  Elinor 89
  Richard 106
  Robert 50,103
Church, John 9,10
Churchill, Anne 102
  Elizabeth 91
  Joseph 91
  Samuel 91,102
  Sarah 91
Clanckerett, Stephen 94
Clapman, Richard 52
Clark/Clarke, Eliza 29
  Elizabeth 14
  Frances 82
  Martha 61
  Philip 82
  Richard 61
  Thomas 41
  William 14,29
  Xpher. 8
Clarles, Henry 21
Claughton, Anne 96,100,113
  James 20,21,40,69,70,79,
  90,118
  John 15,51,69,70,77,79,

Claughton, John (cont'd),
  96,100,113
  Mary 124
  Middleton 70
  Pemberton 113,124
Clay, Robert 120
  William 7,89,113,119
Claybourne, Wm. 120
Cleaves, Ann 8
Cleren, John 105
Clerke, Daniel 94
  Mary 91
  Rebecca 94
  Sarah 114
  Thomas 91
Clifford, Robert 66
Clowes, Phillip 71
Cnibley, Samuel 8
Coat, Elinor 89
Cockerall, Eliz. 58
  John 58
Cockrell, Andrew 13,66
  Edward 111
  John 13,20,34,41,99,111
Codd, Patrick 76
  St. Leger 1,3,4,7,11,48
Cofflin, John 100
Cole, Edward 99,115
  John 106
Coleman, Benjamin 94
  Dorothy 88
  John 88
  Katherine 72
  Stephen 72,78
Coles, Edward 1,3,10,16,
  104,125
  Elinor 3,64
  John 18,35,43
Colgin, Charles 98
Collins, Wm. 47
Colphen, Rich. 89
Colston...84
  Wm. 77
Colton, Isaac 18
Comons, Henry 100
Conaly, Laughly 93
  Sarah 93
Conaway, Dennis 122,125
  John 108,125
Condon, Ann 23
  Edm. 23
Connell, John 104
Conner, Hannah 101
  John 100
  Patrick 84
  Turle 101
  Turlur 104
Conoly, Laughly 113
  Sarah 113
Consedy, Eliza 99
Constant, Peter 25,26
Conway, Christopher 117,
  124,128,129
  Dennis 15,59,70,84,91,
  95,96,117,118,124,127,
  128,136
  Edwin 3
  John 76,84,94,99,101,103,
  106,117,124,128
  Susanna 106
  Winifred 128
Cook, Richard 16
Cooper, George 38,43,45,
  48,49,51,55,68,70,75,80,
  88,91,93,104,120,138
  Mary 8
Cope, John 8
Coppage, Charles 126
  Jane 82,83
  John 83,126,131
  Patience 127
  Thomas 8,9
  Wm. 14,81,83,96,126,127

Coppedge, William 9
Corbell, Clement 122,123,
  128,130,135
  John 8,34,78,81,108,114,
  116,130,135
  Margaret 114
  Mary 122
Corne, Thomas 105
Cornish, Mary 31
  William 7,31,55,68,83,
  87,89,93,136
Cornwell, Dennis 66
Cotanceau, Dorothy 1
  Jacob 1,3,30
  Katherine (also Coutan-
  ceau) 3,50
  William 3
Cotman, Ben. 23
Cotrell, John 132
  Lucretia 132
Courtmell, George 16
Courtnall, George 15,17
Courtnell, George 16,51
  Mary 16
  Phoebe 17
Courtness, George 12
Cout, John 1
Coutanceau, Anne 98,108,
  124,131
  Catherine 57
  Elizabeth 108
  Jacob 38 (also Countan-
  ceau) 38
  John 10,30,38,50,125,131
  Katherine 116,124
  Mary 84
  Peter 44,50,55,57,67,70,
  75,78,79,83,84,85,86,90,
  92,95,102,108,116,117,
  119,124,125,131
  Wm. 38
Couth, Thomas 81
Covernough, Mary 8
Cowe, James 110
Cowland, Margaret 94
Cox, James 72
  Richard 8,13,31,37
  Vincent 66,100,104,117
Cralle, John 24,47,54,61,
  66,75,82,85,107,112,131,
  137
Crane, Thomas 123
Cranstone, John 72
Craton, Richard 11
Craven, John 61,70
Crawford, John 50,51,52,67
Crawley, Miles 8
Cream, James 97
  John 100
Crean, James 40,82
  Jane 88
Creane, James 54
Creel, John 80
Creele, Charles 122
Crinsby, Elinor 58
Crookshank, Wm. 136
Crosby, Daniel 2
  George 59,84
Croshit, John 100
Crosly, George 13
Cross, Richard 99
Crosse, James 17
  Th. 17
Crouch, Mary 94
  Robert 94
Crowder, Fearnot 99
  Fernott 120
  Robt. 121
  Thomas 69,90,99,119,120,
  121,132
Crump, John 110
Culpeper, Lady 97
Cundiff, Rich. 71

Cuning, John 13
Cunningham, James 116
Cursone, Francis 61,69
  William 61
Curtis, Eliza 69
  Geo. 73,129
  Hannah 80
  Henry 69,76,129
  Joanna 97
  John 30,31,53,99
  Pitts 80,97,119,123
  Thomas 8,63,73
  Walter 37
Cushion, Rich. 75

Dabbs, John 16
Dabinett, Jonathan 52,72
Daily, John 73
Dalton, John 72
Dameron, Bartholomew 4,62,
  71,72,76,96,98,99,104,
  109,115
  Christopher 114,134,137
  Elizabeth 115
  George 4,71,76,87,89,98,
  125
  Josiah 138
  Katherine 104,106
  Lawrence 129
  Lazarus 98
  Thomas 104,106,121
Dameronie, Tho. 113
Damison, Peter 11
Damonile, Samuel 117
Dane, Daniel 76
Danielson, Andrew 115
Dank, Anne 62
  Thos. 62
Dankes, Anne 58,66
  John 58
Dare, William 126,127
Dassey, Walton 1
Davies, Thomas 21
Davis, Anne 111
  Charles 119
  David 29
  Elizabeth 111
  Hester 28
  Isabella 93
  Issabell 104
  James 133
  John 28,40,43,44,93,100,
  105,134
  Mary 89,97,111,133
  Matthers 28
  Robert 60,114,132,134,135
  Susannah 135
  Wm. 89,97,113
Dawkins, George 20,28,92,96
Dawson, Ann 91
  Christopher 100,101
  Elizabeth 94,103,112,131
  Francis 82,91,95,101,112
  Henry 14,17,54,66,67,75,
  77,79,86,94,99,103,135
  John 62,78,91,96,103,131
  Katherine 99,103
  Margaret 103
  Sarah 91,103
  William 17,24,25,43,62,
  87
  Xpher 85
Day, John 113,119
  Mary 53,75
  Robert 120
  Sam. 53
  Thomas 88
Deabary, James 8
De Boyes, Henry 17
Deek, Catherine 137
  Joseph 137
de Jerry, Peter 8
Delany, Anthony 104

Delawny, Anthony 132
Demeratt, Luke 58
de Merritt, Luke 54
  Mary 54
Dennis, John 4,76
  Elizabeth 4
  Sarah 76
Denny, Anne 132
  Edmund 132
Depue, David 79
Dermott, Ann 63,70,92
  Charles 63,90,92
  Honor 135
  Hugh 40,135
  Mich. 45
  Owen 40
Deron, Morris 66
Dew, Andrew 133
  Flora 133
  Thomas 8
Dewe, Wm. 130
Dey, Roger 105
Dickenson, Sarah 118
  Tho. 105
Dickinson, Sarah 62
Discoll, Fran. 4
Dobles, Rich. 87
Dobson, Elizabeth 75
Dodd, John 7
Dodson, Anne 100
  Charles 54
  George 100
Doggett, Benjamin 132
  Elizabeth 6
  Mary 132
Donaldson, John 43
Dooly, Dan. A. 23
Dorrell, Elinor 3
  Thomas 3
Dorron, Morris 86
Dorsmundy, Michael 8
Douglas, John 124
Dougle, Richard 118
  William 118
Doulson, John 8
Dowgell, Richard 89
Dowly, John 100
Downes, Mary 8
Downing, Ann 135
  Charles 54
  Eliza 76
  Elizabeth 57,69,73,74,
  82,126,127
  John 4,7,13,20,31,32,33,
  34,35,43,45,48,54,57,69,
  73,74,76,120
  Margaret 19,38
  Mary 18,21
  Samuel 126,127
  Thomas 33,38,50,81,93,
  96,99,113
  William 1,2,3,5,7,18,19,
  21,33,34,35,38,54,55,135
Doyle, Owen 105
Drake, Phil. 73
Duat, Robert 118
Dudly, Elizabeth 53,63
  John 53,63,73
Due, Wm. 119
Duke, John 94
Dukes, Jane 21
  Mary 21
  Thomas 1
Dumlay, James 13
Dun...73
  Walter 72,81
Dunaby, Humphrey 105
Dunaway, Anne 123
  Daniel 114,129,130
  Jane 129
  John 20,54,57,105,115,
  119,127
  Katherine 54,57

Dunaway, Margaret 105,115
  Samuel 123
Dunn, George 9
  Robert 8
  Walter 45
Dunnawan, Wm. 89
Dunne, Walter 76
Durckin, Dorothy 76
  Henry 76
Durkin, Henry 80
Dutton, Mary 34,69
  Thomas 34,60
Dyer, Thomas 32
Dyetfeild, Wm. 104

Earne, Patrick 104
Earth, Jane 136
  Thomas 118,136
Eason, John 71
Eaton, Elizabeth 54
  John 46
  Richard 14,15,41,54,64,
  75,130,132
  Sarah 75
Ecock, Thomas 23
Edes, James 120
Edgar, John 23
Edney, James 16,69
Edny, Anne 125
  James 120
Edward, Nicholas 107
Edwards, Anne 117
  Charles 32,33,34
  Elizabeth 121
  Hugh 134
  Isaac 121,131
  John 73
  Jonathan 131
  Math. 16
  Nicholas 45,79,117,130
  Prudence 33
  William 111
Elinor, Jane 14
Eliphant, Eliza 27
Elliott, Anne 65,66
  Edward 26
  Samuel 4,5
  Wm. 58,66
Ellis, Edward 9
Ellistone, Garvase 57
  Gerv. 29
  George 50
  Jervase/Jervis 114,120
  Mary 114,120
Emberson, John 61
Embry, John 52
  William 52
Emerson, John 49
English, Alexander 9
  John 4,70
  Thomas 70,91
Erimlett, John 56
Eskridge, George 87,93,98,
  100,104,105,106,116,117,
  119,124,131
Ester, Margaret 115
Eustace, Elizabeth 88
  John 18,31,68,74,84,87
  William 74,88
Evans, Alice 76
  Elizabeth 18,30,34
  John 26,30,79,86,116
  Mary 7,89
  Margaret 116
  Philip 10,18
  Thomas 11,92,116
Everard, Thomas 69
Everett/Everitt, Geo. 118
  132,133,134
  Mary 90,133,134
  Thomas 118,134
Eves, Graves 45
  Mary 38

Eves, William 34,38,45
Eycock, Thomas 10
Eyes, Dennis 11,14,15,19,
  29,58,84,94
  Mary 84

Fairefax, Katherine 97
  Thomas 97
Fallen, Dennis 109
  Elizabeth 109
Fallon, Dennis 72
  Charles 84
  Jane 84
Falon, Charles 133
  William 133
Fantleroy, Ann 131
  Griffin 131
  Moor 54
  William 54
Farigon, John 21
Farington, Richard 46
Farmer, Anne 27,39
  William 25,27
Farnefold, John 24,56,60,
  72,78,90
Farragon, John 72
Feild, Edward 13
Feilding, Ambrose 136
  Daniel 91,118
  Edward 2,4,19,50,52,55,
  56,65,124,128,136
  Eliza 52,119
  Hannah 65,93
  John 44,65,73,119,134
  Joseph 33,38,119
  Mary 33
  Rachel 113,119,134
  Sarah 119
  Susannah 65
  William 109,119
  Winifred 124,128,136
Fegan, John 75
Ferne, Allice 72,77
  Lawrence 105
  Mary 72,73,77,79,81
  Robert 75
  Thomas 12,47,66,72,77,
  78,80,81,110
Ferned, James 112
Fernes, Thomas 122
Fernot, James 107
Fielding, Ambrose 19
Fisher, Andrew 105
  Patrick 98
Fitzgerrard, Th. 76
Fitzhugh, Wm. 63,76
Fitzmorris, Margaret 100
Flamagon, Dam. 10
Flanagan, Andrew 102
Flanagon, Andrew 89
Flatman, Anne 78
  Elizabeth 78
  Thomas 78,104
Fleet, Henry 86
Fleming, Alexander 47
  James 98
Fletcher, Diana 93,94
  William 50,53,93,94
Fling, Katherine 104
Flint, Anne 84,116
  James 116
  Jane 84
  Martha 85
  Richard 85,90
  Thomas 84,95,116
Floker, David 97,131
  Joanna 97
Flower, George 5
  Hannah 40
  John 40
  William 2
Flowers, John 25
  William 2,25

Floyd, John 104
Flucker, David 74,79,80
Fluker, Hannah 74,80
  Joannah 79
Flukes, James 105
Flynt, Anne 50,51,54,90,
  97,100
  Martha 85,100
  Mary 17,45,46,62,101,102
  Peter 17,21,30,31,45,46,
  51,60,62,85
  Richard 8,14,21,43,49,
  51,55,60,73,80
  Thomas 21,31,50,54,73,
  85,86,97,100,102
Folio, Edward 75
Ford, John 19
Foreman, Benjamin 136
  Elizabeth 136
Forest, Alexander 82
  Jane 82
  John 126
Fouks, John 47
Foules, James 22
Fowell, John 8,9
Fox, David 11
  Lawrence 75
  William 11
Francis, Joan 4
  Jone 17
Franklin, Hannah 83,93
  Henry 12,39,52,56,59,67,
  79,83,93,99
  Joseph 67
  Susannah 67,73
Frankling, How. 98
  Mary 100
Frarnce, Barbara 18
  Thomas 18
Freeman, John 25
Fryer, Anne 87
Fuker, David 70,131
  Hannah 70
Fulbrook, Lan. 8
Furned, Edward 88
  Lucy 88
Furnett, Edward 32
  Lucy 31,32

Gaines, Daniel 111
  John 109,111
  Mary 109
  Thomas 82,85
Gallington, Edward 115
Gallion, Henry 89
Galway, William 122
Gamar, Jervasse 114
Gamlen, John 28
Gammonds, Philip 23
Gamwell, Lawrence 105
Garling, Xpher. 1
Garlington, Christopher 4,
  5,7,22,52,53,62,64,69,72
  89,106,122
  Joane 1,5
  Margaret 69,106
  Mary 122
Garner, Benjamin 128
  Elizabeth 96,104,112
  John 43
  Martha 105,128
  Parish 96,104,112,136
  Vincent 62,68,76,78,99,
  105,112,128
  William 128
Garrett, Elizabeth 107
  Graves 1
  John 105,107
  Thomas 1
Garrison, Rim 44,61
Garter, John 110
Gascoyne, Henry 8,15
  Josias 8

Gaskeyne, Josias 9
  Thomas 9
Gaskins, Dorothy 94,97,101
  Elizabeth 64,122,125
  Henry 64,94,135
  Isaac 63,125
  Joseph 94
  Josias 40,65,70,97,99,
  101,122
  Martha 122
  Thomas 94,96,98,105,108,
  115,120,122,137
Gater, John 69
  Matthew 137
  Sarah 116
Gator, John 91
Gatton, Mar. 47
  Wm. 47
Gay, Wm. 87
Gayer, Tomson 105
Gaylor, John 118
Gaylord, Ann 13
  James 2,3,12,13
Gaymore, James 95
Gayner, Diana 103
  James 103
Gaynes, Daniel 110
  James 58
  John 110
Gebson, Thomas 47
Gendall, Jos. 57
Genesis, Ezekiel 8,12,18,
  21,22,38
  Rebecca 18
Genn, James 22,65,100,101,
  117
  Mary 100
  Thomas 100,117
George, Elizabeth 22
  Thomas 22
Gerrard, Elizabeth 20
  Samuel 20,37
Gerratt, George 69
Gibson, Jeremiah 10
Gilbert, Harrold 26
  James 7
  Michael 36
  Richard 110
Gill, Ann 17
  David 65,82
  Diana 116
  John 94
  Margaret 84
  Michael 94
  Thomas 7,59,69,76,96,98,
  101,103,112,121,123,129,
  130
Ginn, James 86
Ginnes/Ginnis, James 65,68,
  70
Githagie, William 47
Glover, James 123
Gluge, Wm. 88
Clynne, James 13
Goch, John 35
  Samuel 1,9,12,22,35
Goche, Samuel 21
Goddart, Anne 12
  Thomas 12
Godding, Mary 16
Godnell, Wm. 94
Goldsmyth, Thomas 19
Gording, James 9
Gordon, Robt. 109,129,133,
  137,138
Gould, Jonathan 44
Gouth, John 57
  Mary 105
  Samuel 57
Gouthe, John 105,118,119,
  127
Gradie, Owen 15
Grady, Anne 62,79

Grady, Patrick 54
  Walter 40,43,62,71,85
  William 43,85
Graham, John 26,35,45,52,
  61,73,79,88,92,107,127
  Mary 61,107
  Patience 88,92,115
Cralie, John 100,111
Cralis, John 66
Gralose, John 83
Grant, Alice 3
Grantham, Jeremiah 105
Graves, Elizabeth 97
  George 97
Green, Timothy 27
  William 10
Greene, Ellinor 64
Greensted, Elizabeth 34
  John 28,34,55
  William 60
Greensteed, Jane 64
  John 64
Greenston, Ann 24
  John 24
Gregory, Elizabeth 74
Gridly, Mary 94
  Patience 94
Griffin, Ambraham 54
  Alexander 68
  Corbin 97
  Daniel 16
  Samuel 14,43,48,51,54,
  68,95
  Thomas 97
Grigge, Michael 44
Grimsteed, Wm. 62
Grinstead, John 24
  Thomas 24
  William 24
Grinsteed, Adam 99
  John 129
  Thomas 100
  William 100,128,129
Grinstone, John 15
Grisham, John 117
Grosman, Edward 8
Groth, Matthew 57
Groves, Elizabeth 104,136
  George 63,100,104,136
Gunson, Wm. 58
Gurrill, Joan 58
Guttridge, James 115

Haberfield, Thomas 4
Hack...113
  Mary 108
  Peter 39,43,45,48,50,54,
  57,58,68,70,74,78,79,80,
  88,89,91,92,93,104,105,
  108,137
Hadock, John 136
Hadwell, James 31
  John 78,132
Hales, Richard 3
Hall, Daniel 117
  John 128
  Richard 29
  Thomas 118,128
Hallum, John 7
Hambleton, Elizabeth 36
  George 17,21,25,36
  Roger 20
Hamilton, Elizabeth 1
  George 1,7
Hamlett, John 129
  Mary 129
Hammon, Charles 133
  Peter 61,133
Hamond, Peter 134
Hamons, Margaret 59
Ham't, Mary 31
  Thomas 31
Hanbrooke, Henry 105

Hancock...36
Hand, Margaret 105
Hanks, George 65
  Jane 65
Hanye, Elizabeth 60
  John 58,63
  Richard 58,59,60,61,65
Harcum, Abigail 17
  Hannah 27
  James 17
  John 136
  Lidia 17
  Mary 17
  William 9,17,18,27,38,
  42,52,63,79,93
Harding, Ann 6,113
  Henry 40,60,64,105,113
  Jane 64
  John 40
  Thomas 6,40,41,42,49,61
  Wm. 60,67
Harley, Margaret 4
  Thomas 58
Harmond, Thomas 12
Harris, Anne 80
  Charles 22,23,27,45,50,
  52,56,57,58,59,65,70,72,
  73,74,79,80,113,121
  Grace 2
  Hugh 1,60
  Jane 65,80
  Jer. 20
  John 1,2,3,6,11,13,36,
  57,58,95,109,118,138
  Mary 12
  William 61
Harrison, Alice 103
  Anne 128
  George 128
  Jane 104
  Mary 98,103
  Robert 92,103,104
Harrison, Tho. 98
Harrold, Gilbert 95
  Hugh 56
  James 95
  John 56
  Margaret 130
  Nicholas 56
  Priscilla 56
  Richard 130
  Walter 56
Harsell, Wm. 98
Hart, John 134
  Mos. 10
  Sarah 134
Harte, Thomas 119
Hartey, John 118
Hartley, John 62
Hartly, John 91
Hartney, Richard 73
Harvatt, Wm. 50
Harvey, Edward 29
  Onesephorus 99,119
  Wm. 49,66
Harvie, Wm. 65
Harvy, Allen 67
  Charles 67
  James 67
  Margaret 67
  Mary 67
  William 60,67
Harwood, Ann 37
  Thomas 4,32,37,45,52,
  59,61
Haslass, Wm. 123
Hatfield, Gervase 12,34,
  35
Hatson, Elizabeth 53
  Henry 53
  Wm. 26
Havett, Wm. 53
Hawker, Adam 11

Hawkes, George 90
  Jane 90
  John 90
Hawkins, Elinor 124
  Elizabeth 4
  James 65,70
  John 43
  Sarah 63
Hawson, John 110
Hay, Ann 8
  Daniel 8
  John 105
Hayden, Anne 132
  Thomas 42,69,91,132
Hayer, Roger 8
Hayes, John 75,128
  Thomas 10,43,50,64,108
Haynes, Frances 88
  Edward 68,76
  James 88
  Martha 68,76
Haynie, Anthony 99,109,110
  121,126
  Catherine 133
  Hannah 107,132
  John 1,7,11,18,19,20,24,
  25,33,38,41,42,44,47,49,
  61,89,90,103,107,108,113,
  132
  Mary 108
  Richard 22,26,38,44,93,
  98,101,104,109,130,133,
  135
  Sarah 126,138
  Thomas 103,108
  Thomasin 108
  Thompson103
Head, Walter 4
Heale, Thomas 105
Heard, Elizabeth 4
Heath, Mary 59,81
Henderson, David 51
  William 98
Hendy, John 8
Henley, Wm. 98
Henly, Edward 48,59
  Elizabeth 59
Hester, Isaac 21,22,28,39,
  45,46,119,126
  Margaret 21,119
  Mary 126
Hewes, Richard 101
Hewlett, Thomas 80
  Winifred 97
Hews, Robert 116
Hickman, Esther 70
  Thomas 18,39,70
Hicks, John 43
Higgins, John 3
  Nora 105
  Timothy 89,110
Higgenson, Dorcus 63
Higginson, Dorcas 75,76
  John 31
  Priscilla 106
High, Thomas 26
Hill, Anne 24,28,126
  Ellis 103
  Enoch 88
  Enock 119,135
  Evan 89
  Ezekiel 22,36,38
  Frances 119,135
  George 29,102,103,115
  Hannah 116
  James 38,105
  John 3,70,86,89,101,106,
  116,126
  Mary 102,103
  Robert 36,38
  Thomas 122
  William 9,12,24,28,47,70
  103

Hilliard, Joane 48
  Richard 48,70,112
Hilman, Thomas 29
Hogan, John 84
Hogherd, Anthony 94
Hobson, Anne 70
  Clark 127
  Elizabeth 94,130
  John 129,130
  Sarah 37
  Thomas 2,3,6,8,9,16,20,
    21,26,28,34,35,37,39,43,
    47,50,55,58,59,61,62,64,
    68,69,73,81,83,87,88,90,
    91,98,102,104,107,109,
    110,117,120,122,123,124,
    127,129,130,133
  William 4,70
Holbert, Ellinor 105
Holland, Daniel 93
  Simon 98
Holmes, Ralph 60,76
Holley, Thomas 8
Holly, Jane 112
  Thomas 86,112
Holt, Anne 128
  Joseph 7,111,118,128
  Mary 111
Hooke, Wm. 26
Hope, Thomas 58
Hopkins, Elizabeth 129
  George 129,132
  Grace 2
  Henry 113,116,121,132
  Mary 116
  Thomas 2,21,33
Hornsby, John 85
  Mary 85
Hosier, George 8
Houghton, John 8
Hould, Joseph 89
Hoult, Ann 133,134
  Joseph 32,43,45,52,55,
    56,84,134
  Wm. 123
House, Robert 8
Howard, Dor. 21
  Luy 3
  Patience 2
  Ruth 75,79
  Sarah 125
  Thomas 2,4,7
  William 21,75,70,92,109,
    125
Howe, Richard 98,124,128,
  129
Howell, Elisha 13
  John 96
  Peter 45
  Philip 127
Howing, John 84
Howland, Daniel 75
Howson, Elizabeth 36,84
  Ellin 3
  John 81,82,83,87,88,98,
    111,115,118,130
  Leonard 5,10,11,17,24,
    25,36,80,82,93,95,97,99,
    115,120
  Mary 80,120
  Sarah 92
  Thomas 24
  William 72,73,78,81,82,
    92
  Williamson 3
Huch, Sarah 9
Hudnall, Alice 20,21,22
  Anne 122
  Henry 45,50
  John 2,20,122
  Joseph 120,122,124
  Margery 120,122,124
  Mary 117,122

Hudnall, Partin 22,36,38,
  42,50,95
  Richard 92,117
Hudson, George 20
  Henry 106,109,113
  Isaac 3
Huffe, Robert 123
Hughes, David 8
  George 21,44
  John 24
  Thomas 24,44
Hughlett, Alice 77
  Elizabeth 128,129,132
  Ephraim 120,128,129,132
  John 3,9,10,19,21,49,53,
    55,60,67,73,77,102,103,
    114,128,131
  Katherine 29
  Margaret 106
  Mary 21,55,59,61,103,114
    119,131,132
  Susannah 67
  Thomas 14,43,54,57,59,
    61,62,63,68,90,94,106,
    115,119,133
  William 131
  Winfred 72,77,78,79,80,
    81,110
  Yarrett 128,131
Hughs, George 17,35
  Joseph 118
  Mary 118
  Ralph 93
  Richard 66,74
  Robert 98
  Thomas 35
Hulett, John 60
  Susanna 60
Hulk, John 134
Hulks, Thomas 41
Hull, Anne 56,70
  Elizabeth 14
  John 33,34,36,42,56,70
  Rebecca 121
  Richard 18,19,27,29,31,
    33,35,42,50,57,58,70,79,
    80,104,107,109,113,114,
    121,137
  Sarah 109,113,137
Humphrey, Jos. 57
Hunt, Elinor 104
Hunter, Fra. 4
  Robert 12
Hurst, Dor. 17
  John 73,87,129
  Susannah 73,129
  Tho. 48
Husband, Edward 14
Husk, John 129,138
  Rebecca 138
  Susannah 129
Huske, John 65,112,113,119
  Susannah 65
Hutchins, Sarah 76
Hutchinson, Nich. 98
Hutson, Elizabeth 58
  Henry 58,75,87
Hutt, Richard 46
Hutton, Alice 97,98,100
  Elizabeth 104
  George 1,9,20,24,37,58,
    66,88,104
  Jane 97,98,100
  John 4
  Rebecca 88
  Sarah 58,97,98,100

Ignatius, Hawett 8
Ingee, John 73,86
  Mary 86
Innis, James 87,97
  Katherine 97
Ingram, Charles 87,111,120

Ingram, Charles (cont'd)
  125,134
  John 101,109,111,114,115,
    123
  Katherine 5
  Thomas 6,109
Itrey, John 4

Jackman, Dorothy 32,36
  Mathew 75
Jackson, Andrew 117
  Anthony 89
  Barbara 58
  Charles 15
  Dorothy 117
  George 104
  Thomas 104
  Susanna 46
James, Daniel 61
  James 89
  Joane 48
  John 34,61,62,105
  Mary 61,62
  Parish 128
  Thomas 50,89
  William 48,105
Jameson, John 105
Janes, John 17
Janeway, William 100
Jarsey, James 41,47,52,53
Jeffard, Amos 11
Jefferson, Sam. 17
Jeffery, Robert 11
Jenkins, Walter 71
Jennings, Edmund 92
Jenny, John 22
Jersey, James 4
Jessey, James 40
Jewell, Ashmelew 6
Joanes, Joane 7
  John 43
  Thomas 7
John, James 68
Johnson, Abraham 47
  Benjamin 17
  Elizabeth 111
  James 1,9,17,20,21,27,31
    33,35,47,51,67,71
  Jeffery 26
  Jeoffrey 111
  John 88
Jones, David 77,79
  Diana 77
  Edward 12,55,133
  Elizabeth 87,100,110,117
  Evan 36,94
  Francis 81
  Hugh 7
  James 1,14,32,87,100,101
    110,113,117
  John 36,74
  Margaret 79,98
  Maurice 92,95,96,97,99,
    106,116,122,125,126,131,
    135
  Mary 1
  Owen 89
  Richard 25,27
  Robert 1,66,72,82,92,97,
    116,122
  Samuel 70,77,80,116
  Sarah 66,72
  Solomon 94
  Thomas 17,18,35,36,41,44
    50,56,65
  William 10,12,31,43,46,
    48,49,52,57,69,76479,80,
    98,100,103,111,116,118,
    125
Jonn, James 8
Joyce, Jane 43
Joyne, John 100
Joyce, Abraham 43

Julian, John 17,23
Junn, Katherine 41

Kalleron, Will 105
Kanne, Judith 23
Kaufelaugh, Arthur 104
Kea, Thomas 8
Keady, Michael 87,125
Keaton, Katherine 104
Keen, Elizabeth 24
  John 85
  Thomas 8,70
  William 24
Keene, Anne 86,102
  Elizabeth 108,116
  Wm. 44,78,86,94,102,116,
  119
Kelly, Edward 104
  Giles 123
  Matthew 98
  Michael 105
  Teague 105
  Toby 105
Kenady, Timothy 110,122
Kendall, Edmund 105
Kenner, David 105
  Elizabeth 43,103,106,114,
  117,130,131
  Francis 105,106,110,111,
  114,118,123,125,130
  Hannah 106,114
  Matthew 117
  Rhoden 32
  Richard 3,5,11,17,20,24,
  25,30,32,35,37,43,51,
  102,103
  Rodham 42,45,55,56,58,
  60,62,64,67,68,73,75,
  77,78,89,92,93,101,106,
  113,114,130,131
Kent, John 52,115
  Katherine 52
Kesterson, George 63
Kesterton, Thomas 84
Key, Margaret 85
  Mary 89
  Richard 87,89
Keyne, Thomas 14
  William 11
Kilpatrick, Anne 125
  Edward 125
King, Henry 134
  Tagor 105
  Xper 94
Kingwell, Nich. 39,45,110
  Tho. 110,118
Kirk, Anne 90
  Christopher 19,90
Kirkpatrick, Anne 53
  Edw. 53
Klyne, William 10
Knight, Anne 102
  Elizabeth 85
  George 8,15,27
  Isaac 135
  James 102
  Leonard 85,102
  Mary 122
  Peter 1,2,3,5,12,19,20,
  31,52,68,102
  Thomas 39,89,96,118,122
Knot, William 67
Knoton, Daniel 8
Knott, Abraham 86
  George 14,41,72,78
  Jane 60
  John 9,17,60
  Mary 17
  Wm. 30,68
Knotten, Aug. 10
Kyrke, John 5

Laland, John 100

Lambert, Anne 111
  Elizabeth 92
  Wm. 70,79,100,111,122
Lamprey, Angel 29,34
  Richard 21,22,29
Lancaster, Frances 95
  John 95,103,111
  Nicholas 24,33
Lane, Henry 64
  Mary 104
  Tho. 100
Langdell, Anne 83
  John 83
Langhee, John 104
Langsdale, John 39
Langsdon, Catherine 94
  John 83
  Wm. 94
Lankester, Rich. 62
Lankeston, John 53
Larkins, James 49,51
Larson, Thomas 30
Lastly, Francis 102
Lattemore, Clement 38,68
  Richard 86
Lattimer, Clement 12
Lattimore, Anne 101
  Clement 22,39,49
  Eliz. 127
  Rich. 25,46,57,68,101,
  112,126,127
Laurams, John 24
Lawrence, Dor. 10
  Edward 95
  Frances 96
  John 20,40,42,74,86,92,
  96,98,129,136
  Margaret 89
  Mary 30
  Susanna 136
Lawson, Chris. 85
  Margaret 87
  William 8
Leach, William 13
Leasure, Bartho. 105,113,
  117
  George 65
Leaver, Ann 37
  John 37
Leazure, Bartho. 58,66
  George 66,117
  Hannah 117
  John 66
  Judith 58
Lee, Ann 16
  Charles 25,36,44,71,78,
  86,95,112,120
  Elizabeth 44,65,69,86,
  95
  Han./Hancock 34,69,95,
  98,112,118,120,127
  John 2,16,59
  Leanna 96
  Lettice 100
  Richard 10,100,112,118
  Robert 30
  Sarah 2,127
  Thomas 65,69,92,95,130
  William 24,28,30,33,35,
  37,38,59,62,81
Leech, Eliza 41
  Wm. 41
Leechman, Eliz. 118
  Tho. 102,118
Leefield, Robt. 44
Leethman, Tho. 100
Lehngh, Nicholas 86
Lester, Wm. 117
Letherborough, James 75
Lewis, Ann 50,61
  Charles 68
  Edward 31m50,51,61,68
  Elizabeth 101

Lewis, Ellinor 91
  Frances 12,53
  John 12,17,25,28,30,36,
  37,42,51,53,60,62,71,91,
  101,117,133,137
  Joseph 13
  Lucretia 61
  Mary 42,51,68
  Mutton 106,122,137
  Wm. 50,51,128
Leypott, Margaret 6
Liddon, Wm. 105
Lilley, Mary 104
Limkin, John 69
Limock, Samuel 6
Lindsey, John 76
Linne, John 68
Linsey, John 123
  Mary 123
Linten, Jane 97
Linton...68
  Henry 123
  Isabell 100
  Isabella 82,98
  Jane 65,100
  John 82,87,88,98,100
Lister, Edmund 48
  Wm. 79,88
Listone, Nicholas 85,93
Little, Fran. 15,16,35
  Susanna 35
Littrell, James 69
  Susanna 69
Liver, John 28
Lloyd, Alexander 3
Lock, Tho. 89
Lockman, James 53,73
Lolly, Tho. 105
Long, Christian 18,97,98
  John 82
  Joseph 56,97,98
  Josias 18,21,33,56,97
Longhman, James 89
  Margaret 89
Looper, James 105
Lord, John 55
Love, Alex. 108,129
Lowell, Elizabeth 8
Lowes, John 8
Lowry, Elias 115
Lugg, Richard 7,9,25
Lunce, John 22
Lunseford, Margery 72
  Rebecca 93
  Samuel 93
Lunte, Samuel 60
Lyle, George 8
Lyndsay, Dav. 23
  Robert 16
Lynsfeild, Mary 37
  Rich. 37
Lynton, Anthony 1,9,14,37,
  44,48,76
  Henry 1
  Jane 37
Lyon, John 48,105,130
Lyons, Anne 130
Lynum, John 50
Lyster, Edm. 10
Lyver, John 26,31

MacDonnell, Cath. 64,66
MacGoam, Owen 13
MacGuire, Hannah 10
Mackbeth, James 89
Mackdanell, Geo. 58
Mackdonnell, Cath. 63
  John 88
  Mary 88
MacKenny, Neale 49
Mackfassion, Jane 89
Maclsnahan, John 52
  Mary 52

Maclanchan, Dorothy 80
Macloughan, James 29
Maddox, Thomas 22
Maghby, Jon. 17
Mahallam, Robert 12
Maham, Samuel 54
Mahem, Sam 14
Mahen, Dorothy 97
  Jane 61
  Samuel 2,7,22,47,61,97
Mahens, Dorothy 94
  Samuel 94
Mahon, Samuel 36
Mahone, Elinor 125
  Tho. 125
Mahonny, Dennis 94
Maile, Chris. 118
Maise, Eliz. 117
  Henry 121
Maize, Barbara 47
  Thomas 34,47,50,53,64
Malery, Patrick 130
Maley, Jone 136
  Owen 10
  Patrick 102,136
Mallard, Lucy 66,67,77
  Rebecca 66,77
  Thos. 66,77
Maly, Patrick 8
Man, Elizabeth 63,80
  John 9
  Wm. 46,63,73,74,79,80
Manby, Anthony 15
Mandly, Edmund 55
Manley, Edmund 81
  Hannah 81
Manly, Edmond 104
  Mary 104
Mannon, Luke 4
March, Arthur 83
Marcry, Andrew 42
Mare, John 94
Margill, John 58
Marquant, John 89
Marsh, Arthur 50,55
  John 123,133
  Richard 123
  Robert 102
Marshall, Geo. 40,108
  John 108
  Rachel 40
  Richard 108
Mary, Ann 74
  Henry 65,74,92
  Margaret 65
  William 74,92
Masey, Henry 23
Mason, Isabell 58
  John 94
  Matthew 118
  Solomon 104
  Thomas 110
  Wiliam 111
Massie, Henry 54
Mast, John 76
Mathare, Henry 94
Mathew, Rebecca 22
Matthew, John 14
  Thomas 3,5,7,8,12,20,24
Matthews, Thomas 1,2
Mattley, John 42
Mattocks, Thomas 22
Maudley, Edmond 29,31,35
  Elizabeth 31
  Jane 29
Maursh, Robert 16
Maxfield, Peter 26
Maxteed, Wm. 66
Maxwell, Edward 26
  John 33
  Mary 28
  Peter 21,28
May, Margaret 4,58

Mayhaze, Arthur 79
Mayes, Chris. 64,135
  Elisha 114
  Henry 114,131,135
  Lydia 88
  Mary 131
  Thomas 114,135
Mayre, Henry 72
Mayse, Henry 8,9,118
  Susannah 118
Mayze, Henry 34,76,87,88,96,97
  Litia 76
  Lydia 87
  Thomas 47
McCarty, Daniel 91,93,105,106,108,116,118,124,127,129,130,132,136,137
  Denie 75
  Dennis 55,116
  Frances 116
  Neale 58
McClanichan, Dor. 40
McCormick, Elinor 135
  Francis 135
McDevmil, Hugh 105
McDonnell, Jane 98
McGennis, Nich. 4
McGlaughlin, Dan. 10
McGregory, Robt. 75
McKinall, Wm. 94
McLanna, John 105
Mcray, John 60
Mealy, Alice 105
Meath, John 132,138
  Mabel 132,138
Medcalf, Henry 23,29,100
Medcalfe, Mary 100
  Wm. 82,100,123,125
Medly, John 105
  Margaret 105
Meredith, Dorothy 15
Merrica, Nicholas 125
Merritt, Ellias 6
  Margery 105
Merrydith, John 47
  Mary 47
Merryfeild, John 81,89
Metcalfe, Henry 78,86
  Phil. 76
  Wm. 76,86,102
M'Goon. James 136
Michael, Robert 1
Michleroy, Elizabeth 36
  Patrick 36
Middleton, Edward 8
  Eliz. 78
  John 78,87
Milbanks, Mary 105
Millard, Tho 66
Miller, Lawrence 16
  Mary 137
  Tho. 9,12,22,29,44,61,79,81,100,134,137
Milligan, James 58
Million, John 56,78,96
Milton, Michael 44
Mitchell, James 120
  Robt. 89
  Samuel 105
Monarth, Anne 105
Monteeth, Wm. 97
Montgomerie, Sarah 43
Montgomery, James 23,33,43
Moon, Elinor 132
  John 56,120
  Thomas 132
Moore, Agnes 109
Moor, Anne 19,26
Moore, David 117
  Hannah 110
  James 13,21,22,24,45,46,48,66,109

Moor/Moore (cont'd)..
  John 16,18,29,66,104
  Sarah 8,19
  Sennour 93
  Seymour 93
  Thomas 100
  Walter 8,18,19,26,29
  William 110
Moorehead, Anne 124
  Charles 88,101,102,104,124
  Elizabeth 124
  John 124
  Mary 124
  Wm. 101
  Winifred 124
Moorhead, Chas. 50
Mordam, Isaac 94
Mordey, John 3
More, Sarah 66
  Wm. 103
Morgan, Charles 11,12
  Elizabeth 11
  William 47
  Evan 100
Morning, Peter 11
Morrica, Elinor 63
  Nicholas 63,96,112
Morris, Anthony 13,17,20
  Dorothy 17,20
  Ellinor 105
  Jane 20
  Margaret 105
  Thomas 8,26,27,32
Morrison, Ann 78
  Fenly 78,93
Mortemore, Chris. 123
  James 75,123
Mortimore, James 121
Morton, Andrew 19,38,39,49
  Elizabeth 39
  Mary 19,38,39
Mosely, John 42
  Wm. 42
Mottoone, Frances 12
  John 12
Mottrom, John 1,3,5,7,10,19,20,25,27,32,39,43
  Mary 102,108
  Sarah 79
  Spencer 39,45,48,70,78,92,102,108,134
Moughby, More 17
Mould, Thomas 1
Moulder, James 125
Moult, Joseph 10
Moy, William 4
Muckantion, Jane 64
Mullens, Margaret 105
Mulraine, Alexander 29,38,56,61,69,92,97,98,117,134
  Mary 38
Mulrane, Alex. 114
Mundy, Robert 8
Munkin, Robt. 68
Munsloe, Valentine 119
Munsloo, Vallentine 85
Munslow, Valentine 68
Murdock, Geo. 110,115
  John 128
  Mary 115,128
Murfy, Margaret 98
Murphew, Daniel 132,138
  Jone 89
Murray, David 94
Murrow, Anne 137
  Elizabeth 3
  Wm. 53,126,137
Musgrane, Elizabeth 4
Mutton, John 28
Myer, Matthew 70,80,85
Myere, Matthew 111

Myers, Jane 84
  Matthew 84,122
Mynor, John 32

Nash, Robert 55,105,117
Naster, Patrick 105
Neale, Abner 134
  Anne 137
  Christopher 2,7,19,25,
    30,31,32,34,37,44,46,55,
    67,88,89,90,91,93,106,
    114,125,130,135
  Daniel 4,34,43,45,47,48,
    56,57,76,81,82,92,108,
    124,125,134
  Edward 83
  Ebenezer 108,121,132
  Hannah 55,92,106,125
  Jane 67,93
  John 108
  Mathew 8
  Nathan 124
  Patience 56,92,124
  Richard 105,117,125
  Rodham 92,125,136,137
  Wm. 82,83,88,92,108,121
  Xpher 3,4,5,20
Neele, James 100
Nellagon, Wm. 94
Nelmes, Alice 133
  Charles 133
  Elizabeth 127
  John 25,131
  Thomas 21,22
  Wm. 127
Nelms, Charles 63,90,102
  Elizabeth 102,114
  John 26,96,121
  Richard 15,26,108,116,
    128
  Sarah 116,128
  Thomas 22
  William 35,86,96,110,
    113,114,123,135
Nelson, John 103
Nepper, James 1
Nesbitt, Edward 27,124
Newell, Mary 94
Newman, Alex. 72
  Eliz. 73
  Thomas 17
Newton, Christopher 41,42,
  44,79,88,111,134
  George 105
  Rachel 104
Nicholls, Hancock 115,126,
  129
  John 16,119,120
  Samuel 2
Nickless, Elizabeth 76
  Frances-53,68
  Francis 70
  Hancock 138
  John 41,53,61,65,68,76,
    106,122,133,137
Nipper, James 7,50,51,53,
  57,78
  Jane 57,78
  John 93
Nonner, Andrew 21
Norgate, Anne 128
  Philip 9,12,109,128
Norris, James 79,80
  Wm. 56
Northen, Jane 123
  Samuel 123
Nowland, Margaret 126
  Richard 126
Nusam, Roger 14
  William 14
Nutbank, Susanna 100
Nutt, Ann 135
  Hannah 136

Nutt, Mary 64,95,104,111,
  112,115,124,125
  May 99
  Richard 11,20,23,37,38,
    45,55,79,110,117,120,
    123,124,128,135
  William 11,43,59,64,77,
    95,99,104,112,115,136

Oague, Henry 30
  Israel 39
  John 30
  Mary 39
Oakeley, Samuel 3
Oblin, Katherine 115
Oconoly, Felix 115
  Margaret 115
Ofild, Susanna 8
Ogan, John 58
Oheart, Gilchrist 58
Oldham, Abigail 51,116
  Anne 107
  James 65,82,85,113,116,
    125,126,133,135
  John 2,17,51,82,107,116,
    121,135
  Richard 44,92,116.121,
    125,133,134
  Ruth 133,135
Oldis, Elizabeth 33,34,37
  Joseph 34
  Robert 24,32,33,34
  Sarah 34
Oldoell, Thomas 4
Olds, Edward 7
Olegney, Daniel 94
Olesander, James 8
Oliver, Elizabeth 118
  Ellen 103
  Ignatius 57,63,64,65,76,
    78,103,118
Olliver, Mary 4,104
Ollibo, Wm. 94
Oneale, Arthur 29
  Dennis 52
  Lawrence 94
Roger 46
Onsale, Roger 1
Opie. Thomas 37,54,97
  Susannah 97
Opye, Thomas 15
Orge, Israel 21
Orland, David 27
  Margaret 60
  Richard 27,60,77
Osborne, John 17
Osford, Gilbert 4
Oslen, Rowland 17
Owen, John 76
  Nicholas 1,2,4,5,7,11,
    15,17,23,24,25,34,37
  Thomas 8
Oxe, Thomas 100

Packman, Mary 8
Page, Frances 82
  George 82,108
  Hannah 108
Paine, Ann 3
  Edward 47
  John 32
  Mary 62
  Wm. 42
Palefrey, Jonathan 81
Palfry, Jonathan 100,107
  Mary 107
Palind, William 7
Palmer, Datherine 131
  James 92,129
  John 21,39
  Joseph 24,34,96
  Katherine 116,117,118,
    119,124

Palmer, Marjery 113
  Mary 70
  Robert 96
  Sarah 39
  Thomas 116,117,118
Pan, Anthony 8
Parker, Azariam 14,25,26,
  34
  Eliza 96
  Elizabeth 14,26,33,34,77,
    112
  Fearnot 34
  James 137
  Jane 73
  John 5
  Ruth 29,65
  William 8,23,28,29,35,
    44,47,49,51,54,62,64,65,
    69,73,75,77,90,96,112
Parlar, Wm. 123
Parris, John 44
  Joseph 89
  Nicholas 23
Parry, Henry 87
Parsons, John 94
  Mary 98
Patter, John 50
Pattison, Alexander 14
Patton, Elizabeth 105
Paul, Charles 24
  Edward 99
  Elizabeth 99
Paulson, John 60
Payne, Susannah 129
  William 114,126,129
Peacock, Andrew 88,116,123
  Anne 116
Peannot, Mary 9
Pearce, Anne 119
  Elizabeth 32
  John 44
  Ralph 119
  Richard 32,44,45,73
Pearie, Ralph 62
Pedley, George 4
Pemberton, Elizabeth 96,
  100
  Richard 21,24,25,79,86,
    96,100
Pendrill, Anne 50
  John 50,52,53
  Sarah 52
Perciffold, William 5
Percifull, Eliz. 125
  Kath. 88
  Thos. 88
  William 26,40,82,85,125
Peryne, Alice 20
  Thomas 20
Perriman, Will 2
Perry, James 66
Peters, Edward 75
Peterson, Jane 58
  Matt. 8
Pettigrew, Isabel 9
Petty, Chris. 100
  Thomas 65
Phillips, Elinor 105
  Robt. 76,117
  Tho. 76
Phipp, John 94
Pickering, Wm. 135
Pinckney, Henry 100
Pinkard, Elizabeth 41
  John 4,8,41
  Thomas 68,87,96
Pinley, Elizabeth 70
  Thomas 70
Pithard, John 16
Pitts, Joseph 20
  Josiah 20
  Phillip 6,89
  Rebecca 20

Planner, Wm. 97
Platt, Peter 7,22,89
Plea, Edward 105
Pledjoel, Mary 7
Plodwell, Mary 89
Poggas, Phil. 10
Poiselle, Edmund 29
Polenest, Susanna 105
Pollick, Jane 99
  Katherine 61
  Patrick 21,44,46,64,72, 99
Polundoll, William 19
Poole, Samuel 30,45,112
Poor, John 98
Poore, David 75
  John 104
Pope, Dorcas 76
  James 3,50,58,63
  John 63,75,76,89,93,101, 122,127
Porkey, John 9
Porter, Ann 96
  Elizabeth 95,96,80,132
  John 96
  Thomas 96,129
  Wm. 96
Posakly, Francis 18
Powell, Edmund 36
  Elizabeth 32
  George 71
  John 4
  Morgan 32
  Nicholas 36
  Sarah 36
Presly, Peter 2,7,19,21,24, 5,34,37,39,43,45,47,50, 56,57,59,61,81,91,97,103 113,121,134,138
  William 1,2,3,4,5,7,25
  Winifred 97
Pretty John, Thomas 121
Price, Ann 89
  Benjamin 39
  Eliza 55
  Hugh 105
  John 55,109
  Mary 100,117,123
  Rebecca 135
  Richard 88,100,123
  Thomas 104
  William 89
Prichard, Charles 137
  Richard 61,62,117
Pritchard, Rich. 73
Pritchett, Wm. 94
Probie, Wm. 100
Proctor, Abraham 100
  Stephen 8
Propert, Howell 29
Proverb, Henry 78
  Ruth 66
Pryce, Richard 68
Pue, John 124
  Rebecca 124
Pugh, James 116
Purney, John 68
  Katherine 68

Quick, Thomas 24
Quill, Patrick 105
Quille, Jane 95
  Katherine 104
  Patrick 95,101,104
Quisse, Patrick 100

Rainsford, Edward 94
Randolph, Edward 49
Raney, John 11
Rankin, John 136
Rann. Evan 89
Raskall, Hannah 18
  John 18

Read, Elizabeth 111
  Susanna 87
  William 111
Reason, John 41,54,76,81, 83,89,94,100,113
  Rachel 93
Redish, Thomas 105
Reeves, Robert 91,94,96, 104,105
  William 72
Reine, Margarett 52
Rennelds, William 98
Reynolds, Elinor 21
  William 28
Rhodes, Augustine 1
  Nicholas 25
Rice, Dominic 2,23
  Joan 41
  John 45,112
  Mary 117
  Richard 4,8,25,37,41,44, 45,54,64,84,112,117
Richards, Peter 1
  William 36
Richardson, Charles 85, 130
  Elizabeth 36,77,105,130
  James 77,105,136
  John 80
  Sarah 89
  William 33,36
Rickett, Arthur 8
Ricketts, Benjamin 13
Rider, Anne 19,26
  Henry 18,19,25,26
Roach, John 37,90,104
Roarke, Dennis 104
Roberts, Fra. 85
  John 95
  Mary 96
  Wm. 95
Robertt, Evan 85
Robeson, Ester 52
  Francis 52
Robins, Mary 70
  Symon 66
Robinson, Ann 4
  Annie 6
  Anthony 121
  Elizabeth 119,138
  Frances 67
  Jane 121
  John 2,23,31,83,84,121, 124
  Judith 97
  Martha 84,120,127
  Nicholas 107
  Rich. 63,67,69,82,89, 109,120,121,124,136
  Robt. 61
  Samuel 89,120,127,138
  Symon 90
  Tobert 68
  Thomas 3,13,83
  Xpher 97
Robyson, John 6
Rock, Thomas 104
Rodes, Elizabeth 69
  Hannah 69
  John 69
Roebuck, Robt. 118,126
Rogers, Alex. 128
  Hannah 93
  Isabella 87,88,97,98,100 118,135
  James 66,73,80,82,108, 118,135
  Jane 64
  Joan 10,23,29
  John 10,23,29,59,93
  Phillip 87,88,97,98,100, 101,104,110,118
  Richard 24,34,37,46,59, 64,67,93

Rogers, Susannah 118,135
  William 6,10,15,20,23, 27,29
Roper, Anthony 35
  John 48
  Mary 35
Ross, John 64,86,88,91
  Henry 100
  Mary 86
  Ruth 64
Rosse, Henry 50,57,65,68
Rotherom, John 79
Round, John 50
  Mary 50
Rout, Frances 31,137
  Mary 86
  Richard 31,64,137
  Thomas 18,52,62,64,67, 95,98,123,125
  William 49
Rowland, Luke 61
  Mary 61,68
  Robert 68
  Thomas 6
Rowlands, Anne 61
Rowley, Margery 10
Royston, John 16
  Jonathan 16,18,34,93
  Mary 34,59,69,90,92,93
Rumly, John 8
Runkin, George 58
Russell, Hannah 93,99,123
  James 104
  John 16
  Peter 94,106
  Richard 89,93,99,123
Ruth, Elizabeth 82,96
  Richard 82,96
Ryder, Ann 88
  Henry 88
  Thomas 104

Sabrice, Dorothy 29
Saby, John 121
Sachiverall, Eliz. 131
  Timothy 131
Saddler, Henry 4
  Robert 4
  Thomas 4,19
Sadler, Mary 108
  Miriam 19
  Richard 103,108
  Thomas 89,103,108
Sage, William 8
Salisbury, Andrew 54,57,65
  Barbara 18,47
  John 9
  Mary 65
  Sarah 63,72
  Thomas 47,62,63.72
Sallees, Stephen 27
Sallows, Stephen 4,8,36
Salmon, Alex. 98
  Elizabeth 6
Samford, Samuel 133
Samlers, Henry 7
Sanders...2
  Ebenezer 1,20,23,43,47, 127
  Edwaard 1,20,23,59,84,99 118,127,129,134
  Elizabeth 47,64,70,129
  Ester 61,65,91
  Henry 89
  Joan 4
  John 60,61,62
  Mary 95,98
  Sarah 61
  Wm. 64,70,75,95,98
  Zachariah 61
Sanford, Eliza 26
  Samuel 26
Sarchfeild, Patrick 105

Saunders, Ebenezer 58
  Edward 58
  Elizabeth 58
Savey, Mary 94
Savige, David 100,105
Sax, Hannah 107
  Wm. 107
Schreever, Barthol. 77
Schrever, Barthol. 81
  Mary 81
Scofill, Mary 115
Scott, Anne 91
  John 88,89,91,104
  Robt. 38
Screech, Geo. 89
Screiver, Barthol. 79
  Dennis 79
Screver, Mary 59
Screiver, Barthol. 133
Scriver, Barth. 18,59
  Mary 18,59
Seabourne, Nich. 97
Seabury, Abigail 54
  James 54
Searle, Thomas 24
Sech, Robert 45,46,60
Seddon, Joanna 133
  Thomas 42,100,133
Selfe, Francis 46
  John 78,80
  Rebecca 46
  Susannah 78,80
Sennett, Philip 75
Settswerell, Theophilus 109
Seward, Wm. 94
Shapleigh, Elizabeth 107
  Hannah 94
  Philip 2,3,5,11,19,32, 35,36,39,51,74,94,99, 100,107,114,130
  Thomas 94,107
Sharp, John 53,54
Sharpe, Eliza 67
  John 60,61,63,67,82
  Margaret 61
Sharpless, Cuthbert 110
Shaw, Andrew 40,41,47
  John 18,123
  Rebecca 18
  Shahanna 98
Shea, Daniel 8
Sheares...17
Sheare/Sheares, Abraham 72,105
  Eliza 41
  Thomas 116
  William 1,9,12,20,33,41, 90
Shears, Abraham 16
  Elizabeth 16
Sheere, Abraham 75,77
  Barthol. 75
  Eliz. 72
  Thos. 75,77
  Wm. 77
Sheldon, Hugh 13
Shepheard, Barthol. 85
Shepherd, Robt. 39,107
Sheppard, Eliza 98
Shipard, James 59
Shirley, John 87
  Richard 58,62
  Tho. 37,58
Shirly, Jane 104
Shirsly, Archebald 98
Short, Anne 9,10
  John 90
  Samuel 105
  Thomas 9
  Wm. 102,123
Shorthouse, Thos. 89
Shortman, Mary 7

Showters, William 1
Shreever, Barthol. 81,115
Shrever, Barthol. 62,96
  Mary 62
Simons, James 123
  John 58,60
  Mary 58
Simpson, Mary 82
  Wm. 45,73,82
Sims, Anne 107
  Thomas 35,63,68,94,100, 107
Singer, Edward 136
  Jane 136
Skeles, John 89
Skinage, John 100
Sland, Shoo 21
Smetnan, William 21
Smith/Smyth, Alice 94
  Anne 7,53,98
  Bryan 136
  Daniel 88,89
  Edward 1,54,70,79
  Eliza 55,138
  Elizabeth 36,37,41,56, 72,83,110
  James 104
  Joane 5
  John 25,75,86,97
  Judith 104
  Kath. 58
  Margaret 52
  Margery 88
  Mary 10,116
  Middleton 79
  Rainsford 62,64,69,130, 136
  Richard 4,7,16,23,26,31, 32,34,35,36,39,41,43, 46,56,59,60,72,73,78, 79,86,95,97,100,110,113, 114,116,119,128,137,138
  Samuel 1,3,4,5,24,25,43 51,58,62,64,69,75,94, 123
  Stephen 83,86,90
  Susanna 128
  Thomas 4,12,17,27,39,52, 75,88,118,132
  William 4,7,9,12,29,53, 55
Smithee, Edward 93
  Isabella 93
Smythgill, Anne 11
Soch, Robert 38,45
Southerland, John 9,12,36
Southerne, James 124
Southing, William 18
Southland, Alice 118
Southorne, James 75
Span/Spann, Cuthbert 11,20, 24,25,29,43,44,64,67,72 74,82
  Dorothy 20,82,133
  Elizabeth 66
  John 24,63,67,89,133, 134
  Richard 11,134
  Samuel 133
  Sarah 63,66,67,81
Spans, Davis 90
Sparhatt, Mac. 17
Sparkes, John 23
Speens, David 79
Spellman/Spelman, Clement 109,114
  Hannah 109,114
Spence, Alex. 51
  David 113,126,130
Spencer, Eliz. 79
  Frances 48,108
  Francis 105
  John 88

Spencer, Nicholas 27,48, 88,108
  Robert 118
Spens, David 69,76,81,89, 92,93,95
  Sarah 76,81,89
  Susanna 105
  Wm. 105
Spilman, Mary 13
  Thomas 13
Sprag, Anne 23
Spry, John 89,101,124
  Mary 124
Squire, Jarvis 8
Squires, John 50
Stallin, Gillian 98
Standly, John 42
Staney, Thomas 11
Stanley, John 103
Stanly, James 104
Staplee, Rich. 79
Statham, Sarah 8
Stethan, Mary 48
Stathen, Hugh 55,75,81
  Jane 91
Staton, Jno. 66
Staynie, Hannah 51,94
  Thomas 51,57
Steephens, Ralph 42
Stephens, Mary 58
  Ralph 30,42,46
  Rich. 29
Stephenson, Wm. 100
Steptoe, Anthony 4
  Arthur 84
  John 84,87,103
Steward, Cowen 75
Stone, John 12
Stott, John 76,81
  Thomas 75
Stratton/Streeton, Thomas 112,115,122,124,127,128, 129,132
Straughan, David 60,66,67, 69,72,74,83,90,92,96,100 101,112,117,118,123,124, 128,136,137
  Ruth 66,69,90
Suggett, Rebecca 114,121
  Thomas 114,121
Sullivant, Daniel 97
Sullvant, Daniel 32
Sutherland, Alice 115
  John 115
Sutton, Anne 91
  Henry 80,85,87
  Margaret 80,85
  Rich. 91
Swain, Frances 37
  John 37
  Tho. 37
Swanson, Eliz. 118
  John 22
  Mary 22
  Rich. 106,118,122
Swelter, Mar. 47
  Mathew 47
Swetman, Mary 89
  William 27
Swillivant, Cornelius 117
  Daniel 73,75,79,97,100, 104
  Katherine 78,117
  Owen 78
  Timothy 108
Symmons, John 20
Symons, James 113
  John 7

Talbot, Rich. 126
Talbott, Kath. 104
Talbut, Katherine 65
Tanner, Amb. 10

Tap, Thomas 16
Tapp, Thomas 30
Tapscott, Henry 133
Tarleton, Edward 14
Tarpley, Eliz. 76,80,81
  John 76,80,81,111,112,
  124,125
Taylor, Alice 87,90
  Anne 54
  Elizabeth 111
  Gennett 3
  Henry 23
  John 5,8,87,90,109,111,
  119,125
  Jos. 94
  Lazarus 115,117,118
  Mary 111
  Phebe 111
  Rebecca 93
  Tho. 90,93
  William 24,27,33,54,95,
  111,112
Teaborne...11
Teigne, Robt. 98
Templer, Dorothy 116
Tewes, Robert 17
Thackrell, Tho. 118
Tharte, William 6
Theary, James 104
Thelkeld, Christopher 99
Thewes, Th. 17
Thomas, Arthur 89
  Eliza 23
  Elizabeth 1,136
  David 100
  John 16,46,51,54,55,63,
  79,80,100,101,120,136,
  138
  Mary 1,2,20,23
  Rebecca 20
  William 1,2,20,23
  Zachariah 18,56
Thompson, Dorothy 87
  Jane 58
  John 87
  Marmaduke 81,93,99
  Philip 127
  Richard 12,36,59
  Simon 127
  Tho. 127
  Wm. 100,104
Thomson, Rich. 123
  Simon/Symon 118,122
Thornbury, William 12,13,
  74
Thornton, Wm. 78
Thrapp, Hannah 116
Threlkell, Chris. 132
Tigner/Tignor, Ann 87,91
  Eliz. 109
  Philip 68,76
  Sarah 76
  William 3,8,9,25,87,91
Tillett, Dorcas 73
  Dorothy 68
  Tho. 68,73
Timmons/Timons, Mary 63
  Samuel 96
  Thomas 15,63
Tingcomb, Nathanial 176
Tingey, John 12,13
Tinoth, Sus. 17
Tipto, John 16
Tipton, Edward 35
  Joseph 102,108
  Margaret 35
Tolson, Benj. 57,59
  John 56
  Mary 96
  Tho. 96
  Wm. 125
Topping, John 16,18,20,87
Tosse, James 7

Totton, William 14
Towers, Ann 40
  Dorothy 25
  Sarah 73
  Thomas 9,25,73
Trape, Joyce 59,66
  Mary 67
  Thomas 22,57,59,67
Travers, Rawleigh 51,59,
  66,67,75,78,84
  Rebecca 2
  Samuel 46
  Sarah 84
  William 2
Trea, Lawrence 105
Treskale, William 10
Trimlett, Hannah 51,57,83
  John 44,51,57,83
Trip, Thomas 13,21,22
Trueman, Thomas 116
Trussell, Eliz. 53
  Jane 134
  John 53,106,132,134
  Wm. 106
Tulles, Rich. 66
Tullos, Cloud 18,19,34,39,
  41,43,44,70,71,78
  John 85,88,136
  Mary 72
  Rich. 138
  Sarah 78
Turberville, John 23,34,
  45,46,48,49,57,60,62,
  79,86
Turner, Elinor 123
  John 101,104,123,135
Turrane, John 8
Twyford, James 8,9
Tyney, Wm. 133
Typton, Edw. 34
  Elizabeth 3,9
  Joseph 3,8,9
  Sam. 1,31,32

Urquahart, Tho. 133
Utine, Isaac 85

Vallen, Dennis 104
  Eliz. 104
Vanlandeghan/Vanlandegham,
  Benjamin 57,95,110,111
  Elizabeth 34
  Francis 71,111,119
  Mary 95
  Mich. 25
  Rich. 34,51,110,111,128
Varley, James 16
  John 16
  Xpher. 16
Vaulx, Eliz. 130
  Robt. 130
Vaxon, Rich. 75
Veale, Humphrey 94
Violett, Anne 98
  George 81,98
Vollon, Charles 43,48
Voyer, Francis 72

Wadding, Hannah 126
Waddington, Anne 51
  George 51,62
  Hannah 114
  Ralph 52,103,114,126
Waddy, Andrew 29
  James 15,27,28,36,50,89
  95,98,104,111
  John 6,27,28
  Thomas 4,10,11,36,123
Wade, Mary 17
  Xpher. 17
Wale, George 1,87
  Mary 1
Walford, Ester 25

Walker, Ann 132
  Emmanuel 132
  Jane 95
  John 104
  Joseph 95
  Mary 50,132
  Rich. 132
  Symon 1
  William 2
Walkinsha, John 74
Wall, Benjamine 29,30
  Frances 40,41
  Isaac 40,41
  John 29,129
  Joseph 30
  Ruth 29,30
Wallers, John 71
Wallis, Hugh 136
Walter, John 78
Walters, Diana 16
  Easter 16
  Elinor 23
  Elizabeth 10,19
  Ester 34
  Hester 16
  John 16,25,27,119
  Mary 16
  Phoebe 16
  Roger 59
  Tho. 75,90
Walton, Stephen 8
Warcupp, Sam. 45
Ward, Francis 89
  James 58
  Mary 62
  William 61,62,73
Wares, Fran. 7
Warnaw, Grace 29
Warner, Ann 33
  John 9,12,33,34
  Prudence 33
Warington, Robt. 99
Warrington, Frances 67
  Hannah 124
  John 105
  Ralph 53,67,95,124
Warwick, Wm. 23,41,116
Washi, John 111
Waterman, Isabella 37
  Jos. 37
  Tho. 37
Waters, Elithie 118
  John 111,112
  Thomas 117,118
Watkins, Anne 67,68
  Edward 62,67,68,73,80,85
  114,124,126
  Henry 72
  Peter 72
Watson, Alice 66
Watts, Edward 8
  Elizabeth 30
Wattson, James 33
Waugh, John 2
Waughop, Thomas 13
Way, Edyth 7,9,16
  Eliza. 66,104,133
  John 32,52,54,66,94,104,
  133
  Richard 7,9,32
  Sarah 137
  Wm. 137
Weatherstone, Alex. 46,88
  Jane 88
Webb, Ann 122
  Charity 130,134
  Daniel 32,131
  Elizabeth 56,62,64,69,71
  75,92,109,124
  Ester 95,135
  Francis 127
  John 10,17,27,30,40,46,
  61,62,63,64,71,82,85,94,

Webb, John (cont'd)...
  104,110,118,124
  Mary 9,17
  Rachel 46
  Samuel 95,135
  Susanna 29,35
  Thomas 1,3,7,8,9,16,19,
  20,37,56,60,62,64,69,75
  84,89,118,124,130,134,
  135
  William 10,16,29,35
Wederiffe, Wm. 92
Weeks, Ann 57
  Henry 36,57
  John 57
Wells, Anne 28
  Rich. 53
  Stephen 28
Welsh, Jane 48
  Phil. 8,76
  Rich. 43
  Walter 48
West, John 37,57,77,86,
  112
  Susannah 57,66
  Wm. 77
Westerby, Mary 100
Weston, Edward 91
Wheadon, Edmond 16
Wheeler, Frances 41,90,108
  Francis 104
  John 41
  Mary 104
  Thomas 90,108
White, Alice 104,106
  Edward 5,21,23
  Eliz. 17
  James 48,54,59,80,81,94
  John 16
  Joseph 31
  Lawrence 64,65,66,74
  Simon 109
  Tho. 133
Whitehead, Mary 10,37,61,
  96
  Thomas 37,96
Whitehouse, Lawrence 46
Whitford, David 44,57
Whithers, Erasmus 12
Whittangton, Wm. 97
Whittington, John 8
Whitter, Phebe 105
Wiggan, William 8
Wiggins, Ann 138
  John 138
Wigginton, Frances 131
  Geo. 131
Wilcox, Eliz. 75,94
Wildey/Wildy, Elizabeth
  80,106
  James 86
  Jane 12,13,56
  William 3,12,50,80,106
Wilkes, Elizabeth 31,88
  Thomas 28,31
Wilkins, Jane 55,95
  John 55,56,104
  Peter 136
  Tho. 95
  Wm. 89
Willey, John 29
Williard, Francis 94
Williams, Alice 68,82,98,
  109,115
  David 15,93
  Edward 21,22,25,37,45,
  54,70,75,79
  Elizabeth 63,84,99
  Ellinor 31,33
  Em 63
  Henry 90,93
  Howell 16,31,33,36
  Hugh 89

Williams, John 3,9,73,98,
  99,104
  Katherine 55,75
  Mary 13,76
  Rachel 93
  Rice 27
  Roger 15,51
  Sarah 73,99
  Temperance 22
  Thomas 12,16,18,19,28,
  38,39,68,78,82,84,89,
  98,99,109
  Will/Wm. 17,63
Willgrass, Jos. 100
Willis, Rich. 44
Willoughby, Henry 27
Wills, Hannah 105
  Samuel 1
  Stephen 47
Wilshire, Kath. 103
Wilson, James 54
  John 134
  Letty 134
Wiltshire, Kath. 103,135
  Wm. 103,107,112,135
Winberry, Math. 17
Winder, Elizabeth 65,91,
  103,107,108,120
  Thomas 65,74,77,81,91,
  93,102,103
  Wm. 102,127,129
Winstead, Samuel 63
Winston, Th. 17
Winter, Eliz. 98,129
  Thomas 5,7,16,36,37,62,
  96,98,111,129
Wither, Erasmus 31
Withers, Eliza. 53
  Erasmus 13,53
  Frances 13
Woldridge, Edw. 113
Wollham, Eliz. 94
Wood, William 16,63
Woodland, Mary 48,62,66,
  67
  Wm. 44,48,54,56,59,62
Woodridge, Edw. 68
Woods, Francis 47
Wool, Wm. 76
Woolard, John 4
Wooldridge, Edw. 46,92
  Eliz. 46,92
Wooll, Eliza 98
Wormeley, Chris. 49
Wornom, Elizabeth 61
  John 15,16,19,22,23,31,
  34,44,59,60,61,65,109,
  120
  Mary 115
Wright, Elizabeth 3
  John 110
  Richard 89,96,99,114,115,
  117,124,125,134,136,137

Yarrett, Adam 1,7,14,29,36
  43,46,48
  Jam. 65
  Jane 24,94
  Rachel 1,14,36
  William 24,29,30,36,43,
  53,65,94
Yeomans, Barth. 29
Yoomans, Barth. 22
Young, James 41
  Wm. 125
Yowell, Elizabeth 36
  Richard 36

(Note: List of Tithables not included in this index may be found on pages 5 and 6 in alphabet order.)

www.ingramcontent.com/pod-product-compliance
Lightning Source LLC
Chambersburg PA
CBHW031421290426
44110CB00011B/475